Cleaning Up Greenwash

Cleaning Up Greenwash

Corporate Environmental Crime and the Crisis of Capitalism

Angus Nurse

LEXINGTON BOOKS
Lanham • Boulder • New York • London

Published by Lexington Books
An imprint of The Rowman & Littlefield Publishing Group, Inc.
4501 Forbes Boulevard, Suite 200, Lanham, Maryland 20706
www.rowman.com

86-90 Paul Street, London EC2A 4NE, United Kingdom

Copyright © 2022 by The Rowman & Littlefield Publishing Group, Inc.

All rights reserved. No part of this book may be reproduced in any form or by any elec-
tronic or mechanical means, including information storage and retrieval systems, without
written permission from the publisher, except by a reviewer who may quote passages
in a review.

British Library Cataloguing in Publication Information Available

Library of Congress Cataloging-in-Publication Data

Names: Nurse, Angus, author.
Title: Cleaning up greenwash : corporate environmental crime and the crisis
    of capitalism / Angus Nurse.
Description: Lanham : Lexington Books, 2022. | Includes bibliographical
    references and index. | Summary: "Cleaning up Greenwash characterizes
    corporate environmental crime as an inevitable consequence of neoliberal
    markets and contemporary consumer culture and identifies that traditional
    criminal justice responses may be inadequate to deal with contemporary
    environmental harms"— Provided by publisher.
Identifiers: LCCN 2021045335 (print) | LCCN 2021045336 (ebook) | ISBN
    9781793600547 (cloth) | ISBN 9781793600554 (epub)
Subjects: LCSH: Liability for environmental damages. | Offenses
    against the environment—Law and legislation. | Tort liability of
    corporations. | Environmental law—Compliance costs. | Capitalism—
    Environmental aspects.
Classification: LCC K955 .N87 2022 (print) | LCC K955 (ebook) | DDC
    344.04/6—dc23/eng/20211105
LC record available at https://lccn.loc.gov/2021045335
LC ebook record available at https://lccn.loc.gov/2021045336

♾™ The paper used in this publication meets the minimum requirements of American
National Standard for Information Sciences—Permanence of Paper for Printed Library
Materials, ANSI/NISO Z39.48-1992.

Contents

Acknowledgments

I owe a debt of thanks to a number of people whose support, assistance, and expertise made this book possible. My colleagues in the British Society of Criminology's Green Criminology Research Seminar Network, Tanya Wyatt, Matthew Hall, Nigel South, James Heydon, Harriet Pierpoint, and Jennifer Maher have been invaluable in creating an enthusiastic and supportive environment in which some of the ideas contained in the book have been debated and refined. Several colleagues have also commented on some of the original research from which this book developed and provided opportunities for discussion of ideas to their students during invited guest lectures. These opportunities provided constructive criticism which helped refine several parts of the material into its final form.

I also give thanks to the postgraduate students of Middlesex University who during the academic years 2017–2018 and 2018–2019 studied with me on the *Environmental Politics and Ethics* and *Environmental Crime and Green Criminology* modules I developed and taught at that institution. Our discussions and analysis of contemporary environmental problems gave me additional insight into how issues of corporate environmental crime are viewed from a range of perspectives and how problems are contextualized in different countries.

I am also indebted to my regular research collaborators Tanya Wyatt (Northumbria University), Sam Poyser (Aberystwyth University), Katerina Gachevska (Leeds Beckett University), and Diane Ryland (formerly of the University of Lincoln) with whom I write and discuss issues relating to wildlife crime, miscarriages of justice, environmental politics and security, and animal law/welfare respectively. Sharing ideas with these excellent scholars coming from their respective fields of criminology, international security, and law has undoubtedly exposed me to a broad range of critical and analytical perspectives. Some of the ideas that have arisen in our discussion of issues around crimes against animals, capitalism and markets, criminal justice and criminal investigation, globalization, and international law have influenced me positively during our work on these other topics whilst informing my thinking on some of the ideas in this book from within a broader perspective than my primary criminological and socio-legal focus.

I am grateful to Lexington for commissioning this book and, in particular, to Becca Beurer for pushing me to write something that I have been working on intermittently for around a decade. Becca's support in developing this book from its outline stages to the (hopefully) fully formed text contained within the following pages has been invaluable. I am also grateful for comments from the network of green criminology scholars whose comments at the various green criminology events as I presented work in progress sometimes forced me to refine my thinking or to identify new case examples that would allow me to illustrate the underlying points that form the core part of this book's arguments.

Introduction

This book developed from a series of research lectures entitled *Cleaning Up Greenwash*. The lectures took place sporadically between July 2013 and October 2018 in various forums and formats. Lectures and research talks under the *Cleaning Up Greenwash* banner were delivered as part of the Economic and Social Research Council's (ESRC) Research Seminar Series in Green Criminology (2012 to 2014) and as guest research lectures at various Universities including: Leeds Beckett University; London South Bank University; Northumbria University; Nottingham Trent University; the University of Lincoln; and Utrecht University (the Netherlands). These university lectures variously took place within green criminology and environmental law modules, on modules on corporate crime and corporate governance, and within modules on crimes of the powerful or state crime.

The impetus for the lectures was a long-standing research (and practitioner) interest in corporate environmental "crime" and the noncompliant behavior of corporations. In their book *Environmental Crime*, Situ and Emmons (2000) provided a definition of environmental crime that I have frequently used in teaching and in research discussions around how environmental crime is categorized by legal systems. Their definition (repeated in this book) defines environmental crime as unauthorized acts or omissions that are defined as crime by the criminal law and that are subject to criminal sanctions. As I say in this book (and have said in other publications) this definition is problematic for several reasons. First; the reality of much corporate wrongdoing, even that which contravenes legislation and causes substantial environmental harm is that it is often not defined as "crime." Instead, much corporate wrongdoing and offending is dealt with by regulatory and administrative enforcement mechanisms and the policy and enforcement approach to such behavior is often very different to the approach taken to what is traditionally viewed as "crime." Even where regulators and enforcers have options to deploy criminal sanctions for corporate offending they are allegedly not routinely applied, and regulatory enforcers may instead exercise discretion to use civil and administrative penalties instead of criminal ones. Prior research suggests that this is the preferred approach and that fines and administrative sanctions are thought more effective in dealing with corporate offending than a punitive approach based on criminal law principles (more on that later). The second problem with the definition is that it focuses on crime rather than the extent of environmental harm that is caused and suggests that the criminal law is an appropriate mechanism for dealing with environmental problems. Part of the argument of this book is that this may not always be the case.

From a green criminological perspective, these initial considerations raise questions about how corporate environmental crime is contextualized by justice systems and within the discipline of criminology. Criminology is dominated by discussions of crime as defined by criminal law and the enforcement and sanctioning mechanisms of mainstream criminal justice and sanctioning bodies. A visit to most criminology conferences and examination of mainstream criminology journals will reveal core discussions around police and policing, prisons and penology, crime statistics and quantitative criminology, and gangs and group offending. These are all worthy considerations but as Lynch and Stretesky (2014) and Rob White (2018a) indicate, they do not consider or engage with many environmental harms that are more widespread, more far reaching in their effects and more likely to affect the average citizen than the street and property crimes and crimes of violence that criminology routinely concerns itself with. Thus, the call from green criminologists is that we need to include in our discussions of crime and harm (including the notions of social harm or zemiology put forward by Tombs and others) a green criminological perspective that considers a wider notion of crime and wrongdoing that directly engages with the types of environmental offending that represent a threat to human populations and non-human nature irrespective of whether these are defined as crime by justice systems. Green criminology is thus frequently concerned with environmental *harm* rather than environmental *crime* and seeks to define environmental crime through notions of the impact of anthropocentric actions on the environment and non-human nature. Thus, within the green criminology project, a discourse exists around extending our definition of crime to incorporate not just a strict legalistic definition of crime but to also include a broader socio-legal and more inclusive definition of "crime."

This thinking informed the *Cleaning Up Greenwash* lecture series and the research associated with those lectures that has ultimately led to the writing of this book. Corporate environmental crime is an under researched area within criminology, despite seemingly wide acceptance that corporations cause considerable harm through both legal and illegal activities. There also appears to be quite wide acceptance that illegal activity by corporations is widespread perhaps most cogently encapsulated in Tombs and Whyte's book *The Corporate Criminal* (2015) in which the authors directly state that corporations are inherently criminal, if not outright evil. While I would perhaps not go as far as Tombs and Whyte in calling for the abolition of the corporation, I agree with their analysis that illegal activity has become normalized within many major corporations and that environmental noncompliance is widespread. Arguably this is an inevitable consequence of the operation of neoliberal markets and a corporate culture that prioritizes profits and the smooth operation of market activities over environmental concerns. It is also likely a consequence of the increased political power of the major corporations, some of whom have resources that far exceed those of some nation states and have developed operating practices that illustrate the reality that they can act almost with impunity and where problems do occur, the corporation can literally buy itself out of trouble. This also reflects a political context in which corporations are broadly perceived as being responsible actors. However, a critical exploration of corporate environmental harm requires going beyond the simplistic argument of profit-driven motives as bad. A more nuanced and detailed analysis is required and this is what this book aims to provide.

Within the original lecture series on which this book is based, the exploration of corporate environmental crime incorporated: biopiracy and the rights of indigenous peoples; the behavior of oil companies in African states; the regulation of corporate social responsibility and corporate environmental responsibility; analysis of contemporary environmental legislation and the prosecution of environmental harm, and state-corporate crime and air pollution. A final research lecture on *averting the environmental apocalypse*, dealt with public and state denial that society is sleepwalking towards environmental disaster which current legislative and policy discourse seems unwilling to accept or address. The potential consequence of this is that environmental problems are frequently dealt with in an expedient manner rather than one that deals with the *urgency* of environmental problems. Political considerations sometimes influence such decisions as does the nature of the regulatory and enforcement framework that deals with environmental issues which are often not defined as core policing priorities. Many of these research lectures found their way into this book, in some cases with new case studies that aim to bring the discussions up to date and provide for more in-depth analysis for readers unfamiliar with the history of green criminological discourse and some of the more specialist texts familiar to green criminology and environmental law students and scholars.

The title of this book clearly reflects a discussion of corporate environmental crime as both a symptom of and a cause of capitalism. However, this book's analysis and my general perspective is not one based on an ideological position that the capitalist system is inherently broken and *must* be dismantled. Readers may well come to that conclusion based on analysis of this book's examples, and some of my green criminology colleagues make cogent arguments for dismantling of capitalist systems and a reallocation of resources and creation of new means of production. I agree with many of these arguments and the evidence that capitalism consistently fails through overexploitation of natural resources. I also agree that neoliberal markets routinely fail in their consideration of environmental impacts; the evidence suggests that attempts to achieve a balance between the interests of markets and continued consumption and effective environmental protection have also failed if not actually reached the level of unmitigated disaster. However, it is the *operation* of the systems and markets and how regulatory and enforcement approaches deal with these that is focused on within this book rather than the underlying capitalist systems and structures themselves. This reflects my own background in examining regulatory systems and the operation of regulatory and criminal justice and my interest in the operation of justice systems and enforcement methods to achieve reparation, remediation, and rehabilitation for wrongdoing that harms the environment and non-human nature.

Inevitably there are things that have been left out of this book for reasons of space and because they may not fit with the perspective adopted in writing the book. The case studies chosen to discuss issues are also in part selected through personal interest and to try and avoid covering ground examined by other authors. Some new and interesting cases emerged as the book was in its final stages and where appropriate these have been substituted for older perhaps more established cases.

This book is part of a long-running project shaped by ongoing debates and as it continues to develop I anticipate returning to some of these issues and examining new cases, new policies, and political developments in corporate governance as they appear.

List of Abbreviations

CER: Corporate Environmental Responsibility
CJEU: Court of Justice of the European Union
CSR: Corporate Social Responsibility
ECHR: European Convention on Human Rights
ECtHR: European Court of Human Rights
EPA: Environmental Protection Agency
EU: European Union
GC: Global Compact
GMO: Genetically Modified Organism
GRI: Global Reporting Initiative
ICCPR: International Covenant on Civil and Political Rights
ICESCR: International Covenant on Economic, Social and Cultural Rights
ILO: International Labour Organization
MNCs: Multinational Corporations (see also MNEs)
MNEs: Multinational Enterprises (see also MNCs)
NGO: Non-Governmental Organization
OECD: Organization for Economic Cooperation and Development
SAI: Social Accountability International
UDHR: Universal Declaration of Human Rights
UN: United Nations
UNDRIP: United Nations Declaration on Indigenous Peoples
UNEP: United Nations Environment Programme
UNFCCC: United Nations Framework Convention on Climate Change
UNHRC: United Nations Human Rights Council
UNODC: United Nations Office on Drugs and Crime

Chapter 1

Defining Corporate Environmental Crime

This book explores the contemporary reality of corporate environmental crime, critically examining its nature, scope, and how justice systems and public policy should deal with corporate offending as a distinct phenomenon. Corporate environmental crime might be categorized as accidental wrongdoing, largely considered to be the fault of "rogue" employees or the unintended consequences of governance failures such that blame is laid at the feet of individuals (Bell et al. 2013). In part this reflects societal and policy acceptance of corporations as positive actors who generally provide benefits to society. This paradigm suggests that harm caused by corporations is an aberration in otherwise lawful activity. Accordingly, when corporations cause environmental harm, the corporation may be perceived as victim as much as perpetrator, suffering harm to its reputation and the smooth running of its operations. Thus, the dominant paradigm in corporate governance discourse is one that sees corporations as responsible actors with a vested interest in eradicating environmental harm and corporate wrongdoing. Arguably there is also political reluctance to treat corporations as criminal entities given their contribution to the economy (as employers and taxpayers) and to policy debates. Indeed, in some jurisdictions, criminal prosecution of a corporation as the guilty actor is arguably not possible within the confines of the criminal code and criminal procedure. Thus, in some cases the legal system itself concludes that corporations cannot be "criminals." However, the focus of this book is an exploration of the extent to which corporate environmental offending is almost inevitable and in many cases is a direct consequence of how neoliberal markets operate, and fail to consider the true environmental costs of productivity (Lynch and Strestesky 2014). In particular, this book examines whether the corporate drive for profits and anthropocentric attitudes towards the environment and exploitation of natural resources create a situation where corporate environmental crime is a foreseeable, inevitable,

1

and even *natural* consequence of contemporary neoliberal production and market-driven philosophies. Thus, any enforcement or regulatory approach needs to appropriately consider the behaviors involved in environmental wrongdoing and how best to address them.

Within this book, corporate environmental crime is examined through a green criminological lens, which considers how corporations cause environmental *harm*. Beirne and South define green criminology as "the study of those harms against humanity, against the environment (including space) and against nonhuman animals committed both by powerful institutions (e.g. governments, transnational corporations, military apparatuses) and also by ordinary people" (2007, xiii). This broad definition allows for exploration of both distinctly green crimes, such as illegal trafficking in timber and the trade in endangered species of wildlife, but also "mainstream" crimes such as fraud or regulatory noncompliance that impact on the environment and non-human nature. This is particularly the case when such crimes are linked to environmentally harmful activities such as excessive levels of pollution or illegal dumping of toxic waste. Crucially, most definitions of green criminology identify environmental *harm* rather than crime as a core concern of green criminological enquiry and this is the definitional focus that distinguishes green criminology from mainstream criminology. Lynch and Stretesky suggest that "most criminologists will reject the idea that they ought to be paying attention to the problems of green crime and justice" (2014, 2). Their argument is predicated on the notion that criminology is primarily concerned with crime as it is strictly defined within criminal law and criminal justice systems. This notion of crime reflects the reality that "the focus of official police statistics is street crime, burglary, interpersonal violence—the crimes of the lower working class" (Lea & Young 1993, 89). Arguably, criminology as a discipline is similarly fascinated with and dominated by individualistic and restrictive notions of crime as being anthropocentric, concerned with violent offending and property crimes and focused on mainstream notions of policing and crime prevention as concerned with the detection, apprehension, and punishment of offenders who impact primarily on human victims. These are, of course, important concerns but mainstream criminology risks ignoring a wide range of offending and harmful behavior that has capacity to cause greater harm to human populations. Lynch and Stretesky (2014) assessing National Crime Victimization Survey data that detailed levels of environmental victimization, concluded that "humans are more likely to be the victims of violent green victimizations than they are to be the victims of criminal acts of violence" (2014, 92). The nature of these environmental harms is discussed in more detail later in this chapter; suffice it to say that corporate activity is a significant cause of the alleged violent green victimizations identified by Lynch and Stretesky

(2014) and other authors (Nurse 2016, Sollund 2015, White 2008). In reality, many of these harmful acts will be ignored by mainstream criminology and fall outside the enforcement actions of criminal justice systems; instead being considered by regulatory environmental enforcement structures. Thus, an entire class of offender (the corporation) and of offending (environmental harm) receives scant attention from the mainstream criminological gaze.

This chapter introduces the core focus of this book and identifies that much corporate environmental offending is not characterized as crime but instead consists of a range of wrongdoing, some of which is regulatory in nature or is dealt with through civil or administrative justice systems. This chapter introduces the book's central argument that corporate environmental offending is often *deliberate*, conducted within a corporate landscape where environmental noncompliance can sometimes be a form of business innovation and where regulatory regimes fail to address persistent offending (discussed further throughout this book). Arguably corporate environmental offending is a product of opportunity conditioned by poor monitoring regimes and weak enforcement environments (Situ and Emmons 2000), and a governmental approach to corporate wrongdoing that promotes risk-based or responsive regulation and sees prosecution as a last resort (Gouldson et al. 2009, Tombs and Whyte 2012). Accordingly, corporations understand that they will often be allowed to continue with polluting and noncompliant behavior and that fines and settlements are the likely enforcement response to environmental offending rather than criminal prosecution. Arguably, this is understandable given that corporations are generally legal actors given legitimacy as a consequence of various societal structures (e.g. paying tax on corporate earnings, rules of incorporation, commercial law, and government policy structures). Political considerations (discussed further in chapters 2 and 4) arguably dictate that corporations will generally be treated sympathetically (if not leniently) by justice systems and policy.

THE NATURE OF CORPORATE ENVIRONMENTAL HARM

This book is concerned with identifying and addressing corporate environmental harm in an age where arguably society is sleepwalking towards an environmental crisis (Hamilton 2015, Lynch and Stretesky 2014). The challenges inherent in contemporary green and environmental harm discourse include "industrial pollution of the air, water, and land, toxic waste sites, deforestation, species extinction, excessive pesticides use and pollution, climate change, the excessive use of fossil fuels, acid rain, a growing reliance on coal and oil, the environmental effects of drilling for oil or mining coal, the collapse of coral reefs and fisheries and so on" (Lynch and Stretesky 2014, 11). This list is not exhaustive, but it sets out a wide range of environmental threats and harms many of which are the consequences of lawful corporate activity carried out by corporations operating within legal neoliberal markets. However, Tombs and Whyte (2015) identify a range of activities that harm the environment including "illegal emissions to air, water and land; hazardous waste dumping; and illegal manufacturing processes" (2015, 47). They identify that recent estimates suggest around 800,000 premature deaths from air pollution (Cohen et al. 2005) and that "most pollution is produced by commercial activity" (Tombs and Whyte 2015, 49). Thus, they conclude that "corporations certainly produce most of the air pollution that threatens our health, economy and environment" (Tombs and Whyte 2015, 49).

The reality of corporate environmental harm is that its consequences are wide-reaching, affecting more than just the direct victims of street crime and impacting negatively on ecosystems, future generations, and the survival of many human and nonhuman animal species. Hall (2013) identifies that environmental harm has the potential for long-term negative impacts on human health (citing examples such as the Bhopal disaster, Chernobyl and the Deepwater Horizon Gulf oil spill where direct human harm was an immediate consequence). Environmental harm also has negative long-term economic, social, and security implications and is thus worthy of consideration by criminologists as both direct and indirect threat to human populations. Both Hall (2013) and Lynch and Stretesky (2014) identify that the exploitation of natural resources by corporations and states and the associated harms are often legal or at least distinctly not criminal. Corporations are also implicated in a range of other environmental harms considered externalities from their core activities. The following case study illustrates this point.

CASE STUDY: FRACKING AND ENVIRONMENTAL HARM IN THE UK

Gas extraction company Caudrilla has been alleged to have caused thirty-seven minor earthquakes at its Preston New Road site in Lancashire, UK since it recommenced hydraulic fracturing (fracking) operations in Autumn 2018 (Vaughan 2018). Wilson et al., (2018) identify that the British Geological Survey detected earthquakes just three days after fracking operations commenced at Caudrilla's site following a seven-year hiatus. The company's actions had previously been the subject of a legal action that raised concerns about the environmental damage that fracking might cause. In *Preston New Road Action Group v Secretary of State for Communities and Local Government and Caudrilla Bowland Ltd* [2017] EWHC 808 (Admin) local activists sought to challenge a decision that fracking should be allowed at Caudrilla's Lancashire site. Part of the appeal concerned whether the secretary of state's decision to allow fracking to proceed was flawed by inconsistency because he took into account the benefits of shale gas production but left out of account the harmful effects it would have. The activists also sought a ruling on whether the secretary of state failed to apply the "precautionary principle," in particular by discounting evidence of uncertainty over the possible effects of the development on human health and assuming that the regulatory regime would operate effectively (O'Riordan 1994). While the case involves some technical arguments concerning the operation of the UK's planning system that effectively regulates fracking, it also raises some wider issues concerning the nature and impact of corporate environmental harm. The precautionary principle argument raised by the Preston New Road campaigners relates to the principle of not allowing operations that *could* cause environmental harm to proceed, with the precautionary approach advising decision-makers to act pre-emptively to prevent possible environmental harm by denying approval for activities rather than waiting for conclusive scientific evidence (Laville 2017, Kriebel et al. 2001). The Planning Inspector who examined the initial refusal of planning permission acknowledged that fracking might cause environmental harm but concluded that the harm to the landscape would "only be temporary" (para 15 of the judgment). The environmental activists' legal counsel argued that in principle, there was no reason why the protection from harm afforded by the relevant planning policies should be withheld if the harm, perhaps serious, would last only a short time and then be removed or repaired. In any case, the activists argued that the harm would not be transient. It would last about two and a half years while the exploration works were in place, and the site would only be restored after that if the commercial production of shale gas did not go ahead. The judge in the original trial disagreed commenting that he could not accept an interpretation in which the policy is read as prohibiting *any* harm to the landscape [my emphasis], including temporary harm. Given that mineral development often entails the restoration of the land once extraction is finished, the judge concluded that it would be surprising "if the duration of the development, and the duration of any harm, was irrelevant to the overall assessment of harm for the purpose of [the policy]" (para 16 of the judgment). The appeal judge agreed with this view, acknowledging that while fracking may well cause environmental harm, this harm does not by itself mean that a fracking operation cannot continue. Elsewhere in the judgment, reference is made to the fact that planning policy does not prohibit "environmental impacts that would cause demonstrable harm" noting that if such harm cannot be eliminated, proposals in which harm is "minimized" may still be acceptable (para 27 of the judgment). Later in the same paragraph, there is further reference to environmental impacts being controlled in accordance with "current best practice and recognized standards" acknowledging that corporations' environmental harm can be deemed "acceptable" in a range of circumstances, not least where they relate to other "beneficial" economic activity.

The *Preston New Road Action Group* fracking case study identifies a core concern of corporate environmental harm, namely, the extent to which certain harm is allowed in the interests of production, consumption, and the continued operation of neoliberal markets such as the energy market. Campaigners and activists contend that proper operation of the precautionary principle would dictate that fracking should not be allowed given the uncertainty of its long-term effects (Keeler 2016). Arguably its short-term or immediate effects are already known in respect of the negative impacts of existing operations that have seen communities report problems with drinking water, health concerns, and damage to property (Finkel and Hays 2013, Tuller 2015, Kiely 2014). However, the counter argument is that fracking is necessary or desirable because of the need to identify new sources of energy and thus there are political considerations that favor allowing fracking to take place. In particular, decisions on allowing fracking take place in the context of considerations on the need for reducing high household energy bills and improving UK energy security (Beebeejaun 2013). The UK government is generally in favor of allowing fracking in the UK and encourages this area of corporate activity and investment by energy companies despite concerns about the possible environmental effects (Short and Szolucha 2019).

At an extreme level, corporate activities can cause ecocide (Higgins 2010) which "refers to extensive damage, destruction, or loss of the ecosystems of a given territory" (White 2017, 11). Such harm can be natural for example through pest infestation or naturally occurring environmental problems, or anthropocentric (man-made) activity. Waste crime, for example, has long been recognized as a key environmental issue and has been on the green criminological agenda for some time (Cass 1996, Ruggiero and South 2010). Waste crimes involving the treatment or disposal of waste in ways that breach international or domestic environmental legislation and cause harm or risk to the environment and human health and have also been linked to organized crime (Block and Scarpitti 1985). As a form of corporate economic crime linked to organized crime, waste crime is arguably readily accepted as serious crime or criminal activity requiring a sophisticated response involving criminal and other agencies (Barrett and White 2017). Becker (1968) argues that in any system of punishment, the penalty should be set equal to the net social cost of the crime divided by the probability of detection. His analysis identified that "the optimal amount of enforcement is shown to depend on, among other things, the cost of catching and convicting offenders, the nature of punishments—for example, whether they are fines or prison terms—and the responses of offenders to changes in enforcement" (Becker 1968, 170). Thus, the environmental harm caused by business has many dimensions and incorporates both direct harm; such as that caused by an environmentally damaging process that has immediate or direct effects such as the earthquakes caused by hydraulic fracturing operations (Marshall 2011, White 2011, Pantsios 2015, Vaughan 2018) through to the indirect effects of premature deaths caused by air pollution (Künzli et al. 2001,World Health Organization 2014, European Environment Agency 2016). But defining corporate environmental crime raises some challenges where the lines between harm and crime might be blurred.

Defining Corporate Environmental Crime

Gibbs and Simpson (2008) argue that the problem of corporate crime rates has been the subject of debate, speculation, and operationalization for decades, largely stemming from the complexity of measuring this type of crime. Carrabine (2017, 112) discussing perspectives on white collar crime identified crime as being "almost endemic in national and transnational corporations" suggesting that the range of corporate wrongdoing arguably requires enlarging the scope of criminology to consider a broader range of conduct. From the outset it should be made clear that the phrase "corporate environmental crime" risks being something of a misnomer. The reality of corporate environmental offending is such that much of the activities under discussion as corporate environmental "crime" are strictly speaking not crime but instead fall within a broader conception of corporate wrongdoing and noncompliant behavior. Situ and Emmons (2000, 2) identify a strict legalistic definition of crime as being "whatever the criminal code says it is" and encapsulate a strict definition of environmental crime as follows:

> An environmental crime is an unauthorized act or omission that violates the law and is therefore subject to criminal prosecution and criminal sanctions This offense harms or endangers people's physical safety as well as the environment itself. It serves the interests of either organizations—typically corporations—or individuals. (Situ and Emmons 2000, 3)

This definition clearly identifies environmental crime as solely a violation of existing law albeit it also requires that for something to be classed as an environmental crime it must be subject to criminal prosecution and criminal sanctions. The definition is arguably also confined to only the most serious of environmental offenses and would omit minor or associated offenses such as permit breaches, or other technical offenses that arguably cause no tangible harm and other activities that have somehow escaped the attention of legislators.

However, the reality is that much of the environmental harm caused by corporations would not meet this criminal law definition. Much environmental wrongdoing is carried out by legal actors and is classified within environmental legislation that, strictly speaking does not fall within the criminal law albeit the option for criminal penalties is available within some statutes. As Stallworthy notes, environmental law "is distinctly public law, with widespread regulation of activities, through substantive and procedural constraints; including process controls, emission limits, and environmental quality requirements" (2008, 4). The underlying principles are, thus, not ones of criminalization, instead they primarily allow continued exploitation of natural resources, subject to regulatory control. Thus, an activity could well be permitted but the offense is one of going beyond what the law and permits allow, which becomes a regulatory or administrative breach rather than a crime. Lynch and Stretesky (2014, 7) identify that the law allows corporations to emit certain types and volumes of pollution noting that while this activity may be legal it is not without harmful environmental consequences. Their argument is thus that "just because a behavior isn't defined as criminal behavior doesn't mean that there is no harm, and that the harm is minor, or that the harm is adequately defined in law" (Lynch and Stretesky 2014, 7). Accordingly, Lynch and Stretesky (2014) and indeed other green criminologists argue for a definition of environmental or green crime that considers crime from the perspective of harm and the impact on the environment rather than the narrow legal classification of crime.

The wider consideration of harm is arguably integral to examining and defining corporate crime through legal systems. Uhlmann (2009) identifies the complexity of (US) environmental law, noting that "environmental law raises conceptual and practical challenges even for respected scholars and experienced practitioners. Much of environmental regulation involves sophisticated and technologically advanced industrial processes. As a result, at least from a theoretical perspective, environmental law and criminal law could be difficult to integrate effectively" (Uhlmann 2009, 1232). Cohen (1992, 1059) identifies that "traditional legal theories posit that criminal punishment serves four goals: deterrence, incapacitation, rehabilitation and retribution" whilst noting that many of these goals can be achieved other than by reliance on the criminal law. In his discussion of environmental enforcement, Cohen notes for example that in the Exxon Valdez case,[1] the question of criminal liability was more controversial than that of liability for damage to private property under tort law for damages caused by the spill (1992, 1058). Cohen notes that the debate in this case focused on "whether or not Exxon was morally culpable for the spill" and that "despite the appearance of the spill as an accident the government sought criminal charges" on the grounds that Exxon's culpability went higher than simple negligence. Criminal law through its goal of identifying and bringing an offender to justice and punishing the harm and loss of marine life caused by the Exxon Valdez spill arguably demanded that an offender be made to pay. Thus, criminal prosecution of Exxon "reflected the moral sensibilities of the community" (Cohen 1992, 1059).

In part when defining corporate environmental crime, consideration of the remedy/sanction is appropriate. Cohen (1992, 1059) notes that "torts and crimes also have different remedies. Whereas tort remedies generally involve the compensation of victims and are designed to deter the tortfeaser, criminal convictions generally result in punitive sanctions which are designed primarily to punish." The criminal sanction is, thus, primarily aimed at retribution and deterrence more than it is at remedying harm which raises concerns about its effectiveness in dealing with environmental harm. This is especially the case in corporate environmental crime where a corporation's operation must, by necessity continue in order to generate profits. Thus, one challenge for criminal punishment is whether it can ever be truly effective where the punishment is meted out to individual staff that can be replaced, or where punishment is focused on a corporation that can afford to pay whatever fine is imposed. Evidence exists, for example, that corporations simply absorb the cost of regulatory action and fines as part of the cost of doing business (this is discussed in more detail in chapter 10's discussion of remedying corporate environmental harm). Thus, one question for addressing corporate environmental crime relates to the extent to which law and regulatory mechanisms can keep up with corporate practices (Wilson et al. 2018) and the resources available to the corporate offender. Environmental regulators may, for example, adopt market-based punishments as some of the case examples in this book illustrate.

Green criminology at its best attempts to both challenge and indeed overturn many common-sense notions of crime to reveal and challenge the reality of harms with wider social impact and negative consequences for the environment and human relations (Nurse 2013a). In the specific context of corporate environmental crime, green criminology is uniquely placed to promote news ways of thinking about our attitudes towards environmentally harmful corporate behavior and the illegal exploitation of natural resources as an integral part of mainstream criminal justice, albeit one worthy of dedicated study as a distinct aspect of criminality that goes beyond restrictive notions of deviance perceived as such from within the criminal law (Situ and Emmons 2000, Newburn 2017). However, green criminology is concerned with both crime and harm irrespective of the legal classification given to environmental harms (Hall 2016, Sollund 2015). As Lynch and Stretesky put it "green criminology is based on a premise, justified by scientific studies in a wide variety of disciplines, that green harms are the most important concerns in modern society because they cause the most harm, violence, damage and loss" (2014, 7). That such harms are frequently caused by corporate actors makes a compelling case for including corporate environmental crime and harm within green criminological inquiry (Hall 2016, White 2008). Green criminology's ecological justice perspective (Benton 1998) acknowledges that human beings are only one part of the planet, and that any system of justice needs to consider the wider biosphere and species which depend on nature. Thus, our justice systems need to also extend beyond binary considerations of legal and illegal actors or that of criminal and noncriminal actors, to consider where legal actors such as corporations engage in illegal activity. Within an ecological justice perspective there is scope to incorporate what is referred to as a consequentialist ethic; a theoretical conception concerned with goodness or badness as being more important than "rightness" or "wrongness" (Brennan and Lo 2008).

Thus, for the purposes of this book's discussion of corporate environmental crime, a more expansive definition of "environmental crime" is adopted, adapted from Situ and Emmons' (2000) definition and incorporating wider notions of harm and wrongdoing. Accordingly, this book's definition of corporate environmental crime refers to: any unauthorized act or omission that violates law, regulations, or license conditions and that is subject to penalty or sanction including sanctions imposed by regulatory or administrative measures. Corporate environmental crime in this definition relates to wrongdoing committed by business actors that harms or endangers people's physical safety, infringes on their environmental rights, and/or causes harm to or threatens the environmental itself and non-human nature.

Exploring Corporate Environmental Crime and Corporate Environmental Responsibility

Having established that corporations cause significant environmental harm and that this book is concerned with harm caused by a wide range of unlawful acts or omissions, the remainder of this book examines different dimensions on corporate environmental crime (as defined by this chapter) and what should be done to remedy the harm caused by corporations. Thus, this book explores both corporate crime as defined by the criminal law, and corporate wrongdoing considered by other forms of legislation but which causes substantial harm to the environment itself, ecosystems, and communities. Smith and Pangsapa (2009, 321) articulate the notion that corporations should have responsibility towards those affected by their actions which "was embedded in state regulation before globalization became such a burning issue" but remains a contested issue (discussed further in chapters 2 and 10). Thus, the notion of environmental responsibility under consideration is one that examines the majority of environmental harm, the manner in which corporate wrongdoing is defined by legal systems and how to address corporate environmental harm. These issues can be conceptualized into four key themes that are explored through the remainder of this book's discussion.

The first theme is that of Corporate Environmental Crime as "normalized" activity; the second is concerned with Criminal Justice and Corporate Environmental Harm; the third relates to Corporate Environmental Responsibility (CER) and State Responsibility; and the final theme is of Repairing Corporate Environmental Harm. Through the book's remaining chapters, these themes are examined via analysis of several case studies that illustrate how law and policy seeks to regulate corporate activity whilst simultaneously allowing corporations to exploit natural resources for commercial gain. The case examples discussed in this book also illustrate issues in regulatory and governance failure and raise questions concerning how justice systems should deal with corporate environmental crime.

Chapter 2 discusses what it means to be "green" within criminal justice and explores how corporate environmental crime is defined within green criminological discourse. Situating corporate environmental crime within green criminological debates, chapter 2 begins this book's exploration of the CER and State Responsibility theme by examining the responsibilities on states regarding protection of the environment and dealing with environmental crimes. However, the chapter also notes some problems with regulatory mechanisms used to deal with corporate environmental offending. In this regard, chapter 2 also applies the book's theme of Corporate Environmental Crime as "normalized" activity, noting that regulatory systems often allow corporations to carry on business as normal even when they are caught offending. Global North policy perspectives are also generally reluctant to criminalize corporate wrongdoing that results in environmental harm for both political and economic reasons.

Chapter 3 continues the "normalized activity" theme by examining the causes of corporate environmental criminality and exploring key debates concerning the reasons why corporate environmental crimes and noncompliance occur. The chapter also engages with theoretical discussions on environmental offending and engages with the book's conceptions around "greenwashing." Chapter 3 notes that the distinction between legal and illegal corporate activity is sometimes blurred, but also discusses how the legal frequently facilitates the illegal. Chapter 3 also considers basic notions of corporate environmental responsibility and the influences of neoliberal markets and masculinities as causes of corporate environmental crime.

Chapter 4 firmly develops the book's theme of CER and State Responsibility with a discussion of CER as a distinct concept and potential tool to improve

or develop good corporate environmental practice and environmental governance. The chapter also explores the book's theme of Criminal Justice and
Corporate Environmental Harm. Through a case study of the Gulf oil spill
and the enforcement and policy response to this environmental disaster, the
chapter critically evaluates how CER can be made more effective and examines how justice systems deal with environmental harm.

Chapter 5 of this book continues the Criminal Justice and Corporate
Environmental Harm theme and also examines aspects of the practical
application of CER within offending environments. The chapter examines
the extent to which corporate assertion of environmental credentials is often
a form of criminal entrepreneurship where corporations embrace voluntary
codes of self-practice and self-regulation while internally promoting the
drive for success and profitability and seeking to avoid the true costs of
environmental damage. Chapter 6 of the book further develops this critical
analysis by examining corporate exploitation of natural resources in the oil
and gas industries. It identifies the link between ostensibly legal use of natural
resources and the criminal activity associated with such large-scale corporate
operations as oil and gas exploration and the timber trade. Chapter 6 also illu-
minates the book's theme of Criminal Justice and Corporate Environmental
Harm and the challenges that exist in ensuring effective justice system
responses to corporate environmental harm. Globalization's increased flows
of people, products, and profits allow multinational corporations (MNCs)
to operate freely in Global South countries where regulatory controls may
be weaker than in the Global North and where public institutions (including
government bureaucracy and the judiciary) may be weak and susceptible to
economic pressure (Cox 1997, 51). Chapter 6 considers the extent to which
legal actors commit offenses that sometimes remain hidden as well as examining the general failure of justice systems to prevent or effectively punish
these acts. Thus, the theme of the legal facilitating the illegal is a core concern
of this chapter, examined through a case study of litigation against the major
oil companies for their activities in Africa.

The themes of CER and State Responsibility; and Repairing Corporate
Environmental Harm are discussed in chapter 7 which conducts an examination of biopiracy as a form of corporate environmental crime. In particular,
the chapter examines the actions of biotechnology corporations involved in
the exploitation of natural products with medicinal and healing properties in
a manner where doing so involves the exploitation of the resources of Global
South nations. South (2007) identifies how Western multinational corporations are dominant in exploiting natural resources often at the expense of the
rights of indigenous peoples. Supporters of western corporations' activities
call this "bio-prospecting," while opponents often refer to it as biopiracy
albeit this term is somewhat contested. However, chapter 7 argues that

biopiracy represents a crime of the powerful where illegal or at least unethical means are employed to pursue a corporation's goals, to the detriment of less powerful actors and stakeholders. The chapter also critically examines the advantages and disadvantages of dealing with biopiracy as a criminal justice issue rather than a civil law or commercial (business) law issue.

Chapter 8 continues with the themes explored in chapter 7 with an examination of corporate environmental crime and climate justice. White (2018a, 2018b) has argued for a climate change criminology, noting that climate change is undoubtedly one of the most significant threats facing mankind and represents a major form of environmental harm, placing it firmly within the remit of a broad environmental harm-based green criminology. Yet arguably, criminology has only recently paid attention to the issue despite scientific concern being expressed about global warming over several years. White's (2018b) detailed examination of climate change sets out a framework for considering climate change as a criminological issue, whilst simultaneously considering issues of social and ecological justice, inequality and analysis of power, and social interests at the center of its analysis. Chapter 8, whilst not as detailed as White's (2018b) book length analysis, similarly examines climate change as a criminological issue with a focus on the enforcement and regulation of corporate polluting activities linked to climate change. Tempus (2014) identifies environmental action through the courts as one route through which climate change might be addressed. But the effectiveness of climate change litigation is questionable and court action arguably fails to directly address breaches of greenhouse gas regulations although regulatory action which imposes non-criminal sanctions will likely be the mechanism through which such actions are practically addressed.

Chapter 9 examines the link between corporate environmental crime and infringements of human rights, in particular, the extent to which human rights norms can be applied to private business actors in order to minimize or provide redress for the environmental harms they cause. The chapter considers the extent to which international human rights norms apply to business activities that harm the environment and infringe on environmental rights, particularly those of marginalized and vulnerable communities. While chapter 9 inevitably draws on discussions concerning corporate environmental responsibility and the extent to which states provide for protection against harms committed by corporations, it is primarily concerned with the theme of Repairing Corporate Environmental Harm. Chapter 9 examines the extent to which human rights norms and guidelines concerning business' adherence to human rights principles and access to justice remedies work in practice. It does this primarily through examining how they are enforced and conducting analysis of the use of available mechanisms through which redress can be sought in respect of environmental harms caused by private business. The focus of this chapter is a case study of how contemporary UK and EU law and policy implements UN principles which specify how and why business should observe human rights, but the case study analysis is used to construct an argument concerning how human rights principles should be applied to business activities that infringe on the human rights and environmental rights of the communities in which Global North/Transnational corporations cause environmental harm.

Chapter 10 concludes the book with an explicit discussion of theory and practice concerning remedying corporate environmental crime. The chapter examines the topic of restorative justice as applied to corporate environmental crime and contains a case study of regulatory action taken against the major utilities (water) companies in the United Kingdom, through which regulators have attempted to implement the polluter pays principle which is enshrined in UK and EU law. This case study illustrates the application of market-based regulatory action and summarizes the book's core argument that corporate environmental offending is inevitable given the operation of neoliberal markets and the failure of regulatory systems to prevent and address corporate environmental harm.

The organization of this book and the detail of these chapters are intended to situate corporate environmental crime within green criminological discourse that considers harms and the impact and consequences of anthropocentric activity, rather than the focus on (legally defined) crime that is the traditional focus of criminology. Ragnhild Sollund has written that "because of the multivariate character of problems relating to eco-global crimes, it is necessary to expand the boundaries of criminology as a discipline" (2012). In making the case for green criminology, Matthew Hall (2016) identified that green criminological discourse "has progressed beyond neo-Marxism to embrace concepts of risk, social harm and various models of justice." White (2018a) argues that systemic destruction of the environment is a consequence of global capitalism, and the agents of such destruction are frequently transnational corporations. In reality the nature of capitalist systems is to fragment nature and exploit resources and arguably environmental protection laws are designed to do this, allowing for a balance between protection of natural resources and their continued exploitation. The reality of neoliberal markets and a human-centered view of nature as being a resource for human benefit potentially undermines the willingness of legislators and states to deal with issues such as climate change. As Lynch and Stretesky have previously stated, "the societies that tend to be the least willing to respond to environmental problems are those that cause the most environmental damage because of the economic gains involved" (2014, 23).

NOTE

1. The Exxon Valdez oil spill occurred on March 24, 1989, at Prince William Sound off the coast of Alaska. The oil tanker Exxon Valdez owned by the Exxon oil corporation ran aground on Bligh Sound. The accident resulted in the spilling of nearly 11,000,000 gallons of crude oil. The incident was considered to be a major environmental disaster and eventually polluted around 1,300 miles of shoreline. Piatt et al. (1990) indicate that more than 30,000 dead birds of ninety species were retrieved from the polluted areas by August 1, 1989. Thousands of workers and volunteers were involved in cleaning up the spill which eventually killed a wide range of native wildlife. In addition to birds, otters, whales, bald eagles, salmon, and herring were affected and persistent, toxic subsurface oil exposure continued to kill wildlife more than a decade after the incident (Petersen et al. 2003).

Chapter 2

Critical Perspectives on Environmental Crime, Green Criminology, and Corporate Environmental Offending

Chapter 1 set out the basics of this book's exploration of corporate environmental crime, indicating that environmental wrongdoing has arguably become normalized behavior for corporations. This chapter takes a critical look at environmental crime and corporate environmental offending, exploring what it means to be "green" within criminal justice. The chapter also examines how corporate environmental crime is defined within green criminological discourse where the behavior of corporations and the impact of their actions can be subject to more than one interpretation.

White (2012a, 15) identifies that "the systematic causal chains that underpin much environmental harm are located at the level of the global political economy—within which the transnational corporation stands as the central social force" and arguably corporations have considerable influence over legal and political structures. Transnational corporations are dominant social and economic actors with considerable influence over political and legal considerations on environmental protection. While legislative regimes may not directly reflect *individual* corporate interests, they frequently incorporate the underlying principle that corporations and neoliberal markets should be allowed to continue operating with minimal state interference (Stallworthy 2008, Lynch and Stretesky 2014). This sets up a potential conflict between the need for continued production and the free operation of markets (discussed further in chapter 3) and the desirability of protecting the environment both for its intrinsic value and to ensure the preservation of environmental resources as a public good that should be protected for the benefit of future generations (Weston and Bollier 2013, Curry 2011). The public good of environmental protection may conflict with other societal benefits (e.g. continued consumption) and the extent to which market and commercial concerns cause environmental harm is discussed further in chapter 3. Prior to that discussion, this chapter examines the responsibilities on states regarding environmental crimes and the regulatory mechanisms in place to deal with corporate environmental offending. The chapter provides an overview of western corporate environmental regulatory regimes and examines Lynch and Stretesky's (2014) arguments that environmental crime constitutes the most serious threat to human populations but is largely ignored by criminal justice systems. In their book *Exploring Green Criminology: Toward a Green Criminological Revolution*, Lynch and Stretesky argue that mainstream criminology has all but ignored environmental crime and so has failed to adequately address environmental threats. This chapter's application of green criminological perspectives to the broad context of corporate environmental offending, situates analysis of corporate environmental crime within discussions of the harm caused by corporate environmental wrongdoing and noncompliance with environmental regulations. It also considers how some activities are defined as crime while others are not.

THE MEANING OF GREEN

Green criminologist Rob White identifies that concern with environmental crime requires considering the local and the global "and to ponder the ways in which such harms transcend the normal boundaries of jurisdiction, geography and social divide" (2012a, 15). White's analysis identifies that "green crimes" are frequently transnational in nature although criminology arguably lacks a clear definition of what is meant by "green" crimes. Definitional problems exist not just because of the wording of legislation, but also because of socially constructed notions of the acceptable use or exploitation of nature and natural resources. Thus, what is illegal environmental exploitation in one state may be acceptable use of natural resources in another. Accordingly, legal systems do not consistently define environmental harm as "green crime" as perceptions of crime can vary from one jurisdiction to another. Lynch and Stretesky (2003) also identified that the term "green" was not always clearly defined even in green criminological discourse. Potentially any crime of a distinctly environmental nature (e.g. wildlife trafficking, pollution) and that has a direct green characteristic would be incorporated into a definition of green crime. However, arguably any crime that indirectly affects the environment or non-human nature or that has links to the environment could also potentially be defined as a green crime. Thus, arguably all unlawful actions of water utility companies whose remit is to provide safe and clean drinking water and to manage water as a valuable natural resource risk being green crimes given the company's reason for existence is a distinctly environmental one. One could argue, for example, that tax fraud committed by a water company is a green crime as by definition the company's actions all relate to the environment. However criminal justice systems and environmental law likely consider a narrower definition, one that is shaped by legal classification of environmental crime according to Situ and Emmons' (2000) definition discussed in chapter 1.

Critical analysis of corporate environmental crime and understanding of its contemporary characteristics requires a more detailed analysis of such concepts and definitions. Attfield (2016, 1) identifies that not everybody means the same thing when they talk about the "environment," thus defining corporate environmental crime and what criminal justice systems mean when discussing the environment and environmental harm requires clarification. Stallworthy (2008, 2) turns to European law for clarification of how the environment is defined, using the following definition of a:

Combination of elements whose complex inter-relationships make up the settings, the surroundings and the conditions of life of the individual and of society as they are and as they are felt. (EC Council Regulation 1872/84, Action by the Community Relating to the Environment, 1984)

This definition is arguably all-encompassing, including Attfield's notion of the "global environment" which means all natural systems of the planet rather than just the environs or surroundings (2016, 3) as well as other definitions that include ecosystems and non-human nature, or landscapes (Greider and Garcovich 1994). Accordingly, this book's starting point for considering the meaning of green within definitions of green crime and green harm incorporates a broad conception of interrelationships albeit criminal justice systems are generally reluctant to consider the environment as a crime victim or of having "interest" in environmental cases (Starik 1995, Stone 1985). However, Stallworthy (2008, 4) argues that the dominant feature of environmental law is "widespread statutory regulation of activities, through substantive and procedural constraints: including process controls, emission limits, and environmental quality requirements," measures that all appear somewhat regulatory in nature. Accordingly, "permitting, inspection, sanctioning and enforcement" are the key legal tools being deployed (Stallworthy 2008, 4) rather than the detection, apprehension, and punishment tools routinely employed by criminal justice systems. These measures are arguably appropriate to the behaviors of legal actors such as corporations. Such regulatory measures are potentially assigned to assist corporations with understanding legal principles that are designed to offer a level of environmental protection whilst still providing corporations with the ability to operate freely within neoliberal markets.

To illustrate how environmental legal systems work in practice, Stallworthy (2008) next turned to the United Kingdom's Environmental Protection Act 1990. The Act's broad remit is to provide for improved control of pollution arising from commercial activities. The Act also contains measures relating to the collection and disposal of waste and restates (and clarifies) the law defining statutory nuisances. It also seeks to improve measures for dealing with such nuisances, to make provisions relating to such waste; to restate the law defining statutory nuisances and improve the summary procedures for dealing with them, to provide for the termination of the existing controls over offensive trades or businesses, and to provide for the extension of the (UK) Clean Air Acts to prescribed gases. The environmental protection regime in the UK is complex but the Environmental Protection Act 1990 essentially deals with pollution and associated harm as an environmental protection problem. There is a basic international law principle that states should protect human rights (discussed later in this chapter and in chapter 9) which can include a right to peaceful enjoyment of one's property.[1] Arguably the state does have a role in environmental protection and associated environmental rights through monitoring and enforcement of environmental protection legislation such as clean air acts or noise nuisance provisions, breaches of which could impact on peaceful enjoyment of property. The UK's Environmental Protection Act 1990, for example, while not explicitly human rights legislation creates regulatory and enforcement frameworks to deal with emissions and other environmental harm caused by nuisance. Such domestic legislation generally allows regulators to act where a corporation fails to adhere to pollution or emission limits. Thus, regulators have tools that allow them to require remedial action, such that corporations may need to modify their processes to reduce environmental harm. Local authorities have an environmental monitoring role under the Act such that affected citizens can claim that their "environmental rights" have been breached and can ask local authorities to take enforcement action without incurring costs themselves. Thus, arguably environmental statutes provide for a remedy in respect of certain environmental rights and may contain criminal and civil sanctions although "civil penalties are most typically involved as the legal remedy against environmental wrongdoers. Criminal penalties are usually invoked only when environmental statutes have been willfully or knowingly broken" (Situ and Emmons, 2000, 38). While practical enforcement of such measures may be predominantly directed at low-level emissions such as fumes or smoke that exceed permit levels, they provide a means for enforcers to address harms such as pollution and nuisance activities that have a cumulative effect and negative impact on the right to live in a healthy environment (see discussion in chapter 10).

Lynch and Stretesky (2003) identify that various definitions of "green" can be involved in discussions of "green crime" including a definition closely aligned with corporate interests and considerations surrounding green environmentalism. A contrasting environmental justice definition (Schlosberg, 2007) is arguably concerned with equality in respect of access to justice and access to environmental resources. The environmental justice movement that originated in the United States (Schlosberg 2007, Bullard 1994) has concerned itself with environmental inequality and environmental racism (Taylor 2000, Cole and Foster 2001) and the power of social movements to incorporate race, class, and gender elements into environmental justice. In particular, the environmental justice movement has sought to end the types of discrimination that have been visited upon vulnerable communities, such as communities of color and indigenous communities who are disproportionately affected by corporate activities that cause pollution (Mohai et al. 2009, Bullard 2000). Previous research (Nurse 2016, Cole and Foster 2001) identifies that various commentators have used the term "environmental racism" to denote the manner in which ethnic minority groups and indigenous people disproportionately suffer from lack of access to environmental resources. Ethnic minority groups are also disproportionately affected by the location of toxic factories, pollution, and waste sites in their neighborhoods and the degradation of their environment which sometimes represents the *deliberate* targeting of communities of color for environmentally damaging operations (Chavis 1991). Environmental racism contends that negative environmental consequences of business activity frequently impacts communities of color more than Caucasians despite the general principles of environmental law that are intended to provide for equal access to the environment (discussed further later). Hall et al. (2017, 1) identify that the criminal law is increasingly used to regulate environmentally harmful activities and thus "a mainstream administrative criminology has had to acknowledge such crimes within its remit" whilst green criminology has continued to grow as a discipline and to develop its consideration of corporate environmental crime.

Key Aspects of Environmental Law

International law is of significance in respect of identifying shared values between states; particularly the basic idea that the environment should be protected, and that excessive environmental damage should be subject to some form of sanction. Thus, environmental law, particularly in the form of treaties, sets out general expectations as well as specific commitments that states are required to abide by and should implement in national legislation. Nurse (2015) identifies that a range of international environmental law measures seek to achieve everything from preventing the international transfer of toxic waste through to protecting migratory wildlife and requiring states to take measures to ensure such species survival. However, Stallworthy (2008,

8) argues that "environmental commitments under international law are typically in the form of "soft" law, which has no binding effect and lacks both specificity and enforceability." Stallworthy also suggests that international environmental law is primarily aspirational; setting out principles that might develop into specific laws whilst allowing national sovereignty and a socially constructed notion of environmental protection to be retained. National sovereignty remains important given that states are often required to implement international law through their own domestic legislation which can filter international principles to take account of cultural and social sensibilities. Thus, laws on pollution may well differ between countries, but so too may their enforcement in terms of the agencies employed, the wording and nature of offenses and the sanctioning regime. Environmental enforcement might consist of a mixed (civil and criminal) approach in one country or a strict criminal approach in another; dependent on the perceived level of the problem, the influence of lobby, and political groups and nature of the justice system itself.

Legal instruments such as international treaties are rarely self-sufficient (Pirjatanniemi 2009), requiring implementation through national legislation before they become effective. As a result, arguably states comply with international environmental law only to the extent to which doing so serves national interests and local governance needs. Accordingly, flexibility exists in how states approach their international environmental law obligations and how they implement the requirements of law commensurate with the idea that states have autonomy and discretion over how best to exploit national resources (Nurse 2015, Stallworthy 2008). This is especially true in respect of "soft" international law which is not directly enforceable, but which sets out shared standards or aspirations for states, albeit these may be subject to varied interpretations commensurate with state interests. For example, White and Heckenberg (2014) identify that in relation to wildlife trade, the function of law is to define legal notions of harm and criminality and not to provide for the health and well-being of animals. In this regard, the logic of international wildlife law "is not simply to protect endangered species because they are endangered; it is to manage these 'natural resources' for human use in the most equitable and least damaging manner" (White and Heckenberg 2014, 133). Thus, exploitation of natural resources is generally legal (Stallworthy 2008) and offenses occur primarily when such exploitation exceeds the limits set by laws and regulations or fails to comply with the specific requirements of governance systems, often dominated by licensing and permit systems. In this regard, political sensibilities also govern the regulation of corporate activities that might harm the environment, requiring a balancing act between corporate and political interests and environmental protection. Such sensibilities also govern what actions are criminalized. Ruhl (1997) set out (six) basic principles of environmental law which contend that 1) environmental law should be based on principles of libertarianism (freedom of contract and markets). Thus there should 2) also be limited acceptance of regulatory restraint, while 3) regulatory approaches should balance (market) interests with minimizing environmental harm. Ruhl's principles also indicate a preference for 4) the operation of substantive environmental law through the use of sustainability and precautionary principles and 5) an adherence to environmental justice and the sharing of costs and benefits among citizens. Ultimately Ruhl proposed 6) a deep green perspective prioritizing ecological over human interests which arguably is enshrined in the basic texts and principles of international environmental law.

Environmental Protection and International Law

International environmental law provides a framework setting out the obligations on states in respect of legal standards for environmental protection through both "hard" law in the form of written agreements or principles which are directly enforceable by national or international bodies; and "soft" law—a range of different measures including codes of conduct, resolutions, agreements, commitments, and joint statements. In considering how environmental law constrains the actions of corporations, there is a need to consider both hard and soft law measures including: international environmental protection treaties; EU or state law and policy; national environmental and biodiversity law and national and local environmental policy. In addition, societal expectations, public opinion, and political considerations influence the legislative and regulatory environment that corporations will operate under.

While it is beyond the scope of this book to provide for a comprehensive analysis of environmental law, some principles are worth setting out to explain the policy environment in which corporate activity operates and ultimately is regulated. The need for international environmental protection was recognized in the 1972 UN Declaration on the Environment (the Stockholm Declaration).

- Principle 1 of the Declaration states that man has the fundamental right to freedom, equality, and adequate conditions of life, in an environment of a quality that permits a life of dignity and well-being, and he bears a solemn responsibility to protect and improve the environment for present and future generations.
- Principle 2 states that the natural resources of the earth, including the air, water, land, flora, and fauna and especially representative samples of natural ecosystems, must be safeguarded for the benefit of present

and future generations through careful planning or management, as appropriate.
- Principle 5 of the Declaration specified that: the nonrenewable resources of the earth must be employed in such a way as to guard against the danger of their future exhaustion and to ensure that benefits from such employment are shared by all mankind.

These provisions create a basic framework linking man's fundamental rights and freedoms with the quality of the environment. This arguably creates the principle of sustainable development and identifies that while exploitation of natural resources is generally permissible, such exploitation needs to consider limiting any use that impacts negatively on future generations and causes serious depletion of natural resources. For oil and gas extraction industries, for example, Principle 5 could be interpreted as meaning that production should be limited to that which can be sustainably managed. Principle 17 of the Declaration identified that: appropriate national institutions must be entrusted with the task of planning, managing, or controlling the environmental resources of states with a view to enhancing environmental quality. Thus, states are required to put in place governance procedures to ensure that environmental resources are not just maintained at existing levels but can be improved. A principle of limiting corporate exploitation of natural resources is indicated as a necessity, and the principle articulates the need for planning and managing environmental resources in a sustainable way. Principle 21 of the Declaration specifies that: states have, in accordance with the Charter of the United Nations and the principles of international law, the sovereign right to exploit their own resources pursuant to their own environmental policies, and the responsibility to ensure that activities within their jurisdiction or control do not cause damage to the environment of other states or of areas beyond the limits of national jurisdiction.

The Universal Declaration on Human Rights expands on this with three specific articles:

- Article 22 states that everyone has the right to social security and is entitled to realization of the economic, social, and cultural rights indispensable for his dignity and the free development of his personality.
- Article 25 states that everyone has the right to a standard of living adequate for the health and well-being of himself and of his family, including food, clothing, housing, and medical care and necessary social services.
- Article 27 specifies that everyone has the right freely to participate in the cultural life of the community, to enjoy the arts, and to share in scientific advancement and its benefits.

While the Universal Declaration on Human Rights does not provide for a specific environmental right its practical application (linked to the principles of the 1972 Declaration) has been one of positive interpretation that considers how standards of living and right to access the benefits of society are inextricably linked. This being the case, the right to live in a healthy environment and to have an adequate standard of living that is dependent on a healthy environment can be strongly inferred and has been directly written into some state's constitutions.

Following on from the 1972 Declaration, the UN General Assembly adopted a World Charter for Nature in 1982 which contains the following five principles of conservation:

1. Nature shall be respected and its essential processes should be unimpaired;
2. Population levels of wild and domesticated species should be at least sufficient for their survival and habitats should be safeguarded to ensure this;
3. Special protection should be given to the habitats of rare and endangered species and the five principles of conservation should apply to all areas of land and sea;
4. Man's utilization of land and marine resources should be sustainable and should not endanger the integrity or survival of other species; and
5. Nature shall be secured against degradation caused by warfare or other hostile activities.

In principle, the UN Charter provides a mechanism for protecting the environment (and animals) from harm by providing a conservation framework that requires *active* protection of nature. Similar to the provisions of the 1972 Declaration, the principles of the UN Charter provide the framework for legislation or regulation that limits excessive exploitation of natural resources and provides that any commercial use of natural resources should be sustainable. However, in practice implementation of the Charter relies on national environmental protection and biodiversity laws that contain conservation enforcement mechanisms. However, Sections 21–24 of the Charter provide authority for individuals to enforce international conservation laws that could provide for some environmental protection and has been used by NGOs as a basis on which to conduct direct action to prevent animal harm (Nurse 2013, Roeschke 2009).

Regional environmental legislation also exists. For example, the Treaty on the Functioning of the European Union provides a framework for environmental protection across the EU. Minimum rules exist on penalties for environmental offenses in accordance with Article 175 of the Treaty establishing the EC. Member States have to ensure that any act committed intentionally or out of serious negligence which breaches community rules on protecting the environment is treated as a criminal offense. EU legislation includes provisions prohibiting the following: the unauthorized discharge of hydrocarbons, waste oils, or sewage sludge into water and the emission of a certain quantity of dangerous substances into the air, soil, or water; the treatment, transport, storage, and elimination of hazardous waste; the discharge of waste on or into land or into water, including the improper operation of a landfill site; the possession and taking of, or trading in protected wild fauna and flora species; the deterioration of a protected habitat; and trade in ozone-depleting substances.

The EU's policy environment for protection of the environment is one that aims to set general quality standards related to the state of the environment and that guide the overall development of coherent policy approaches internationally. The European Environment Agency (2015) also identifies that EU environmental policy seeks to set overall targets related to environmental pressures (often including a breakdown either by country or economic sector, or both) and to formulate specific policies that address pressure points, drivers, sectors, or standards. This action aims to identify environmentally harmful activities or threats to environmental protection and to implement policy to address these harms. EU environmental protection policy is broadly set out in Article 174(1) of the EU Treaty[2] which specifies that European Union policy on the environment shall contribute to pursuing a range of objectives including: preserving, protecting, and improving the quality of the environment; protecting human health; prudent and rational utilization of natural resources; and promoting international measures aimed at dealing with regional or worldwide environmental problems. The Treaty identifies climate change as a particular focus of policy attention, indicating its importance as a perceived contemporary environmental threat. EU policy on protection of the environment also aims for what is described in the Treaty as a "high level of protection" but one that takes into account diversity within the European region and the reality that the needs of environmental protection will differ in the 27 Member States.[3] The EU Treaty makes clear that a principle of EU policy is that EU environmental protection policy is based on the precautionary principle and on the principles that preventive action should be taken, that environmental damage should as a priority be rectified at source and that the polluter should pay for the environmental harm they cause.

The body of EU environmental law—also known as the environmental acquis—amounts to more than 300 directives, regulations, and decisions. Recent EU environmental policy initiatives address climate change, loss of biodiversity, unsustainable use of natural resources, and environmental pressures on health. Article 3 of the Treaty on the European Union specifies that the EU "aims to work for the sustainable development of Europe based on balanced economic growth and price stability, a highly competitive social market economy, aiming at full employment and social progress and a high level of protection and improvement of the quality of the environment." Arguably this is an aspirational approach, but the EU's 7th Environment Action Programme goes further stating that:

> In 2050 we live well, within the planet's ecological limits. Our prosperity and healthy environment stem from an innovative, circular economy where nothing is wasted and where natural resources are managed sustainably and biodiversity is protected, valued and restored in ways that enhance our society's resilience. Our low-carbon growth has long been decoupled from resource use, setting the pace for a safe and sustainable global society.

The policy framework outlined here has implications for the activities of corporations by creating a policy and enforcement environment that broadly seeks to achieve environmental protection alongside economic growth, thus the EU's 7th Environmental Action Programme sets out as its key objectives: to protect, conserve, and enhance the Union's natural capital; to turn the Union into a resource-efficient, green, and competitive low-carbon economy; and to safeguard EU citizens from environment-related pressures and risks to health and well-being. To achieve these goals, EU policy intends to achieve better implementation of legislation whilst seeking better information by improving the knowledge base and more and wiser investment for environment and climate policy. This also requires full integration of environmental requirements and considerations into other policies thus EU law routinely imposes a framework of planning and reporting obligations on Member States. Member States must plan for implementation of their environmental obligations; they must report on their performance, explaining failures to comply, as well as the lawful use of derogations and exceptions to the primary compliance obligation; and they must explain how compliance will be maintained or achieved in the future. The plans and reports are public documents which are sent to the European Commission.[4] These responsibilities pervade EU environmental law (Lee 2017). The EU requires criminal penalties to be effective, proportionate, and dissuasive and to apply both to persons convicted of breaching community law as well as persons involved in such offenses or inciting others to commit them. Thus, an obligation exists on states to ensure effective environmental protection and which arguably regulates Member State environmental protection and failure to provide such protection. In the field of international environmental law, a range of different laws both national and international prohibit specific actions deemed to harm the environment (Schaffner 2011). However environmental laws also incorporate the idea of sustainability a concept that identifies that use of natural resources is permitted only so far as those resources (including wildlife) are not exhausted. Generally, states have an obligation to prevent environmental crime and to create a system of sanctions (or punishments) in respect of environmental crime and to also provide for a system of monitoring and investigating environmental offenses (as EU policy illustrates). The extent to which a state has effective environmental law, regulation, and enforcement systems is crucial in addressing environmental crime given that weak enforcement regimes are considered a primary cause of environmental crime (Situ and Emmons 2000).

Environmental Offenses and Human Rights

While often not specifically enshrined in the criminal law, rights relating to the environment are spread across a number of instruments including: the Universal Declaration on Human Rights; the International Covenant on Economic Social and Cultural Rights; the International Covenant on Economic Social and Cultural Rights; the Convention on the rights of the child and within various case law and national legislation. These and other instruments contain the following broad environmental rights:

1. Right to ecologically sustainable development
2. Right to an adequate standard of living including access to safe food and water
3. Rights of children to live in an environment suitable for physical and mental development
4. Right to participation in environmental decision making.
5. Right of access to education and information including information on the links between health and the environment

Principles 1 and 2 of the UN Declaration on the Environment (1972, referred to earlier in this chapter) set out a basic framework linking man's fundamental rights and freedoms with the quality of the environment. While the environment is not mentioned as a specific right within the Universal Declaration on Human Rights, the Declaration has been interpreted positively to consider how standards of living and right to access the benefits of society are inextricably linked, as the following quote illustrates:

If you deliberately dump toxic waste in someone's community or disproportionately exploit their natural resources without adequate consultation and compensation, clearly you are abusing their rights. . . . changes in the environment can have a significant impact on our ability to enjoy our human rights. In no other area is it so clear that the actions of nations, communities, businesses and individuals can so dramatically affect the rights of others—because damaging the environment can damage the rights of people, near and far, to a secure and healthy life. (Office of the UN High Commissioner for Human Rights 1996–2019)

Thus, a conception that environmental crime impacts negatively on human (environmental) rights exists, so too does concern about disproportionate exploitation of natural resources. Generally, under human rights conventions, states are required to act to positively uphold rights or to ensure that they are interfered with only so far as is necessary. Thus, human rights conventions and national human rights law potentially provide additional weapons in the environmental protection toolkit. The European Convention on Human Rights, for example, does not specifically provide for a right to live in a healthy environment but manages to achieve this goal by engaging several of its individual rights. Article 2 (right to life), Article 8 (respect for privacy and family life), Protocol 1, Article 1 (the right to peaceful enjoyment of possessions and property), and even Article 6 (the right to a fair hearing) have all been used in cases before the European Court of Human Rights (ECtHR) to develop the idea of a right to a healthy environment that public authorities (e.g. the state and local government) are required to uphold. These issues and the application of human rights norms to corporate activity are discussed in more detail in chapter 9.

Crimes of the Powerful and Corporate Environmental Crime

Sutherland identified "white collar crime" as being a crime committed "by a person of high status in the course of his occupation" (1949, 9). The principle can be applied to organizations as well as individuals and can include the activities of lawful corporate actors who engage in unlawful activities. Corporate environmental crime is often a crime of the powerful, committed by corporations, organized crime groups, and others who constitute powerful social actors with access to capital and the benefits of globalized markets (Lynch and Stretesky 2014, South and Wyatt 2011). Situ and Emmons (2000) identify that environmental crime is predominantly a civil matter; in other words, fines and administrative penalties are the main technique for dealing with environmental crime. The reason given for this is a perceived lack of effective international law and the reliance on national (state) legislators to define what environmental crime is and how it should be dealt with. The result is often that environmental crime is not seen as a priority criminal justice issue. However, Lynch and Stretesky (2014) point out that "green harms are the most important concerns in modern society because they cause the most harm, violence, damage and loss." While environmental harm is frequently the result of lawful activity, Lynch and Stretesky argue that the wide-reaching impacts of environmental harm makes it worthy of dedicated criminological attention which it seldom receives.

As White and Heckenberg (2014) indicate, state failure to effectively protect the environment is or should be criminal. A wide range of environmental obligations are imposed on states under international law and are also implicit on states as part of customary international law which sets out expected levels of state action in various areas (Bodansky 1995). Thus, a failure to provide for effective environmental protection arguably represents a state crime. National justice systems are primarily concerned with individual offenders and are rarely adequate to deal with state failures thus an international justice system has been created. However, the extent to which that system effectively deals with state failures is questionable given that it often relies on other states to be affected and on their willingness to bring an action at an international level.

Green Environmental Crime as "Normalized" Activity

Chapter 1 identified that environmental harms committed by corporations are a core concern of green criminology. This book explores the theme of corporate environmental crime as normalized activity noting that corporate environmental harm is widespread, even though such harm is not always the consequence of crime or illegal activity.

However, where crime does occur, corporations may engage in a variety of explanations to justify illegal activity. Hall (2015, 86) explains that Sykes and Matza's (1957) neutralization theory "has been applied to corporations to explain their use of techniques to deny responsibility, along with any injury and victimizations, caused by their activities." Matza's drift theory (1964) also provides an explanation for how and why delinquents often accept a moral obligation to be bound by the law but can drift in and out of delinquency. Matza suggested that people live their lives fluctuating between total freedom and total restraint, drifting from one extreme of behavior to another. While they may accept societal norms, they develop a special set of justifications for their behavior which allows them to justify behavior that violates social norms. These techniques of neutralization (Sykes and Matza 1957, Eliason 2003) allow delinquents to express guilt over their illegal acts but also to rationalize between those whom they can victimize and those they cannot. This means that offenders are not immune to the demands of conformity but can find a way to rationalize when and where they should conform and when it may be acceptable to break the law. Arguably such considerations also apply to corporate activity. Indeed, Hall suggests that Braithwaite (1991) applied a form of strain theory "to the corporation arguing that corporations will employ dubious and illegal methods to maximize profits when more legitimate methods are closed to them" (2015, 86).

Chapter 3 discusses the causes of corporate environmental crime in more detail.

NOTES

1. This right is contained in Article 1 of the First Protocol of the European Convention on Human Rights. This imposes an obligation on the state not to: interfere with peaceful enjoyment of property; deprive a person of their possessions; or subject a person's possession to control.

2. In the Official Journal of the European Union (Volume 51), original Article 174 of TEC becomes Article 191 of the Consolidated Versions of the Treaty on European Union and the Treaty on the Functioning of the European Union (2008/C 115/01).

3. The number of EU Member States is correct as of time of writing in July 2021, following the UK's departure from the EU.

4. The European Commission is the EU's executive arm which implements the decisions of the European Parliament and the Council of the EU. The Commission is responsible for drawing up legislative proposals and enforcing EU legislation.

Chapter 3

The Causes of Corporate
Environmental Crime
and Criminality

This chapter examines the causes of corporate environmental criminality by examining key debates concerning the reasons why corporate environmental crimes and noncompliant behavior occur. The chapter also engages with theoretical discussions on environmental offending; applying criminological theory and prior research to corporate environmental crime. Conventional criminology is perhaps dominated by discussions of street crime and serious offending related to crimes of violence, sexual offenses, and the activities of organized crime. It is also largely anthropocentric in nature, primarily focused on human concerns and human victims. By contrast, much environmental crime is corporate in nature and concerns the behavior of legal actors, legitimate corporations engaged in lawful, state-supported activities albeit these activities cause harm to the environment and non-human nature. Thus, immediate differences can be found between corporate environmental crime and mainstream crime in conceptions of both offender and criminality. Offenders in mainstream crime are generally regarded as deviants by both society and criminal justice agencies, whereas corporate environmental offenders are frequently characterized as having committed technical, regulatory offenses and are often not subject to the attention of mainstream criminal justice agencies (Stallworthy 2008). This chapter discusses these issues, noting that the distinction between the legal and illegal is sometimes blurred, but also noting that the legal often facilitates the illegal. This chapter discusses corporate environmental offending primarily in respect of pollution and hazardous and toxic waste although brief preliminary mention is made of corporate wrongdoing associated with the oil and gas extraction industries, the timber trade, and biopiracy (which are covered in later chapters). The chapter explores the influences of neoliberal markets and masculinities as causes of corporate environmental crime.

CONCEPTUALIZING CORPORATE OFFENDING

Crime is arguably a social construction where what gets classified as crime is subject to a range of social and political considerations. Thus the criminal law "is an aspect of public law and relates to conduct which the state considers with disapproval and which it seeks to control and/or eradicate" (Slapper and Kelly 2017, 8). Definitional issues may also be important and "the processes of criminalization and decriminalization impact on perceptions and responses to environmental harm" (White 2008, 113). Thus, activities that might be considered to be part of the "normal" functioning of corporations are unlikely to be prohibited by law as crimes. But deliberate acts by individual actors for personal gain or with clear intent to harm the environment may well be criminalized. Actions that interfere with legitimate property rights (e.g. poaching of game) are also likely to be criminalized. Our definitions of "crime" thus take into account a range of purposes and in the environmental sphere can incorporate protection of the environment and non-human nature, limitations on the exploitation of environmental resources, and the prohibition of specific acts considered to be harmful or undesirable. Accordingly environmental crime definitions change over time.

In 2005, the UK's House of Commons Environmental Audit Committee conducted an analysis of corporate environmental crime in the UK. The Committee noted that the causes and nature of corporate environmental crime were varied and that:

> The crime may occur because the business concerned is ignorant of its environmental obligations. It may also occur all too often as a result of negligent behavior, for example, where businesses are poorly managed, staff are inadequately trained or equipment and infrastructure has not been maintained to the required standard, allowing a pollution incident to occur. But perhaps the most depressing cause is when corporate environmental crime is the result of a deliberate and intentional illegal act, a decision taken in the full knowledge that the act is illegal and will result in environmental harm. (House of Commons Environmental Audit Committee 2005, 9)

The primary focus of the Committee's consideration was pollution events, with attention paid to pollution by UK water companies (among others). The Committee's consideration identified the varied nature of corporate environmental offending, including the reality that offenders likely fall into several different categories rather than having shared motivations or behavioral characteristics. Previous research (Nurse 2011, 2013) into wildlife offenders identified that far from environmental (wildlife) offenders being one homogenized group, a range of offending types and behaviors exist. Thus, understanding the psychology of offenders, the economic pressures that affect them, and the sociological and cultural issues that impact on offending are integral to developing policies to address offending behaviors and conditions that lead to environmental crime (Nurse 2011, 2013). The analysis of previous research identifies that some offenses are motivated by purely financial considerations, some by economic or employment constraints (Roberts et al. 2001, 27) and others by predisposition towards some elements of the activity such as the exercise of power or the opportunity to engage in thrill-seeking behaviors. Analysis for this book contends that many of the elements identified in relation to wildlife crime as one form of environmental offending are also true in relation to corporate environmental crime. Nurse (2011, 2013, 69–70) identified a typology of offender as follows:

1. Traditional profit-driven Offenders
2. Economic Criminals
3. Masculinities Criminals
4. Hobby Offenders
5. Stress Offenders

The analysis from this previous research (Nurse 2011, 2013) can be adapted and applied to corporate environmental crime, behaviors involved in offending; the rationalizations employed by offenders and the public policy response. The five models of offender outlined above relate to profit-driven offending, employment-related offending; offending driven by masculinities behaviors; offending linked to hobby or compulsion; and offending caused as a reaction to the pressure the offender is under (Nurse 2011, 2013). Thus, in respect of wildlife crime; some offenses incorporated the taking and exploitation of wildlife for profit (wildlife trade) others involving the killing or taking or trapping of wildlife either in connection with employment (e.g. bird of prey persecution) or for purposes linked to field sports (e.g. hunting with dogs). Nurse (2011, 2013) concluded that for organized crime groups, wildlife trafficking is primarily a profit-driven offense, undertaken to gain maximum revenue for a group without the punitive consequences and overt law enforcement attention that accompanies the trafficking in drugs, weapons, or human beings. South and Wyatt (2011) similarly concluded that different types of activity were involved in organized crime activity such that policy needed to consider different types of organized crime groups engaged in wildlife offending, rather than responding as if hierarchical mafia style groups were the only offenders. Similarly, when examining corporate environmental crime, varied offending patterns and behaviors are in evidence. At the level of the corporation (i.e. the corporate entity as offender) much corporate environmental offending fits within the first category of profit-driven offending where environmental crimes, whether by act or omission are frequently committed in order to ensure profits for the corporation. White (2008, 146) notes that the law "holds the corporation 'criminally responsible' when its acting mind and will exhibit wrongful intention" although this can be difficult to prove in a large corporation. However, activities involving excessive or illegal exploitation of natural resources for profit (e.g. in the oil, gas, and illegal timber trading industries) for example, might be carried out at corporate level where there is a clear "controlling mind" that dictates the form of an operation that clearly goes beyond the permissible limits of any permits or licenses.

However, at the level of the individual employee, environmental offending can be complex such that offenders may fit within several different categories and be subject to various motivations as Table 3.1 illustrates.

Individualistic behaviors within corporate environmental crime can fit within the economic criminal category where offenders are motivated to commit their offenses by a range of economic and social pressures, but the primary object is not direct (personal) financial benefit. Examples of this include those involved in (mostly legitimate) commercial production activities (discussed further later) who may be driven to their offending behavior through the need to meet targets where this would be problematic if fully complying with environmental regulation. In the economic criminal model,

Table 3.1. Motivating Factors and Offending Type

Type of Criminal	Ignorance of the Law	Pressure from Employer or Commercial Environment	Financial Gain	Feeling of Power	Excitement, Thrills, or Enjoyment	Low-Risk Crime	Keeping Tradition or Hobby Alive or Fulfilling a Compulsion
Traditional Criminal	No	No	Yes*	No	Yes	Yes	No
Economic Criminal	No	Yes*	Yes	No	No	Yes	Yes
Masculinity Criminal	No	No	No	Yes*	Yes	Yes	Yes
Hobby Criminal	No	No	No	No	Yes	Yes	Yes*
Stress Offender	No	Yes	No	Yes*	Yes	Yes	No

* indicates the primary motivator

Source: Nurse 2011, 48.

the offender's motivation comes in part from external pressures (e.g. an employer or a perception of market pressures) and in part from association with others within his sphere of employment or social circle who have also committed offenses (Sutherland 1973). The offender is most likely aware that his acts amount to offenses under existing legislation or environmental regulations but because of pressures brought to bear he may continue to commit the offenses. The causes of crime for the economic criminal are directly related to outside pressures and a lack of controls on their activities. Crime is arguably likely in any situation where an individual is encouraged to commit a crime for fear of losing his employment if he does not do so and this provides a powerful motive for some environmental crimes. Nelken (1994) describes such "white-collar crime as being typified by a situation where 'successful business or professional people are apparently caught out in serious offenses, quite often for behavior which they did not expect to be treated as criminal, and for which it is quite difficult to secure a conviction" (Nelken in Maguire et al. 1994, 355). Nelken suggests that white-collar criminals are responsible people and that the crimes that they commit raise questions such as why do they do it when they have so much to lose? how likely are they to be caught? and what is the true level of crime in their area?

The nature of the offender as an otherwise law-abiding individual allows the "economic" environmental offender to be contextualized within traditional criminological literature that describes white-collar crimes as those that "involve evasions of regulations and violations of laws carried on as part of an occupation or business in order to secure greater profit and without concern for the injury inflicted on the public" (Vold and Bernard 1986, 331). However, the pressure brought to bear on the individual (discussed further in chapter 5) is important in distinguishing otherwise law-abiding actors who are subject to influence, from those engaged in deliberate offending for personal gain.

For some activities, offending behavior also fits into the masculinities offender model, where crimes are committed to reinforce notions of power and masculinity and are rarely committed by lone individuals (Nurse 2013, 75). For example, corporate offending that involves risk-taking activities and the challenges of subverting regulation or frustrating enforcers may be attractive to the male offender, employed (and often rewarded) for risk-taking activity. Sykes and Matza's neutralization theory (1957) provides contextual understanding of the justifications used by offenders that gives them the freedom to act (and a post-act rationalization for doing so) while other theories explain why environmental offenders are motivated to commit specific crimes.

A community element has been identified in some environmental offending (Nurse 2013) especially where the environment is one that encourages offending behavior and where informal controls or neighbors to exert essential controls on offending may be absent. Arguably corporate offenders exist within a community or subculture of their own which accepts their offenses, given that anthropocentric views of environmental resources as a commodity to be exploited exist within subcultural groupings of offenders, e.g., corporate teams with a shared target and shared interest in avoiding costly environmental regulation. Corporate environmental crimes often attract only fines, regulatory sanctions or lower-level prison terms which reinforces environmental crime as "minor" offenses unworthy of official activity. In addition, Sutherland's (1973) differential association theory helps to explain the situation that occurs when those involved in organized groups learn their activities from others in their community or social group (Sutherland 1973). Indeed, corporate culture itself may rationalize an appeal to higher loyalties (profits and others in the group) and reinforce the view that there is no harm in continuing with an activity that simply represents another form of risk-taking behavior that is prized within some corporate environments. Awareness of the illegal nature of their actions leads some corporate offenders to use the justifications outlined by Sykes and Matza (1957) but the association with other offenders, the economic (and subcultural) pressures to commit offenses and the personal consequences for them should they fail and let down the group (or their employer) are strong motivations for corporate actors to commit environmental crimes, responding to strains that determine noncompliant behavior to be the solution to their problem (Merton 1968). Discussion of masculinities as a factor in crime and criminal behavior are relevant to any analysis of environmental crime, given the largely masculine nature of the corporate world. Consideration of the different aspects of masculinities show how masculine stereotypes can be reinforced and developed through offending behavior (Goodey 1997) are important factors in addressing offending behavior which may sometimes be overlooked (Groombridge 1998).

Corporate Environmental Crime, Greenwashing and the Treadmill of Production

Treadmill of production theory provides an exploration for environmental harm as an inevitable consequence of continued commercial production and the exploitation of natural resources. Arguably capitalism is an ecologically destructive means of production because it is concerned primarily with the profits to be made from continued use of natural resources and with the human benefits derived from continued production, rather than considering any limits on production in the interests of maintaining a healthy environment (Lynch et al. 2013). The purpose of production and the operation of markets that allow for production is to produce goods, with environmental resources primarily existing in the service of such production and the needs of the market. Lynch et al. (2013, 998) suggest that "the ecological disorganization approach draws attention to the ways in which human preferences for organizing economic production consistent with the objectives of capitalism are an inherent contradiction with the health of the ecological system." Schnaiberg's (1980) treadmill of production theory suggests that changes in production accelerate environmental degradation, or the erosion of the natural environment and the destruction of ecosystems. Environmental degradation is thus a consequence of production when the means of production negatively impact on the environment. Long et al. (2012, 330) explain, for example, that "in the case of coal production, environmental degradation occurs when mining operations contaminate ground water through the chemicals used in mining practices and when strip-mining operations such as mountaintop removal mining alter the landscape which can lead to loss of species." While the object of the mining exercise is to obtain coal for fuel, the impact of the operation is environmentally damaging; even though this may be an unintended consequence of an otherwise lawful activity.

White (2008, 46) identifies that "the social construction of environmental problems relates to the place of human rights and human interests in shaping issues." Thus, "when it comes to environmental harm, what actually gets criminalized by and large reflects the efforts of claims-makers to make an issue of the harm in question" (White 2008, 46). The extent to which claims of environmental harm may conflict with other considerations and perceived environmental benefits and are accepted as an important area of public policy is also a factor. Lynch (1990) has argued that capitalism contributes to various types of environmental crime and deviance that are unevenly distributed according to race and class. Arguably, the processes of producing and consuming goods *must* generate ecological disorganization by consuming and polluting nature in part because of changes in manufacturing production that have enhanced the forms of ecological degradation (Schnaiberg, 1980).

Capitalism's ecologically destructive tendencies are seen in the processes of ecological withdrawals and ecological additions where increasing levels of pollution and natural resource extraction are related to Western capital that has been invested in chemical-and energy-intensive technology. Ecological withdrawals are defined as the resource harms capitalism produces in the process of extracting raw materials (Lynch 2014). Chemical and technological developments have arguably increased the extent to which environmental harms are caused in the process of extracting materials from the natural environment. At the same time, increasingly mechanized and technologically advanced processes have become more efficient in withdrawing resources. Thus, intensification of the ecological withdrawal process accelerates ecological disorganization by increasing the destruction of nature (Lynch 2014).

Ecological additions consist of the emission of pollutants into the ecosystem which can arise from the legal operation of production processes. White and Heckenberg (2014, 157) identify that "the problem of pollution is directly related to how humans use and dispose of natural resources in systemic processes of production and consumption." Over time as the treadmill of production accelerates, it generates larger quantities of ecological additions, and emits increased (and more concentrated) quantities of pollution. It has been claimed that "just 122 corporations account for 80 per cent of all carbon dioxide emissions. And just five private oil; corporations—Exxon Mobil, BP Amoco, Shell, Chevron and Texaco—produce oil that contributes some ten per cent of the world's carbon emissions" (Bruno, Karliner and Brotsky 1999, 1). Ecological additions also produce ecological disorganization by changing nature and accelerating other ecologically destructive tendencies (e.g. climate change caused by additions).

Gould et al. (2008) suggest that the treadmill theory is structurally deterministic, focusing on production rather than consumption. Arguably a focus on consumption would obscure power relations, which are the shaping force of consumer behavior. While consumers have the power to reject particular products, they have no influence over capital allocation or over the means of production. Thus, while consumers can in some small ways influence what we consume in relation to environmental problems (for example by boycotting environmentally damaging products or demanding a reduction in wasteful packaging), consumer behavior is unlikely by itself to substantially reduce levels of consumption. Ecological modernization theory suggests that the economy benefits from moves towards environmentalism with "continued industrial development as offering the best option for escaping from the ecological crises of the developed world" (Fisher and Freudenburgand 2001, 702). However, Gould et al. (2008) indicate that green technology, greater efficiency, and market reforms have all failed to reduce increased consumption trends. Spaargaren and Mol (1992) also contend that restructuring the processes of production and consumption is only a partial solution. They suggest that any change to ecologically sound patterns of production and consumption is limited by the dimension of the contemporary environmental crisis. This crisis is endemic to production and consumption patterns based on nature as sustenance-base thus changes to production and consumption patterns do not by themselves provide a solution to problems related to the changing role of nature as "intuited nature" and how citizens "deal with" the environmental crisis within everyday life (Spaargaren and Mol 1992). Green technology is only effective if associated with an overhaul of the funding and orientation of business innovation and of societal responses to the environmental crisis. Arguably, corporations have no major incentive to depart from methods that are arguably working and providing continued profits. Similarly, increased efficiency through green technology is ineffective because arguably it supports continued economic expansion and persistent use of natural resources rather than instigating a change in consumption and production patterns at a fundamental level.

Treadmill of production theory draws attention to the ways in which the state, the private sector, and labor interact to facilitate ecological disorganization under post–World War II capitalism. Globalization policies have arguably forced localities to subordinate ecological concerns to attract business interests and to take advantage of global trends towards increased consumption. While some localities have opted out of the global trading system with a view to creating more sustainable local economies (Wheeler and Beatley 2014, Seyfang 2006), this is currently at too small a level to address the overall drive for consumption.

Concerns about the harm caused by production impact on corporations where they face a backlash in respect of the perceived harm they cause in production processes and in marketing environmentally "harmful" goods (Dauvergne 2008). As a result, the 1990s saw a rise in environmental claims where manufacturers saw the benefit in distinguishing themselves from the competition and negative environmental campaigning by asserting the environmental benefits of their products. However, firms faced backlash when false environmental claims were exposed by environmental NGOs activists and journalists. The term "greenwashing" which broadly refers to the dissemination of false or incomplete information by an organization to present an environmentally responsible public image became commonplace in newspaper reporting in the early 21st century. Use of the term peaked "in 2009 at more than two hundred articles mentioning the term per year in the United Kingdom. In 2008 seventy-three articles mentioned greenwashing in the *New York Times* alone (with seventy-one in 2009)" (Bowen 2014, 18).

Discussion of greenwashing is relevant to this book's analysis of corporate environmental crime, environmental harm, and corporate environmental responsibility. This book identifies greenwashing as both a *symptom* of environmental harm where corporations seek to disguise their environmentally harmful actions, and potentially a *cause* of environmental harm where corporations actively seek to push responsibility for environmental harm onto individual staff and use corporate environmental responsibility reporting and policies as a tool to shield the corporation from attention from environmental activists and enforcers (see the further discussion in chapters 4 and 6). Conventional greenwashing definitions separate a firm's communications from "actual environmental impacts" (Bowen 2014, 32). Marquis and Toffel (2012) suggest that increased pressure to report environmental impacts has resulted in selective disclosure, "an attention deflection strategy whereby firms seek to gain or maintain legitimacy by disproportionately revealing relatively benign performance indicators to obscure their less impressive overall performance." Thus, organizations seek to conceal potentially negative information about their activities to appear more legitimate. Walker and Wan (2012) indicate the basic conception of green-washing (discrepancy between green "talk" [claims] and green "walk" [action]) differs from green-highlighting (concentrated efforts of the "talk" and "walk"). Bowen (2014, 3) refers to "symbolic corporate environmentalism" to describe the "shared meanings and representations" surrounding changes made within corporations; described as being primarily for environmental reasons. Hamann and Kapelus (2004) identify a need for sincerity and accountability in sustainability reporting and policies in order to avoid such policies from simply becoming greenwash and in their study of the mining industry identify gaps between true accountability and fairness and CSR activities. Laufer (2003, 254) argues that the problems and challenges of ensuring fair and accurate corporate social reporting mirror those accompanying corporate compliance with law. Corporations have some incentive to comply with legislation in the form of the threat of prosecution or regulatory sanction if they do not. But "some corporations will hold themselves out as fully committed to compliance when the commitment is in fact absent. Without metrics for assessing compliance effectiveness, regulators and prosecutors often rely on little more than corporate representations" (Laufer, 2003, 254). As chapters 4 and 6 indicate, voluntary adherence to CSR and CER tools is not, by itself, evidence of compliance or of responsible activity. One aspect of this book's analysis is the extent to which regulatory scrutiny and enforcement is adequate to address wrongdoing that results in environmental harm. As Laufer notes "regulators, prosecutors and courts may be able to determine that a firm has adopted the prescriptive steps in the Guidelines, but this may be quite different from assessing effectiveness. It is not surprising that many corporations are equally clueless." Holcomb (2008) goes so far as to suggest that corporate greenwashing actively thwarts retributive and restorative justice processes where public relations campaigns and conflicting information on the internet obscure the reality of corporate environmental crime and stifle attempts to call for corporate environmental accountability.

Discovering the "Corporate Environmental Criminal"

As the earlier discussion illustrates, corporate environmental crime is "a product of motivation and opportunity conditioned by the quality of law enforcement" (Situ and Emmons, 2000, 67). Indeed, the House of Commons Environmental Audit Committee concluded that "unless there is a real threat of being detected, the offender will continue to offend. We cannot stress strongly enough the importance of the threat of detection as a deterrent"

(2005, 4). Criminological deterrence theory contests the notion that threat of detection alone is sufficient (Wright et al. 2004, Paternoster and Simpson 1996). Arguably general deterrence occurs when potential offenders in the general public (or corporations) are stopped from committing crime because they are aware of the possibility of punishment and have knowledge of particular individuals who have been punished. Publicity given to sentencing is essential in establishing general deterrence, as the public must be encouraged to believe that punishment *automatically* follows the commission of a crime. But general deterrence is extremely difficult to evaluate because it is impossible to measure and identify those potential offenders who do not commit crime for fear of punishment, although common-sense logic dictates that punishment will have general deterrent effects and the publicity given to sentencing is a core function of this deterrence function. Individual deterrence occurs when an offender is caught and punished and finds the experience sufficiently unpleasant that they resolve to never offend again. However, one of the main problems with deterrence theory is that it assumes that offenders are rational and responsible individuals who calculate the risks associated with crime before deciding whether to commit an offense. This is a questionable conclusion to come to as many offenses will not achieve full publicity and it is unlikely that offenders conduct a full assessment of their offending behavior before the commission of an offense. But were this to be the case, offenders may be aware of relatively low clear up rates for certain offenses (Wasik in Stockdale and Casale 1992, 123). In an area such as timber trafficking where much activity takes place outside of the gaze of justice agencies, offenders are aware both that the remote nature of the activity shields them from detection and apprehension, and that there are potentially problems in distinguishing illegal logs from legal ones. The deterrent effect is therefore limited if a rational offender concludes that his chances of being caught and receiving the punishment are minimal. Thus, deterrence is particularly problematic within the contemporary environmental regulatory environment where arguably the chances of detection and punishment are also slim. The problem is likely compounded by corporate knowledge that regulatory control mechanisms are not designed to be overly punitive or to prevent continued corporate activity. Gunningham and Sinclair (2007) suggest that:

> The deterrence strategy emphasizes a confrontational style of enforcement and the sanctioning of rule-breaking behavior. It assumes that those regulated are rational actors capable of responding to incentives, and that if offenders are detected with sufficient frequency and punished with sufficient severity, then they, and other potential violators, will be deterred from violations in the future. The deterrence strategy is accusatory and adversarial. Energy is devoted to

detecting violations, establishing guilt and penalizing violators for past wrong-doing. (2007, 3)

By contrast, they suggest that an "advise and persuade" or "compliance" strategy may be preferable because it "emphasizes cooperation rather than confrontation, and conciliation rather than coercion" (Gunningham and Sinclair 2007, 3). The benefits of such an approach are that it seeks to prevent harm rather than punish transgressions which is arguably less confrontational and more acceptable to business and regulators. There is also an inherent conflict between drivers to make money and the costs of regulatory compliance which are recognized by UK Government in the Hampton and Macrory Principles of *risk-based* regulation (Hampton 2005, Macrory 2006). Black (2005, 513–515) suggests that "risk-based regulation arguably conflates two ideas. The first 'refers to the regulation of risks to society: risks to health, safety, the environment, or less usually, financial well-being'" (Black 2005, 514). This perception examines whether or not an activity should be regulated and what preventative measures firms should take. Black's second conception on risk-based regulation considers "regulatory and institutional risk" (2005, 514) including whether a regulator or company will achieve its objectives. This also considers issues around developing "decision-making frameworks and procedures to prioritize regulatory activities and the deployment of resources, principally inspection and enforcement activities" (Black, 2005, 514). Thus, regulators make choices around when and how to conduct enforcement activities within a policy environment that arguably assumes that corporate norms and the "natural" drive of corporations to behave ethically will *automatically* provide for self-regulation. Within this paradigm, regulation is arguably responsive rather than preventative and fines and administrative sanctions are considered more effective than prosecution.

While the deterrence strategy and the compliance strategy are arguably extremes that require some adjustment to work in practice, environmental regulation is arguably closer to the compliance strategy. Contemporary policy in jurisdictions that wish to promote business (e.g. the UK and US) favor a modified form of compliance model.[1] Thus, the presumption is that inspections and other regulatory activity should take place only when necessary—i.e., enforcement activity should be lessened to reduce the regulatory burden on business. In addition, the intention is that sanctions for business should be proportionate and meaningful and should not overly seek to criminalize business activity. Thus, where enforcers may have a range of tools at their disposal, settlements' and allowing corporations to amend their behavior are favored approaches to effective regulation with criminal prosecution generally being a last resort. However, for the more serious offenses and those that fall squarely within the criminal law, criminal prosecution might be employed. The following case study illustrates the challenges of regulatory enforcement.

Case Study: General Electric and the Hudson River

During a 30-year period ending in 1977 General Electric (GE) was involved in the discharge of polychlorinated biphenyls (PCBs) into the Hudson River in New York. Two plants owned by GE, one at Fort Edward and the other at Hudson Falls were involved. Cooling drainage, steam condensation, detergent washing processes, and a network of interconnected diffuse sources supplied PCB from one of the plants to the river (3). A significant portion of the PCB derived from the other plant was discharged to the river from a municipal sewage treatment plant (Brown et al. 1988). Claudio (2002, 184–185) comments that research has shown that "exposure to PCBs is associated with a wide range of toxic developmental, reproductive, endocrine, and carcinogenic effects." In addition, PCBs "have been designated as persistent organic pollutants and are of special concern because they remain for many years in the environment and in the tissues of animals exposed to them" (Claudio 2002, 185). Brown et al. (1985, 656) identify that results of fish monitoring activities conducted by the New York State Department of Conservation (DEC) identified high concentrations of PCBs, beyond that allowed by the tolerance levels identified by the Food and Drug Administration. In 1975, two capacitor manufacturing plants owned by GE were identified as the primary cause of the contamination and fishing was banned in the (Upper) Hudson in 1976. The Environmental Protection Agency classified PCBs as "probable human carcinogens" and banned their production in 1977 under the Toxic Substances Control Act (Claudio 2002, 185). Brown et al., (1985) indicate that legal action was brought against GE for infringements of New York State Environmental Conservation Law. Cray (2001) identifies that in 1976 an initial settlement was reached between GE and the state of New York that limited GE's liability for polluting the Hudson River to $3 million. The settlement also provided for a reduction in PCB discharges by the GE facilities and expenditure of approximately "$7 million to assess both the contamination problem and possible remedial action" (Brown et al. 1985, 656). However, in 1984, the EPA listed the Hudson River as a national "Superfund" site placing 200 miles of river, between Hudson Falls and the Battery in New York City on the EPA's list of most contaminated hazardous waste sites, although at that time the EPA recommended no action on dredging of the site. In 1991 GE allegedly began a campaign to oppose dredging as the EPA reconsidered the 1984 decision.

GE also allegedly delayed the cleanup at the site. A cleanup plan was put forward by the EPA in 2002 which involved dredging 2.65 million cubic yards of sediment from a 40-mile stretch of the Hudson. However, GE contested the dredging plan on the grounds that it was unnecessary because "naturally occurring processes in the river have and will continue to rid the ecosystem of PCB contamination" (Claudio 2002, 186). The company also argued that there was insufficient evidence that PCBs are toxic to humans. Initially GE opposed the EPA plan arguing that dredging would stir up the pollutants and cause them to flow downstream, embarking on a "huge advertising and lobbying campaign to weaken the plan" (CBC News 2001). While GE signed a consent decree with the EPA in 2005 to perform dredging to reduce PCBs in the fish, water, and sediment, three years after the EPA decision, GE was reported to be dragging its feet on the cleanup (Sullivan and Schiavo 2005) while at the same time promoting itself as a company that cared about the environment via its "ecomagination" initiative of environmentally friendly technology (Reed and Neubert 2011). The company had allegedly hidden behind a "veil of cooperation" doing the minimum that regulators asked for while at the same time disputing the EPA's decision, seeking legal means through which to challenge it and delaying the start of the cleanup which was initially pushed back from 2005 to 2006. The company challenged the cleanup plan in federal court "trying to strip the government of its authority to order companies to deal with hazardous waste" (Sullivan and Schiavo 2005, np). While publicly agreeing to what regulators asked, GE also challenged the EPAs powers in federal court. In 2000, GE filed suit in the United States District Court for the District of Columbia challenging the Comprehensive Environmental Response, Compensation, and Liability Act (CERCLA) and its Unilateral Administrative Orders (UAO) regime. In its amended complaint, GE alleged that the statute violates the Fifth Amendment to the United States Constitution because it "deprive[s] persons of their fundamental right to liberty and property without constitutionally adequate procedural safeguards." According to GE, "[t]he unilateral orders regime imposes a classic and unconstitutional Hobson's choice: because refusing to comply risk [s] severe punishment [i.e., fines and treble damages]," Thus, UAO recipients' only real option is to "comply before having any opportunity to be heard on the legality and rationality of the underlying order." GE also alleged that it "has been and is aggrieved by CERCLA's fundamental constitutional deficiencies because it has repeatedly received UAOs and is likely to receive them in the future." The Supreme Court in *General Electric Company, Appellant v. Lisa Perez Jackson, Administrator, U.S. Environmental Protection Agency and Environmental Protection Agency, Appellees No. 09–5092*, rejected GE's arguments that the provisions of CERCLA relating to UAOs are unconstitutional.[2]

GE began its sediment dredging operations to cleanup the PCBs on May 15, 2009, with the cleanup removing approximately 300,000 cubic yards (230,000 m³) of contaminated sediment in a phase one operation that ended in October 2009. Phase two of the cleanup commenced in 2011 and sought to address approximately 2,400,000 cubic yards (1,800,000 m³) of PCB-contaminated sediment from a forty-mile section of the Upper Hudson River. The project was subject to monitoring and review by the EPA although its success remains contested. Stempel (2019) reported that "New York state officials plan to sue the U.S. Environmental Protection Agency for allowing General Electric Co to stop clearing the Hudson River of PCB contamination before the cleanup work was finished." GE is reported to have spent an estimated $1.7 billion over eight years on cleanup, including six years of dredging and in 2019 the EPA issued a "certificate of completion" in respect of the remedial action that allows GE to stop dredging until further studies show whether the company has done enough cleanup (EPA 2019). The EPA states that "the certification is an acknowledgment that the dredging and associated construction work specifically required of GE under the Consent Decree was properly carried out" (EPA 2019, 4). However, Stempel (2019) identifies that New York State officials considered GE's work at the site to be "incomplete" and noted that in December 2018, New York state's Department of Environmental Conservation found PCB levels in fish in the upper Hudson after dredging "essentially the same as before" (Stempel 2019).

The GE (Hudson River) case demonstrates how self-regulation fails where different perspectives held by corporations and regulators impact on effective resolution of environmental complaints. Rather than accepting liability for the harm once found culpable, GE's behavior typified aspects of Sykes and Matza's (1957) neutralization theory; the company denied responsibility, contested the legitimacy of the enforcer (through legal challenges to its continued use of enforcement powers), and refuted the necessity of legal action. Further examples discussed within this book show that these are regrettably common behaviors.

Conclusions on the Causes of Corporate Environmental Crime

As this chapter illustrates, corporate environmental crime and noncompliance are substantially caused by the drive for profits and opportunity to commit crime potentially conditioned by a weak enforcement regime. However, this chapter also identifies a range of varied offending behaviors involved in corporate environmental crime. A broad typology of offending shows that while the basics of corporate environmental offending are established as some profit or advantage to the business enterprise, there is a need to consider the detail of offending behavior, motivation, and rationalization for different types of corporate environmental crime. Gunningham and Sinclair (2007, 4) suggest that "in terms of general deterrence, the evidence shows that regulated business firms' perceptions of legal risk (primarily of prosecution) play a far more important role in shaping firm behavior than the objective likelihood of legal sanctions." Attitudes towards corporate environmental responsibility and the importance of environmental protection are also a factor, as the next chapter discusses.

NOTES

1. In the UK a Code of Practice for Regulators was established by the Legislative and Regulatory Reform Act 2006, extended by the Enterprise Act 2016. In the foreword to the Code the Minister for Business states that the Government is "committed to reducing regulatory burdens and supporting compliant business growth through the development of an open and constructive relationship between regulators and those they regulate."

2. It should be noted that at the time the Supreme Court rejected GEs arguments in 2010 the company was involved in response actions at seventy-nine active CERCLA sites where UAOs might be issued, including the cleanup of some 200 miles of the Hudson River stretching from Hudson Falls to the southern tip of Manhattan. However, the Supreme Court noted that the EPA had yet to issue GE a UAO for the Hudson River at that time although the agency reserved the right to do so.

Chapter 4

Cleaning Up Greenwash

Corporate Environmental Responsibility and Environmental Crime

This chapter explores the concept of Corporate Environmental Responsibility (CER) a distinct aspect of Corporate Social Responsibility (CSR) and the phenomenon of "greenwash." The chapter explores CER as the mechanism through which corporations monitor the impact of their business practices and assess whether the corporation is acting responsibly and sustainably, minimizing the harm to the environment from its practices. However, it identifies that while most corporations have CSR and/or CER policies that can usually be found either in the corporation's annual reports, special CSR/CER/ Sustainability reports, or on their websites, CER remains largely voluntary and many corporations with stated CER policies still continue to commit environmental crimes. As examples, both BP and Shell have good CER policies yet have been variously responsible for major oil spills and other upset events which have devastated the environment and impacted negatively on human populations, arguably causing human rights violations. This chapter explores corporate environmental responsibility for environmental harm via a case study of the Gulf oil spill and the enforcement and policy response to this environmental disaster.

CONTEXTUALIZING ENVIRONMENTAL RESPONSIBILITY

Koppell (2005) suggests that there are five dimensions of accountability: transparency; liability; controllability; responsibility; and responsiveness.

Moore, Greiber, and Baig (2010) define accountability as the requirement for actors to accept responsibility and answer for their actions, while Bovens (2007, 450) defines accountability as "a relationship between an actor [accountor] and a forum [accountee], in which the actor has an obligation to explain and to justify his or her conduct, the forum can pose questions and pass judgement, and the actor may face consequences." Accountability can also be considered through the notions of vertical or horizontal accountability. Vertical accountability "is characterized by a hierarchical principal-agent relationship" (Biela 2014, 4, cited in Nuesiri 2016, 5), through which "citizens, mass media and civil society seek to enforce standards of good performance on officials" (Stapenhurst and O'Brien 2005, 1). *Horizontal* accountability is "where the accountee is not hierarchically superior to the accountor" (Schillemans 2011, 390), such as when the executive branch of government has to give account to the legislature.

Environmental Responsibility is broadly defined via two key concepts:

1. Caring for an environment comprising the natural world including life support of which humans are an integral part
2. Ensuring accountability for harm or wrong done to the environment

Sharpe (1996, 270) suggests that in respect of the environment "value extends beyond the immediate present, that balanced and thriving ecosystems are valuable both intrinsically and as conditions for continued human and nonhuman existence." Accordingly, corporations should operate in a manner that avoids environmental depletion (through unsustainable practices of habitat destruction, species extinction, stratospheric ozone depletion, and air and water pollution). Sharpe's notion argues that consideration of the impact of corporate behavior should have a primary place in environmental risk assessment and reduction, and that unsustainable practices are remedial by the choices of those living today. This thinking links to the principles of new environmentalism (Steer 1996; O'Riordan 1991) that argued that implementing sustainable principles and finding harmony between economic development and the preservation of the natural environment required a new approach to corporate activity. The ten principles of new environmentalism broadly operate as follows:

1. *Set priorities carefully*—Broad, shallow, and expensive approaches should be avoided in the interests of prioritizing environmental problems. Priority-setting exercises should be grounded in proven studies and analyses.

2. *Make every dollar count*—In addressing environmental problems cost-effectiveness is vital, allowing for much more to be achieved with limited resources. It requires a multidisciplinary approach.

3. *Harness "win-win" opportunities*—Some gains in the environment will involve costs and trade-offs. Others can be achieved as by-products of policies designed to improve efficiency and reduce poverty.

4. *Use market instruments where feasible*—Arguably market-based incentives to reduce environmental damage are best in both principle and practice. Innovative approaches involving emissions and effluent charges, harvesting permits, market-based extraction charges, and tradable permits are some examples.

5. *Economize on administrative and regulatory capacity*—Emphasize on self-enforcing policies and other instruments (such as taxes, bans, fees, etc.) with less intervention. This envisages a greater role for NGOs and community groups.

6. *Work with the private sector, not against it*—This reflects the reality that governments are switching from a control-dominated attitude towards the private sector to one that involves dialogue and negotiated, monitorable programs. Self-enforcement and independent certification schemes (discussed later in this chapter) arguably now play a greater role than standard coercive enforcement approaches.

7. *Involve citizens thoroughly*—This principle indicates that a country's environmental problems are better addressed and the chances of success greatly enhanced if local citizens are involved.

8. Invest in partnerships that work—Encourages stakeholders working in partnership. NGO involvement in priority-setting exercises, and tripartite relationships, (the government, the private sector, and the community organizations) are becoming increasingly common.

9. *Remember that management is more important than technology*—The old-fashioned, technology-driven approach to the environment is giving way to a recognition of the crucial role of good management and importance of improved management practices.

10. *Incorporate the environment from the start*—Prevention is much cheaper—and more effective—than cure. Assess and mitigate potential damage from new infrastructural investment. (Adapted from Steer 1996)

These principles represent a change to how environmental policies, programs, and projects are formulated and implemented. The new environmentalism (Steer 1996) links economic activities and environmental problems together suggesting that the approach to environmental problems requires a range of actors and for actions to be taken at various levels to solve environmental problems. Arguably the principles of new environmentalism can be deployed as governance tools that encourage greater precision and consideration for environmental costs and benefits into policy making. In respect of the corporate social responsibility movement, these principles have begun to be incorporated into formal governance structures as the next sections discuss.

CORPORATE ENVIRONMENTAL RESPONSIBILITY AS CORPORATE GOVERNANCE

Corporate Social Responsibility[1] policies can be integrated into a business model that theoretically provides for adherence to the law, ethical standards, and international norms of business behavior and accountability. CSR provides a means for corporations to promote their brand as ethically and socially responsible and operates mainly on the basis of self-regulation, where corporations are trusted to voluntarily adhere to non-legally binding standards of ethical behavior, with no single commonly accepted definition of the principle (Mazurkiewicz 2002). Generally "every corporation has a policy concerning CSR and produces an annual report detailing its activity" (Crowther & Aras 2008, 10), yet the central problem in assessing appropriate standards of CER is that a range of approaches to CER (within the broad CSR framework) exist and thus the effectiveness of CER and the extent to which corporations integrate CER into their practices as a tool to minimize environmental harm varies.

Many major transnational corporations have good CER policies on paper but continue to commit environmentally damaging (and sometimes criminal) acts albeit sometimes unwittingly. Thus, the issues for green criminology to consider in examining criminal entrepreneurship are how should good standards of CER be enforced? Assessing this requires considering whether this solely consists of defining what is legal or illegal or requires going further to include regulated standards of behavior and expectations of corporate behavior that the public will accept as ethical compliance. Harris (2011) highlights that corporations may adopt CSR/CER for a variety of reasons, principally:

1. Acting ethically is the right way for the company to behave
2. Doing what is right and fair is expected of an organization
3. Acting ethically is in the organization's best interests. (Harris 2011, 39)

The extent to which one (or all) of these reasons applies and provides the corporation's motivation for integrating CER can have an effect on whether CER is adopted as part of operational practices. This influences corporate consideration of the impact and wider implications of its activities and the extent to which CER is enforced internally or whether (and how) CER becomes solely an aspect of marketing, brand management, and becomes a PR tool. The need to combat negative publicity or damaging perceptions of a corporation and its valuable brand may, for example, lead to the adoption of CER purely to obtain benefits for a MNE's public image. There may even be inconsistency within a MNE about the extent to which CER should be observed or apply to its operations, especially where there is no clear chain of CER ownership at board (strategic) level and CER reporting is outside of core corporate governance, external scrutiny, or stakeholder audit.

An organization's reporting of environmental compliance and its adoption of CER strategies are immaterial if the strategies are not adhered to in practice and make no impact on decision-making. The validity of CER policies can also be questioned if CER is in conflict with operational practices that prioritize profit over environmental law compliance whether overtly or by implication. McBarnet argues that one approach to legal compliance is creative compliance where "practices that might be illegal, indeed criminal, if legally structured in one way could be legally repackaged and claimed to be lawful" (2006, 1091). Alternatively, active embracing of monitoring and auditing process can provide a means through which the appearance of compliance is achieved.

CER adoption may therefore suit the needs of a corporation's stakeholders or the development and protection of its brand, rather than being adopted as part of an ethical operating strategy that minimizes the impact on communities affected by their actions. However, it may fail as a practical tool to encourage legitimate compliance allied to entrepreneurism because of the lack of an enforceable, independently verified CER standard against which an organization's performance and the accuracy of its reporting can be assessed. Thus, CER voluntarism by itself may be inadequate and legal controls may be required to enforce CER although this can itself be problematic.

Green criminology has documented the persistent nature of lawbreaking in respect of pollution, disposal of toxic waste, and misuse of environmental resources (Lynch & Stretesky 2014, Pearce & Tombs 1998). It has also challenged corporate definitions of good environmental practice and provided a means through which corporate wrong doing can frequently be considered as deliberate criminal acts (White & Heckenberg 2014, Lynch and Stretesky 2003). In addition, Crowther and Aras (2008) argue that corporations do not truly account for the environmental impact of their activities so that externalities are routinely excluded from corporate accounting with the true costs of corporate environmental damage being met by communities. Corporations may thus add "misleading the public" or fraud to their environmental activities through poor or negligent corporate environmental reporting.

Corporate directors already have a number of incentives to align their behavior with accepted standards and routinely claim to be operating responsibly, taking account of the needs of communities. Alcock and Conde (2005) argue that further legislation to regulate responsible corporate behavior is unnecessary, but numerous cases highlight the failure of corporations to remedy the harm they have caused (see for example persistent pollution incidents such as those at Shell's Deer Park refinery 2003 to 2007 discussed as a case study later in this book) suggesting the failure of self-regulation and voluntary compliance with ethical standards. Using perspectives on corporate governance; environmental law & regulatory justice this chapter's contention is that corporate environmental damage should be the subject of regulatory restorative justice, in effect forcing corporations to comply with a set of CER principles and negating the harmful impacts of criminal entrepreneurship. The "polluter pays" principle should be a core feature of the law and potentially a market-based form of enforcement and regulatory action to ensure that corporations take (private) responsibility for and remedy their environmental damage. The following section defines how this principle is implemented in notions of CER.

Mazurkiewicz (2002, 6) explained that by 2002 there had been "over 300 CSR codes, principles performance standards, management standards developed by governments, business associations, or academia" and also a wide range of individual companies' codes of conduct or different reporting mechanisms or initiatives. While international corporate sustainability initiatives like the Global Reporting Initiative (GRI) have become widely recognized, the challenge for monitors, consumers, and other stakeholders is to know the standard by which companies should be held to account, a problem complicated by the lack of an absolute CER standard agreed upon by NGOs and corporations, and by MNEs adopting and promoting different CER perspectives dependent upon the industry and legal/regulatory environment. Research by a network of Canadian environmental NGOS (ENGOs) concluded that "ENGOS view environmental commitment and awareness as key components of CER but expressed difficulty in discerning genuine environmental commitment from public relations exercises bordering on green wash" (Jamison, Raynolds, Holroyd, Veldman & Tremblett 2005, iv). The ENGOs concluded that the following key components were essential in achieving CER:

1. Environmental commitment and awareness
2. Stakeholder engagement
3. Measuring, reporting, and auditing
4. Transparency
5. Commitment to continuous improvement

6. Going beyond compliance

However, while corporations might easily put in place some form of measuring, reporting, and auditing and include this in CSR, or CER policies, and
annual reports; engagement with stakeholders and going beyond basic compliance presents difficulties for all but the most environmentally conscious
corporations. While this is not to suggest that all corporations are predisposed
towards environmental crime; when the drive for corporate success (in terms
of greater profits or lower costs) greatly exceeds the legitimate or profitable
means for achieving it, the "structural groundwork for motivation is laid"
(Situ and Emmons 2000, 67). Where this is combined with opportunity and
a weak regulatory structure, corporations fearful of decreasing profits or
increasing costs may seek to circumvent environmental legislation even while
publicly making pronouncements of environmental responsibility. Where
corporations may be dealing with multiple environmental performance
demands and expectations from stakeholders and investors, the requirement
to set protection and restoration of the environment as a strategic priority may
result in a conflict between the interests of the corporation, environmental
interests, and those of the wider community. The Australian Senate Standing
Committee on Legal and Constitutional Affairs (1989) summarized the potential conflict as follows:

> To require directors to take into account the interests of a company's employ-
> ees, its creditors, its customers or the environment, as well as its shareholders,
> would be to require them to balance out what would on occasion be conflicting
> forces. To make it optional for directors to take into account the interests of a
> company's employees, its creditors, its customers, or the environment, as well
> as its shareholders, again would mean that directors would be in the position of
> weighing up the various factors. It would also limit the enforceability of share-
> holders' rights if directors were able to argue that, in making a certain decision;
> they had been exercising their option to prefer other interests. (Senate Standing
> Committee on Legal and Constitutional Affairs 1989)

This potential conflict and a belief that corporate norms and the natural drive
of corporations to behave ethically and responsibly provide for automatic
effective self-regulation, are at the heart of movements to resist further regulation of CSR and CER. Yet while the concept of CSR is still evolving and,
as yet, there exists no globally-accepted binding definition of CSR (Kercher
2007) there is evidence that even corporations that actively promote themselves as engaging with communities and being ethically responsible still
cause significant harms to the environment. Seemingly, self-regulation and

voluntary compliance with the norms of corporate behavior and ethical business practices is not working.

CSR STANDARDS AND MECHANISMS

Several CSR mechanisms exist and while it is beyond the scope of this chapter to assess them all, a brief outline of key measures is provided in the following section.

The United Nations created the Global Compact (GC) 2000 which incorporates 10 norms on environmental sustainability and anticorruption in business. The GC is nonbinding but employs principles derived from the Universal Declaration of Human Rights, the Fundamental Principles on Rights at Work (provided by the International Labour Organization), the Rio Declaration on Environment and Development and the UN Convention against Corruption. Arguably the GC is the largest CSR program which at time of writing (mid 2019) lists on its GC website that it has been signed up to by 9.913 companies from 161 countries and has resulted in 63,630 public reports (UN Global Compact 2019). The ten principles of the GC are intended to guide business to act responsibly and, at a minimum, meet fundamental responsibilities in the areas of human rights, labor, environment, and anticorruption. Accordingly, the two human rights principles require businesses to make sure that they are not complicit in human rights abuses and to support and respect the promotion of international human rights standards (discussed further in chapter 9). The four labor standards indicate that business should uphold the freedom of association and the effective recognition of the right to collective bargaining; eliminate all forms of forced and compulsory labor and work towards ending child labor whilst also ending all forms of discriminatory practices in respect of employment and occupation. The three environmental principles require business to support a precautionary principle approach to business activities and to undertake initiatives to promote greater environmental responsibility whilst also encouraging the development and diffusion of environmentally friendly technologies. There is also an anticorruption principle that requires businesses to work against corruption in all its forms, including extortion and bribery. Kell (2013) identifies that the GC's success is arguably in managing to incorporate UN-endorsed principles into the global corporate responsibility movement. However, the extent to which the Compact is successful in practice, depends on four factors defined as: *continued relevance of the initiative's underlying idea, sustained institutional leadership support, governmental support (political back-up)*, and *operational viability* (Kell 2013, 31). UN endorsement is likely a factor in companies joining the GC with Cetindamar (2007) identifying that companies gain both ethical and economic benefits from GC membership. However, Williams (2004) identified that at least in its early stages, corporate buy-in to the GC was uneven with major US companies seemingly reluctant to join the GC. While the position has arguably changed somewhat in the last fifteen years, analysis of GC membership during research for this book identifies that as of mid-2019 only 574 US companies are listed as GC members, compared with 507 United Kingdom companies, 826 Brazilian companies and 1240 French companies. The relative size of the countries and nature of their commercial operations raises questions concerning why the US and UK have such similar numbers.

The UN has also produced Draft Norms on the Responsibilities of Transnational Corporations and other Business Enterprises 2003 which incorporates model guidelines and voluntary self-imposed corporate codes provided by trade unions and NGOs. While these and other corporate guidelines exist they are largely voluntary and MNEs are not required to comply with any of the guidelines which remain largely advisory. In addition, these standards are not routinely incorporated into legal systems and are thus not legally enforceable, instead they are monitored through voluntary international frameworks such as the GRI, an international reporting standard for corporations to use when reporting on the economic environmental and social impacts of their business. Corporations may also use Social Accountability International (SAI) a voluntary auditing standard which monitors whether codes of conduct are being met. SAI uses SA8000 as a social certification standard that measures social performance in eight areas considered important to social accountability in workplaces. The Standard reflects provisions contained within the Universal Declaration of Human Rights and International Labour Organization conventions. SAI states that SA8000 helps secure ethical working conditions for around two million workers (Social Accountability International 2019).

Crucial to the success of CSR/CER mechanisms are the extent to which they are rigorously enforced and their principles internalized by corporations. Runhaar and Lafferty (2009) suggest that measures such as the GC are perceived as minimum requirements that do not provide any incentive to corporations to behave better. Accountability guides the actions of power-holders in corporations towards more socially and environmentally sustainable results, by ensuring that the voice of citizens and potentially affected people enter the decision-making process. But the CSR mechanisms identified above are generally led by corporations with some discretion over how they choose to work on these.

As chapter 2 indicates; international laws and standards identify states as the primary actors with accountability for natural resource use and environmental protection. Arguably, governments and international organizations would rather formulate symbolic environmental regulations and hesitate to enforce strong regulations because they do not wish to offend powerful actors in business (Matten 2003, Baker 2007). Accountability is a central principle for good governance, including governance of natural resources, because it serves to prevent or mitigate negative social and environmental impacts, and protects against abuses of power (Ottinger 1969, Koppell 2005, Bovens 2007) but in practice there is a lack of enforcement standards and mechanisms to impose CSR/CER on corporations.

CASE STUDY: THE GULF OIL SPILL

The Gulf oil spill (also known as the Deepwater Horizon spill) is considered one of the worst environmental disasters of the early 21st century. On April 20, 2010, the Mississippi Canyon 252 Deepwater Horizon oil well exploded linked to a failure in the blowout preventer system. Eleven people were killed in the explosion and the rig eventually sank on April 22, 2010. Oil flowed from the site for 87 days, following several unsuccessful attempts to stem the flow by: attempting to close the blowout preventer valves; placing a containment dome over the largest spill; pumping drilling fuels into the spill and attempting to seal it with concrete; and diverting the flow to a containment seal. Eventually a relief well was drilled and a replacement blowout preventer was installed. BP originally estimated a flow rate of 1,000 to 5,000 barrels per day. The resultant oil spill covered 28,958 square miles, an area the size of South Carolina. Schnoor (2010, np) identified that the spill "is the first to emanate from 5000 ft beneath the sea. It is the first to make major use of dispersants at the source of the leak, and it is the first to result in a major submerged plume." Goldstein et al. (2011) suggest that the Gulf oil spill's "magnitude, duration of release, source of emission (the deep-sea floor), and management techniques used (dispersants and controlled burns)" put the spill in a different category than other spills (1334).

In addition to the harm caused to marine wildlife Solomon and Janssen (2010) identified that the Gulf oil spill posed a direct threat to human health from inhalation or dermal contact with the oil and dispersant chemicals, and indirect threats to seafood safety and mental health. BP was considered to be "grossly negligent" in respect of the offshore rig explosion.

The case involved both civil and criminal issues. Civil claims were made by businesses and persons affected by the oil spill with the spill and subsequent pollution having destroyed the livelihoods of several businesses relying on the marine environment. Transocean who owned the rig were the subject of class actions for financial losses under the Oil Pollution Act. Seventy-seven cases, including those brought by state governments, individuals, and companies were eventually heard in the U.S. District Court for the Eastern

District of Louisiana under Multi-District Litigation docket MDL No. 2179, captioned *In re: Oil Spill by the Oil Rig "Deepwater Horizon" in the Gulf of Mexico, on April 20, 2010.* In September 2014 a federal judge ruled that BP was primarily responsible for the oil spill as a result of its deliberate misconduct and gross negligence. Criminal cases included a US Department of Justice claim that sought to establish that BP "was grossly negligent and engaged in willful misconduct in causing the oil spill." The government's investigation concluded that BP had operated "a culture of corporate reck-lessness" and indicated that the company took risks with pressure tests that if conducted correctly could have stopped the oil flow before the blowout.

The case was eventually the subject of an estimated $20 billion settlement, which included $5.5 billion in civil Clean Water Act penalties and billions more to cover environmental damage and other claims by the five Gulf states and local governments. Mufson (2012) identifies that BP agreed to plead guilty to 14 criminal counts, including manslaughter, and will pay $4 billion over five years in a settlement with the Justice Department over the April 20, 2010, drilling disaster in the Gulf of Mexico that killed 11 people and unleashed the worst offshore oil spill in U.S. history. Transocean Deepwater also agreed to plead guilty to violating the Clean Water Act and to pay a total of $1.4 billion in civil and criminal fines and penalties (US Department of Justice 2013).

CORPORATE ENVIRONMENTAL
CRIME AND ENFORCING CER

In principle, strong CER mechanisms already exist. The GC, for example is arguably a robust mechanism that contains ten principles that have social responsibility at the heart of their provisions. The specific measures on human rights and the environment also contain clear indicative guidelines to drive corporate activity. However, as with many areas of regulation and legislation it is in the enforcement of these principles that problems occur.

The Gulf oil spill illustrates several CER and regulatory justice issues. At the time of the accident, the company arguably had a robust CER system in place and was engaged in sustainability reporting and publicly had policies in place to act sympathetically in the communities in which it operated. But as the case study demonstrates, governance structures cannot cover everything and the implication of a culture of recklessness, raises questions about the extent to which CER was effectively integrated into practices and monitored within the companies involved.

Potential problems can be due to weak political will on the part of government given that governments are often reluctant to make powerful actors comply with formal accountability standards. In some cases there is also weak local capacity for collective action. This is particularly the case where local people and communities are poor, marginalized, and disenfranchised from the political process of a country for a significant period of time, they tend to be weak at collectively organizing to demand accountability from powerful actors (Eyben 2011, Mansuri and Rao 2013). In Global South countries there may also be a lack of resources for civil society organizations. NGOs and social movements play a key role as change agents, but those from the Global North are often better resourced compared to their counterparts in the Global South. Weak regulations and sanctions to move business towards accountability are also a problem.

Corporations who break environmental laws and fall short of accepted standards of behavior are not always prosecuted via the criminal law but are sometimes subject only to civil or administrative sanctions. Strong environmental legislation, regulation, and environmental awareness is often driven by the activities of high profile NGOs who work to ensure that prosecution of companies for environmental damage becomes an established part of the legal landscape (Nurse 2013). The legal responsibility of MNEs for injury to workers and environmental damage arising from their operations is increasingly exercising the interest of courts, governments, trades unions, and NGOs globally and is beginning to be recognized by both civil and criminal justice systems, offering hope that an efficient mechanism for enforcing CER can be established.

However Slapper (2011) identifies that there have been modest developments in the use of the civil law to address corporate abuses (2011, 95) and that "apart from a growth in domestic criminal liability of corporations" there has been an increase both in civil litigation against companies "but also the advent of domestic liability for corporate torts that are committed abroad" (2011, 95). Thus, while international law may not yet have caught up with transnational corporate environmental abuses, domestic law might, in some cases, provide a civil remedy. The Gulf oil spill shows application of both criminal enforcement and civil remedies in respect of remedying the harm caused to affected communities and individuals and the implementation of a compensation scheme.

Slapper's point is also illustrated by US civil law in the form of the *Alien Tort Claims Act 1789* which allows action to be taken against companies for their actions overseas (Slapper 2011, 95). The *Act* confers on US federal courts jurisdiction over "any civil action by an alien for a tort only, committed in violation of the law of nations or a treaty of the United States." Thus, where corporate acts which are the subject of litigation raise international concerns and constitute a crime against humanity, a remedy potentially exists for victims of corporate abuses able to bring a case in US courts. Cases can also be brought in the EU against a parent company resident in the EU where it can be shown that the relevant management decisions (i.e. those which influenced or caused the local incident) were made at parent company level. Fagan and Thompson identify class actions as being the primary legal mechanism feared by US corporations, which Hodges (2008) identifies as being based on a model where "one individual claim is asserted to represent a class of others, whose owners are bound by the result of the single claim unless they opt-out of the class and procedure" (2008, 2). The class action procedure allows for punitive damages and requires parties to meet their own costs (Fagan & Thompson 2009, 56–57).

The existence of CER policies can also be a factor in litigation. The International Council for Human Rights Policy notes that many company CSR codes are little more than public relations exercises. But, where worded with sufficiently clarity "they can also have legal significance because they set out the values, ethical standards, and expectations of the company concerned, and might be used as evidence in legal proceedings with suppliers, employees or consumers" (2002, 70). Fagan and Thompson (2009, 55) identify that litigation has already been brought against companies such as Walmart and Nike for publishing allegedly misleading CSR materials. Nike was the subject of litigation after having allegedly lied in PR materials about the mistreatment of workers in its supply chain, while Walmart was sued for a failure to enforce its supplier standards. Thus, while international human rights norms or international environmental law might be difficult to enforce against companies (discussed further in chapter 9), CSR materials can, in the US at least, be used as evidence of the standards that a corporation *claims* to meet. Fagan and Thompson argue that consumers might be able to bring misrepresentation claims against corporations if they can demonstrate that they have suffered recoverable loss as a result of the claims made (2009, 55). The threat of such litigation might encourage a change in corporate behavior and when combined with criminal action such as that employed in the US Foreign Corrupt Practices Act (and also within UK legislation) of providing incentives for corporations to work with enforcers in order to avoid criminal prosecution and to settle cases through civil mechanisms (Hatchard 2011, 153–155) can provide a remedy.

Simpson et al. (2013) identify that informal controls are an important part of the regulatory environment while Hatchard argues that the threat of prosecution allied to self-reporting may prove effective in dealing with transnational corporate crime (2011, 153). The UK's Law Commission in its consultation paper on wildlife law reform (Law Commission, 2012) argues that any regulatory approach should adopt the risk-based approach of the Hampton (2005) and Macrory (2006) principles. In essence these argue that prosecution should only be resorted to where *necessary* and, in the case of corporate offending, should be a last resort where informal methods might yield results. The practical implementation of such mechanisms can be seen in cases such as the Serious Fraud Office's initiative to allow corporations to self-report corruption and negotiate a civil settlement as a means of avoiding prosecution (Hatchard 2011, 155). The effectiveness of such initiatives in part depends on whether the harm caused to corporations by any prosecution outweighs the financial benefits of noncompliance with environmental standards. Arguably where criminality is an endemic part of corporate behavior (Nurse 2011) self-reporting or negotiated settlements are unlikely to succeed.

NOTE

1. From this point on, the abbreviation CSR will be used when referring to general CSR or sustainability policies and reporting while the abbreviation CER will be used when referring to specific environmental responsibilities and Corporate Environmental Responsibility reporting.

Chapter 5

Creative Compliance, Constructive Compliance

Corporate Environmental Crime and the Criminal Entrepreneur

Chapter 4 identifies some of the core elements of CER and their relevance to examining whether corporate behavior is responsible for or causes environmental harm. However, this chapter notes that while corporations may generally embrace the *concepts* of social and environmental responsibility, numerous examples exist to show corporations claiming to act sustainably and responsibly, while simultaneously causing considerable environmental damage and impacting negatively on communities. As this book's title illustrates; one conception of greenwashing is that claims of environmental responsibility mask the reality of corporate environmental offending. Chapter 4's analysis shows how CER can operate as a form of positive environmental branding even where environmental noncompliance may be endemic within corporate practice. This chapter argues that such noncompliant behavior can constitute criminal entrepreneurialism (Baumol 1990) where both creative and constructive compliance combine to subvert environmental regulation and its enforcement. Thus, corporate assertion of environmental credentials is itself often a form of criminal entrepreneurship where corporations embrace voluntary codes of practice and self-regulation while internally promoting the drive for success and profitability and/or avoidance of the costs of true environmental compliance that are deemed to be too high.

CORPORATE INNOVATION AND CRIME

Baumol identifies a distinction between productive corporate innovation and unproductive activities such as organized crime (1990, 893). However, within corporate environmental crime discourse, this distinction is not absolute. Corporate compliance with environmental regulations operates along a continuum from absolute compliance to total noncompliance consistent with Hobsbawm's view that private enterprise has a bias only towards profit (1969, 40). Accordingly, noncompliance with environmental regulations and entrepreneurship which *actively* subverts or minimizes the costly impact of regulatory compliance can represent a form of innovation that arguably benefits some corporations by maximizing profit. Embracing green credentials, reassuring consumers and governments that they take their social and environmental responsibilities seriously are legitimate means through which corporations demonstrate alertness to opportunity, creativity, and respond to consumer demand for ethical corporate practice (Werther and Chandler 2005, Becker-Olsen et al. 2006).

Evidence suggests that the majority of corporations show at least surface adherence to social and environmental responsibility through the production of CSR or CER reports and by making these and environmental policies publicly available. Thus, arguably a contemporary CSR movement exists which is encouraged by market forces and recognizes CSR as beneficial to corporations (Vogel 2005). CSR has also become an area for academic study within business and management studies, law and governance studies and environmental ethics and management study. Yet green criminology identifies that corporate environmental crimes are widespread and "often eclipse the scope and reach of the criminal law" (Sollund 2012, 3). The global operations of Multi National (business) Entities (MNEs) can have significant negative consequences for the communities in which they operate and the wider environment yet are often legal given the relative lack of regulation for corporate practice in relation to environmental harm (White & Heckenberg 2014).

While there has been widespread adoption of CSR policies by businesses in Global North countries in the last 20 years, business activities are often not subject to international law or human rights norms (discussed further in chapter 9). As chapter 4 shows, CSR remains largely voluntary and while CSR and CER are routinely embraced by business, the question remains as to what extent this is just business proclaiming what people expect it to do while at the same time continuing to act either unethically or unlawfully.

Corporations armed with the knowledge of a weak environmental regulatory regime (both nationally and internationally) and the preference of Governments to use administrative or civil penalties as tools to deal with corporate environmental offending embed noncompliance into their operating practices. In doing so some corporations actively embrace the tools of corporate environmental responsibility, auditing and monitoring as structural mechanisms through which corporate offending can be neutralized (Sykes & Matza 1957). They may achieve this by blaming "rogue" individuals within the company, challenging the activities of law enforcement when aimed at corporate environmental crime and even blame environmental victims themselves.

Following on from chapter 4's discussion of the nature of corporate environmental responsibility and its core principles, this chapter considers the impact a relative lack of regulation has over corporate compliance with environmental regulation. This issue is explicitly explored within this chapter by a case study which assesses the contemporary corporate environmental responsibility landscape against the reality of corporate environmental offending. The case study illustrates repeated corporate offending (and non-compliance) against a backdrop of apparent environmental monitoring and scrutiny of corporate environmental practices. The chapter thus explores a context in which corporations might repeatedly be the subject of regulatory enforcement action, yet continue to embed noncompliance into operating practices with fines being simply the cost of doing business. Accordingly, this chapter queries whether Baumol's legal/illegal distinction remains valid in relation to corporate environmental offending. In doing so it asks whether responsibility for environmental damage is both a corporate *and* social responsibility issue, taking into account the nature of "illegal" actions by legal actors, and argues that it should be the subject of regulation to ensure corporate responsibility for environmental damage.

EXPLORING CORPORATE ENVIRONMENTAL RESPONSIBILITY AND ENVIRONMENTAL DAMAGE

While a range of activities that cause harm to the environment are subject to national and international law, there is no single definition of environmental damage for which corporations should be held responsible. In addition to the definitions contained within specific legislation, the social legal perspective argues that some acts, especially by corporations, "may not violate the criminal law yet are so violent in their expression or harmful in their effects to merit definition as crimes" (Situ & Emmons 2000, 3). In effect:

> The social legalist approach focuses on the construction of crime definitions by various segments of society and the political process by which some gain ascendancy, becoming embodied in the law. The strict legalist approach, without

denying this dynamic emphasizes these final legal definitions of crime as the starting point of any analysis because they bind the justice system in its work. (Situ & Emmons 2000)

While the environmental (and criminal) justice system focuses solely on those acts that are prohibited by legislation, definitions of environmental crime and corporate liability for these acts also needs to consider how criminal acts manifest themselves and consider those acts not yet defined as crimes but which go against the norms of society. Lynch and Stretesky explain that from an environmental justice perspective a green crime is an act that "(1) may or may not violate existing rules and environmental regulations; (2) has identifiable environmental damage outcomes; and (3) originated in human action" (2003, 227). They explain that while some green "crimes" may not contravene any existing law, where they result in or possess the potential for causing environmental and human harm, they should be considered to be crimes. In relation to CER; this requires a corporation to consider not just minimum legal standards but also the extent to which it may need to go beyond basic compliance and engage with communities and other stakeholders.

White (2012a) identifies that "much environmental harm is intrinsically transnational" (2012a, 15) and is by its very nature mobile and easily subject to transference. He further argues that "the systemic causal chains that underpin much environmental harm are located at the level of the global political economy" (White 2012a, 15). Thus, the global reach of MNEs is situated within international markets and systems of production, requiring a system of understanding and addressing environmental harm that incorporates appreciation of its international dimensions (Beirne & South 2007). However, business activities are often not subject to international law or human rights norms designed to enforce environmental rights and thus there is some confusion over precisely what legal and human rights norms apply to a corporation's activities and over the precise CER policies or standards they should observe. Harvard Professor John Ruggie (Special Representative to the UN Human Rights Council) identified that "the failure to enforce existing laws that directly or indirectly regulate business respect for human rights is often a significant legal gap in state practice" (United Nations Human Rights Council 2012, 8). Thus, not only is judging appropriate standards of corporate behavior problematic but so too is enforcing such standards and remedying environmental/human rights problems caused by corporations (discussed further in chapter 9). Business activity that harms or impacts on the environmental rights of communities is subject to a mixture of voluntary compliance, regulatory activity, and victim litigation primarily driven by national legislation.

Failures in Voluntary Compliance

Situ and Emmons (2000) identify that environmental crime is predominantly a civil matter; in other words, fines and administrative penalties are the main technique for dealing with corporate environmental crime rather than rigorous criminal justice enforcement (White & Heckenberg 2014, Stallworthy 2008). The reason given for this is the lack of effective international law and instead reliance on state (national) legislators to define environmental crime according to the requirements of national criminal or civil justice codes. The result is often that it is not seen as a priority criminal justice issue and often falls outside of the remit of the main criminal justice agencies.

However, as chapter 2 discusses, there are a number of international environmental conventions, mechanisms put in place to require states to provide for effective environmental protection. Voiculescu and Yanacopulos (2011) identify the United Nations as being at the forefront of devising universally acceptable standards to embed "respect for human rights norms and abstention from corrupt practices" into business and transnational corporations' operating practices (2011, 4). Their observation is based on the idea that much environmental damage is committed by corporations falling outside the remit of much criminal law as in reality countries have different laws and "frequently quite different approaches to dealing with environmental crime" (White 2008, 184). Environmental crime is also not always dealt with by police or criminal justice agencies and in many countries falls within the jurisdiction of the enforcement arm of the state environment department, rather than being integrated into mainstream criminal justice. Indeed, some jurisdictions do not provide for corporate criminal liability within their justice systems. As a result, CER becomes a matter of voluntary compliance and in practice is often enforced primarily by NGOs (Nurse 2013, 2011). Yet voluntary compliance with good standards of CSR and CER is often dependent on the composition of a corporation's board, the extent to which it is willing to comply with good standards, and the size and power of that corporation.

Friedman theorized that the main responsibility of the corporate executive is "to make as much money as possible while conforming to the basic rules of the society" (Friedman 1970). Crowhurst (2006) identified that while responsible industry usually welcomes certainty in environmental legislation and clarity in CER, there are corporations that actively seek to avoid "costly" legislation. Global corporations which produce harmful environmental effects and who have the economic power to do so deliberately, may invest in "pollution havens" (countries with low levels of environmental regulation) so that as standards of environmental liability become stricter in the EU and other western countries, global companies allegedly move their investments and harmful environmental activities out of the reach of the tougher regulatory systems (Neumayer 2001).[1] This represents a form of criminal entrepreneurship.

Creative Compliance, Constructive Compliance, and Criminal Entrepreneurship

Obschonka, Andersson, Silbereisen, and Sverke (2013) identify entrepreneurs as individuals with a propensity for action, risk-taking, and a desire to push against traditional structures and rules. Scholarship on green entrepreneurism also alludes to the importance of "creative destruction" where entrepreneurs promote change in part by challenging old ways of operating (Farinelli et al. 2011, 43). Thus, a notion of noncompliance and testing the boundaries of structures can be incorporated into the accepted behaviors of entrepreneurs and should be considered within broad understandings of what constitutes the "criminal" entrepreneur.

Gottschalk and Smith argue that the criminal entrepreneur's task is "to discover and exploit opportunities, defined most simply as situations in which there are a profit to be made in criminal activity" (2011, 300). In the case of environmental harm, this is illustrated by situations where multinational corporations pursue profit without regard to relevant CSR/CER matters (Kercher 2007). When caught in environmental wrongdoing, multinational corporations dispute the extent of the environmental damage they cause or the measures required to resolve the damage applying the same techniques of neutralization applied by other white-collar criminals to deny the criminality of their actions (Sykes and Matza 1957). Thus, criminal entrepreneurship is sometimes embedded in the behavior of legal organizations who become the victims of such third-party actions committed by employers and managers which cause loss to the corporation (Gottschalk and Smith 2011, 304). However, corporations become perpetrators of crime when [financial] crime is committed within the context of a legal organization (Gottschalk and Smith 2011).

As previous chapters illustrate, this applies equally to environmental crime where "greenwash" is employed as a tool to publicly promote CER while a corporation privately continues to pollute and subvert environmental regulations as a tactic. Corporate responsibilities (Friedman 1970) also require executives to consider: the harm to a company's reputation (and profits) if it is repeatedly the subject of enforcement action and required to meet the costs of environmental remediation, the increased legal bills that a corporation may face in fighting lawsuits; consumer action and regulatory justice, and the increased likelihood of further regulation and scrutiny if corporations are found to be promoting CER while causing environmental damage. Thus, if based on perceptions of rational choice theory (Cornish and Clarke

2014), individuals (and corporations) weigh up the costs of environmental compliance and regulatory obedience and then choose the alternative likely to provide the most satisfactory outcome for them. In some cases, corporate environmental crime arguably represents an appropriate choice and various techniques might be employed to facilitate this whilst minimizing risk to the corporation.

Creative compliance involves the use of techniques which can be argued to be "perfectly legal" despite the purpose and impact of such techniques being to undermine the whole purpose of reporting and regulation and in practical terms using the letter of the law to defeat its spirit, arguably "with impunity" (McBarnet 2006, 1091). Thus, the use of "pollution havens," mentioned earlier, allows a corporation to operate a lower level of environmental protection than might be allowed or expected within its home jurisdiction. Linked to this, corporations might also use dummy or subsidiary corporations, especially overseas subsidiaries in order to divert responsibility from the parent corporation. Corporations might also develop environmental monitoring and auditing processes that shift responsibility away from the corporation and onto individual staff. Thus, in the event of a regulatory problem, the company can point to the existence of its environmental policies and argue that the subsidiary corporation or individual "rogue" employees are at fault rather than the parent company being responsible for any identified environmental harm linked to the corporation's practices.[2] McBarnet suggests a tension between conflicting responsibilities such that creative compliance becomes "something to be emulated rather than reviled" (2006, 1092) and is considered clever rather than deviant. McBarnet suggests that when deploying creative compliance, practices that might be illegal if not actually criminal, if structured in one way, can be legally repackaged and claimed to be lawful (McBarnet 2006, 1092). Accordingly, the essence of creative compliance is that it can be defended as *not* noncompliance (McBarnet 2006).

By contrast, constructive compliance refers to a process where corporations appear to be compliant with regulation, but this may not be the case. Sustainability and other forms of CER reporting can be constructed in a manner that suggests regulatory compliance whilst the reality is one in which it becomes impossible for staff to comply with environmental policies and practices and meet corporate (and personal) productivity targets. Such action may exploit staff propensity for risk-taking and a desire to push against traditional rules and structures (Obschonka, Andersson, Silberseisen, and Sverke 2013). In this scenario, testing the boundaries of compliance becomes incorporated into dueling with a weak environmental enforcement regime where repeated offending "builds in" the cost of responding to regulatory enforcement and prosecution and settlement costs arising from litigation and enforcement activity.

McBarnet primarily refers to "clever and imaginative legal problem solving" (2006, 1096) and the use of legal mechanisms to make potentially unlawful mechanisms and practices lawful. However corporate practices that embed environmental compliance within policies that can be referred to in the event of regulatory investigations but which in practice may not be effective also represent a form of creative compliance. Gallicano refers to active "greenwashing" where individuals are actively misled about a company's environmental practices (2011, 1). In a broader sense, inconsistency between a company's environmental claims and its actual behavior also represents a form of "greenwashing" as the following case study illustrates.

Case Study: Ineffective Justice: The Case of Shell's Deer Park Refinery

As indicated earlier weak environmental law enforcement allows corporate environmental crime particularly within competitive markets where the benefits of noncompliance may significantly outweigh the limited risk of detection and apprehension (Situ and Emmons 2000) identify. Heckenberg (2010) identifies that global environmental harm is part of a complex process of transference which can be "externalized from producers and consumers in ways that make it disappear from their sight and oversight" (White 2012a, 21). Movement of environmentally damaging products within global markets becomes difficult to police, especially given disputes over what is defined as environmentally harmful and what gets defined as a crime (White 2012a, 22). Thus, corporations seeking to maximize profits and minimize costs within lucrative global markets subject to ineffective laws and weak regulatory structures may seek to circumvent environmental legislation even while publicly making pronouncements of environmental responsibility. The context in which such incidents may occur is one in which the regulatory regime is designed to allow corporations to continue operating and to put problems right whilst the regulatory enforcement system operates alongside corporate activity.

The US Clean Air Act 1970 controls routine emissions at petroleum refineries, by creating limits and penalties for excess emissions. The Act makes provision for "upset events," air emissions released because of unforeseen or unavoidable circumstances, if companies report the emissions and take corrective action (Ozmy and Jarrell 2011). Deer Park, Texas, is home to a Shell chemical plant, one of the largest oil refineries in the US and which has been the subject of numerous alleged environmental violations primarily of the Clean Air Act. For example, in June 1997 an ethylene explosion at the plant was heard and felt up to 25 miles away. In 2008 environmental organization the Sierra Club filed a federal lawsuit against the Shell Oil Company and its subsidiaries over an estimated 1,000 incidents of pollution between 2003 and 2007 at the Deer Park refinery and chemical plant (Seba 2008). The pollution levels at the plant exceeded the levels allowed under permits issued by Texas regulators, amounting to a total of five million pounds of air pollutants into the atmosphere, "including toxic chemicals like benzene and 1,3-butadiene, as well as sulfur dioxide and oxides of nitrogen" (Mouawad 2009). Although Shell had been cited by regulators and had paid fines for some of the incidents, its alleged failure to take any action to resolve ongoing pollution concerns at the plant led to the Sierra Club and Environment Texas initiating the lawsuit to force enforcement of the Clean Air Act's provisions. Joshua Kratka of the National Environment Law Center (representing the Sierra Club and Environment Texas) stated that Shell was paying to pollute alleging that "Shell is factoring these fines into its costs of operating these facilities" (Seba 2008).

Yet publicly Shell had embedded sustainability and environmental best practice into its operating procedures since 1997. The company states that all of its operations "must take a systematic approach to managing environmental impacts" (2008, 21). The company further states that "Shell's groundbreaking first sustainability report *Profit and Principles—does there have to be a choice?* issued in 1998 after Shell's reputation and internal morale had suffered as a result of Brent Spar and human rights issues in Nigeria" set the benchmark for scrutiny of the company's practices (SustainAbility 2010). Thus, at the time of the problems at Deer Park, Shell had already instituted a CSR process with external scrutiny of sustainability issues and annual reporting. Since 2005 its sustainability reporting has been subject to the scrutiny of a committee of external experts and the company states it followed the GRI's guidelines. An external review committee assesses Shell's sustainability reporting content and processes; details of committee membership and reports are openly published by Shell online. For example, the 2011 committee includes experts from; the Indigenous Peoples Working Group of the Social Investment Forum, a barrister working with the International Finance Corporation, an Environmental Policy Advisor to Rio Tinto plc (who was also a visiting professor at Imperial and University Colleges, London), and the co-founder and CEO of policy think tank Civic Exchange. The committee thus arguably boasts considerable expertise independent of Shell's corporate structure; its 2011 report indicates Shell's engagement with sustainability issues but is also mildly critical of Shell's failure to achieve long-term sustainability action.

While it is not suggested that Shell was in any way influencing committee decisions, an overly critical committee risks its own survival and external advisors may well be diplomatic in the manner in which criticisms are couched. Other corporations use external auditors for their sustainability review (BP for example has used Ernst and Young). Shell's 2008 report, comments that "we have a structured company-wide approach for listening to our neighbors, for working with them to reduce negative impacts from our operations and produce local benefits" (Shell 2009, 26). It further comments that "all our refineries and chemicals facilities, as well as all upstream operations where impacts on the community could be high, have social performance plans in place" (Shell 2009, 26). The reporting further notes that Shell has instigated a "multibillion dollar program to end the continuous venting and flaring of natural gas at oil production facilities" (Shell 2009, 29) and noted improvements in energy efficiency at Shell chemical plants since 2001. Yet in the case of Deer Park the concerns and impact on residents were seemingly not directly being addressed either through the regulatory mechanism or the company's own monitoring process.

Connelly and Smith (1999) suggest that collective action is often the necessary solution to environmental problems where civil action can be used to seek a remedy in ways that criminal action often fails to. The failures in formal (state) enforcement action in Texas required citizen groups to sue to stop illegal air emissions arising from so-called "upset" events: equipment breakdowns, malfunctions, and other nonroutine occurrences. Luke Metzger, Director of Environment Texas explained that "despite repeat violation notices and fines, the Texas Commission on Environmental Quality never got to the root of the problems at Shell Deer Park" (Environment Texas/Sierra Club 2009). The lawsuit was subject to a settlement agreement in April 2009 requiring Shell to remedy the faulty processes at the plant which were causing pollution problems and to pay a civil penalty which would be used for further environmental measures (see below). Arguably it illustrates a means through which the impacts of creative compliance and corporate noncompliance can be addressed by justice systems, as the following section discusses.

Reparation for Environmental Damage

Combating those practices which may view the continued payment of fines as preferable to the costs of remediation or organizational change requires a change in regulatory approach. The use of the "polluter pays" principle for environmental damage was adopted by the OECD in 1972 as a background economic principle for environmental policy (Turner 1992). By making goods and services reflect their total cost, including the cost of all the resources used, the principle required polluters to integrate (or internalize) the cost of use or degradation of environmental resources. However, environmental damage is not solely an issue of cost and increasingly legislators, regulators and the courts apply the basic principles of restorative justice which include the "repair of harm" principle and mediation or contact between victim and offender as tools to remedy or mitigate corporate environmental damage.

Parker (2004) identifies a model where regulators are able to directly address creative noncompliance by imposing enforceable undertakings which allows regulators to employ their own creativity in recommending remedies for harm caused by corporate wrongdoing. The ideal for such effective restorative justice is that offenders are held to account for what they have done, realize the harm that they have caused and are encouraged to both remedy that harm and change behavior. Such mechanisms can work within the market by allowing regulators to impose market-based penalties that avoid the escalation of legal justice and its associated costs and delays (Marshall 1999). For example, a regulator may award compensation to consumers commensurate with the profits gained by noncompliance or require some form of reinvestment in facilities (see for example, the Southern Water case study in chapter 10). Applied to environmental damage restorative justice provides for legal enforcement of CER and moves beyond the general criminal law approach of punishment to embrace civil law's focus on remedying injustice such as environmental harm. It potentially provides for targeted enforcement action that negates the creative noncompliance of criminal entrepreneurialism.

The settlement negotiated by Shell in relation to the Deer Park pollution provides a model for negotiated settlements using restorative principles. The settlement required Shell to; reduce emissions from air pollutants from its plant by 80 percent within three years, upgrade chemical units and reduce gas flaring, and is also accompanied by a $5.8 million civil penalty. The settlement agreement between Shell and the environmental groups was subject to review by regulators (the EPA and the Justice Department) and also required the approval of the US District Court for the Southern District of Texas providing a measure of judicial oversight of the settlement. While it is impossible to achieve the ideal of putting the community back in the position it would have been in had the harm not occurred, the penalty will "be used to finance environmental, public health and education projects in Harris County including a project to reduce diesel emissions from school buses, and another to install solar panels on public buildings" (Mouawad 2009). Thus, Shell's damage to the environment at Deer Park is at least partially offset by positive environmental action.

CONCLUSIONS

While corporations may achieve voluntary compliance with CER and have appropriate CER polices at least on paper, it is essential that the application of CSR and CER principles are part of the legal and regulatory justice system. This is preferable to that system being applied only after environmental harms have occurred and disputes arise over corporate liability and appropriate remedies. Failures in voluntary compliance are inevitable where enforceable standards are lacking and there are disputes between NGOs, corporations, and communities over the responsibilities of corporations and the extent of stakeholder engagement. Where commercial imperatives override wider environmental responsibilities and are also associated with weak enforcement and regulatory regimes crime or noncompliance is more likely to occur. There are undoubtedly some cases (or types of environmental damage) for which negotiation between communities and corporations, or corporations and NGOs is inappropriate and where self-regulation and voluntary CER policy-compliance fails. In these cases; enforcers should be able to enforce CER through the imposition of remedial measures, reserving the right to move to formal prosecution action even though this may not provide full redress for the consumer.

Legislation needs to keep pace with persistent CER failures, corporate criminality, and creative criminal entrepreneurship; EU (and UK) legislation provides one means through which this can be achieved using restorative justice principles within the environmental law regime. The UK's *Environmental Damage (Prevention and Remediation) Regulations 2009* allows UK enforcers (generally the Environment Agency, the relevant local authority, or Natural England) to require corporations to remedy their environmental harm. In addition the UK's *Regulatory Enforcement and Sanctions Act 2008* allows for restorative principles to be applied to some cases of damage to the environment (including under the *Control of Pollution Act 1974*, the *Clean Air Act 1993*, the *Environment Act 1995, Water Industry Act 1991,* and *Water Resources Act 1991*) through the use of enforcement mechanisms that are designed to repair the harm caused by business practices (particularly through discretionary restorative notices and enforcement undertakings) rather than simply punishing offenders.

As Slapper (2011) indicates, US law now also provides a model that might be applied to enforcement of failed CER where CER compliance claims are found to be untrue or exaggerated and have the effect of misleading consumers. Such claims will primarily be the subject of civil action and it should be noted that the use of class actions is commonplace in the US but less so in the EU. But at least in theory, legislative and regulatory frameworks now exist that have not only moved firmly towards the "polluter pays principle" but which also allow for the actions of MNEs to be measured against their CER promises and an implied standard of behavior. Thus, those that are responsible for environmental damage may not only be subject to criminal enforcement activity and/or civil litigation but open themselves up to judicial scrutiny of their corporate governance procedures through legal processes. This falls short of achieving a global legal enforceable standard for CER. However, the availability of several routes through which CER failures can be enforced may not only make the polluter pay; but may also make the polluter stop and think before making unfounded claims of environmental responsibility while engaging in creative environmental noncompliance.

An earlier version of this chapter appeared as Nurse, A. (2015) "Creative Compliance, Constructive Compliance: Corporate Environmental Crime and the Criminal Entrepreneur" in Gerard McElwee and Rob Smith (eds) Exploring Criminal and Illegal Enterprise: New Perspectives on Research Policy and Practice*: 5 (Contemporary Issues in Entrepreneur Research), Bingley: Emerald Publishing. ISBN 978-1784415525. The chapter has been substantially revised for this book but its origins in the Exploring Criminal and Illegal Enterprise project are hereby acknowledged.*

NOTES

1. The "pollution havens" debate is a somewhat contested one with some writers such as Manderson and Kneller (2012) questioning the robustness of evidence that "dirtier" multinational enterprises (MNEs) are more likely to locate in host countries with lax environmental policy than cleaner MNEs. Other writers (Neumayer, 2001; Wheeler, 2006) identify that Global South countries can be said to provide a "pollution haven" if their environmental standards are below their efficiency levels or if they fail to enforce their standards in order to attract foreign investment. This raises the possibility that an easier operating environment and financial incentives may be allied to operating in a "pollution haven" rather than a deliberate attempt to avoid Global North environmental standards.

2. Parent company liability was, for example a contested issue in the Bhopal chemical disaster when on December 3, 1984, more than forty tons of methyl isocyanate gas leaked from a pesticide plant in Bhopal, India, immediately killing at least 3,800 people and causing significant morbidity and premature death for thousands more. Broughton (2005) suggests that parent company Union Carbide attempted to distance itself from legal liability and placed responsibility for the disaster on its Indian subsidiary. US litigation arising from Bhopal in part clarified that parent company Union Carbide was not responsible for the disaster (Hosein, 1993; Baxi, 2010). Environmental activists and others might argue otherwise and suggest that as a minimum the parent company has a moral responsibility for the harm caused by its actions. The Bhopal disaster has been analyzed extensively in academic papers and books from a range of different perspectives and it is beyond the scope of this book to examine the case in detail. However, some suggested material is included in the further reading list at the end of this book.

Chapter 6

Corporate Exploitation
of Natural Resources

(Oil and Gas and the Timber Trafficking Industries)

This chapter examines the exploitation of natural resources and the link between ostensibly legal use of natural resources and the criminal activity associated with such large-scale corporate operations such as oil and gas exploration and the timber trade.

Globalization's increased flows of people, products, and profits allow MNEs to operate freely in developing countries where regulatory controls may be weaker than in Global North countries and where public institutions (including government bureaucracy and the judiciary) may be weak and susceptible to economic pressure (Cox, in McGrew, 1997, 51). As earlier chapters indicate, neoliberal markets also tend to ignore or minimize externalities, particular the wide range of environmental harms that arise from ostensibly lawful activities which may result in pollution incidents such as oil spills (Lynch and Stretesky 2014, 8–10).

This chapter discusses the link between illegal exploitation of natural resources and human rights violations (discussed further in a later chapter) and the theme of legal actors committing offenses and the general failure of justice systems to prevent or effectively punish these acts. Thus, the theme of the legal facilitating the illegal is a core concern of this chapter, particularly in respect of (mostly western) MNEs who dominate the oil and gas extraction industries and are able to exert considerable economic power in Global South countries where they operate.

The chapter contains a case study of litigation against the major oil companies for their activities in Africa, discusses allegations of corruption raised against some major oil companies, and the challenges for affected communities in bringing legal action against major corporations.

GLOBALIZATION AND THE
EXTRACTION INDUSTRIES

This chapter continues with this book's application of a green criminological perspective to corporate environmental crime and the question of how to address environmental and social harms caused by the oil and gas extraction industries (with brief mention also of the timber trade). Sykes and Matza's neutralization theory (1957) is used in identifying the justifications used by corporations when committing crime or environmental harm. In addition, differential association theory helps to explain the situation that occurs when potential corporate offenders learn their activities from others in their community or social group (Sutherland 1973). As McBarnet's (2006) analysis identifies, corporate culture may rationalize an appeal to higher loyalties (profits and shareholders and continued market activity) and reinforce the perception that there is no harm in continuing with an activity that represents standard or widespread industry practice even where it suggests noncompliance with regulatory structures.

In the oil industry, for example, commentators have suggested that failure to address oil spills or mitigate the harmful effects of activities such as gas flaring are relatively commonplace (Ubani and Onyejekwe 2013, Ukala 2011, Bassey 2008). Baumüller et al. noted that

> negative impacts of the oil industry are a major concern in sub-Saharan Africa (SSA), threatening not only the health of local communities, but also the livelihoods they depend on. (2011, 1)

Decades of oil exploration in the Niger Delta have resulted in pollution of much of the region's vegetation, fishponds, and drinking water, undermining farming and fishing livelihoods. These effects are sufficiently severe to meet green criminology's expanded definition of what should be classed as crime by virtue of constituting significant environmental harm (White 2008).

Whereas Baumol (1990) distinguished between legal and illegal actors (see chapter 5), this chapter acknowledges that MNEs involved in oil extraction are legal actors but that oil extraction may result in harmful consequences for ecosystems which may fall outside the strict legalistic definition of crimes (Situ and Emmons 2000) where these are unintended or accidental consequences of a lawful activity. Remedying such activities often proves problematic for a variety of reasons, not least the inherent failure of justice systems to deal with corporate environmental harms and the ongoing conflict between the profit-making demands of neoliberal markets and the relative weakness of environmental law enforcement regimes. As indicated earlier, enforcement actions are often predicated on regulatory control rather than harm or crime prevention. Arguably there is inevitable conflict between the legitimate actions of MNEs in the oil and gas extraction industries, and the needs of local communities. Awareness of the "illegal" or noncompliant nature of their actions leads corporations to employ the justifications outlined by Sykes and Matza (1957).

White (2007) identifies inequality as a significant aspect of environmental justice, particularly the manner in which ethnic minority and indigenous communities suffer at the hands of western forces. Rachman (2009) identifies energy derived from oil as significant for the world's largest economies (the EU, US, China, and Russia), none of which are entirely self-sufficient in oil thus relying on sources other than their own to meet energy needs. Considerable incentive, and economic benefit, thus exists for MNEs operating in the oil and gas industries to continue their operations. This also gives major oil companies such as BP, Shell, and Exxon considerable power when negotiating with governments, particularly within developing nations in Africa where oil resources are integral to a country's economy (Amnesty International 2011, 2009). Some oil companies wield considerably more economic power than developing world governments particularly within African countries where "administrative neglect, crumbling social infrastructure and services, high unemployment, social deprivation, abject poverty, filth and squalor, and endemic conflict" present enduring problems (Amnesty International 2009, 9) despite the natural resource wealth and income that might be derived from oil and gas reserves.

Similar concerns exist in the timber industry. Myburg (2011) suggests that the illegal timber trade is worth as much as US$7 billion per year, (unreported and unregulated) fisheries trade alone was valued at between US$4.2 billion and US$9.5 billion per year. Figures reported by the United Nations Office on Drugs and Crime (UNODC) put the trade in illegal timber from South-East Asia to the European Union and Asia as worth an estimated $3.5 billion in 2010. Economic considerations drive much environmental crime; particularly profit-driven crimes fueled by demand for forest products or where wildlife has negative economic impact on producers such that its destruction or removal and destruction of habitats becomes desirable to achieve or maintain economic benefit (White 2008). Timber markets, for example, demonstrate the relatively simple mechanics of supply and demand. Where demand for such products is high and lawful supply is limited, illegal logging is likely to occur particularly to fuel the demand of an international market where end consumers and participants in the trade may be "flexible" concerning the source of products and where historically weak trade rules have allowed the trade to continue (Smith et al. 2003). Rhodes et al. (2006) identify problems of illegal logging as primarily being based in economic concerns where loggers with uninhibited access to source woods are able to supply the market irrespective of the wider costs of any illegal activity they conduct.

Kishor and Lescuyer (2012) in their discussion of illegal logging argued that "little has been done so far to specifically fight illegal logging in the domestic markets of the tropical countries" (2012, 8) although some recent initiatives arguably seek to address this. Concerns remain that little has been done in consumer countries albeit consumer-based social crime prevention is emerging as a potential solution to illegal timber trafficking and endangered species trade. Thus market-based approaches can address the demand for and supply of timber products targeting prices and markets for timber products and substitutes such as sustainable harvested resources.

CORRUPTION IN THE OIL AND GAS INDUSTRIES

Oil extraction in Africa and the behavior of MNEs typifies a number of elements common to corporate crime and white-collar crime discourse, particularly regarding corporate noncompliance and crimes of the powerful (Ruggiero and South 2013). Nieuwoudt (2007) has suggested that bribery by MNEs in seeking to win exclusive drilling and processing or prospecting licenses has resulted in payments to the overseas accounts of government ministers or payment of such things as their children's private school fees. Claims of corruption in the granting of exclusive drilling or prospecting rights are also relatively common (Casertano 2013, Rees 2011, Rosenstein 2005) especially in those countries generally considered to be poor but which are oil rich, providing them with valuable natural resources to be exploited. Unlike mainstream criminology where mostly illegal actors are involved in activities defined as crimes by the criminal law, exploitation of natural resources often involves legal corporations operating with tacit or explicit approval of states who often benefit economically and politically from their actions (Situ and Emmons 2000). However, legal markets facilitate illegal ones, allowing organized crime to also operate under the cloak of legitimized markets and transnational flows of products (White and Heckenberg 2014, Lynch and Stretesky 2014, Ruggiero and South 2013). Corporations are able not only to exercise considerable economic power to subvert regulations and avoid prosecution but are also able to exploit legal systems in ways that impact negatively on the ability of local communities to enforce their environmental rights or to combat the legal resources available to MNEs (Hobson 2006).

Neoliberal markets and an anthropocentric view of nature as being a resource for human benefit undermine the willingness of legislators and states to deal with environmental harms while simultaneously identifying how criminology's techniques of neutralization (Sykes and Matza 1957) are employed as tools to nullify culpability for environmental harm and minimize enforcement actions intended to address these. As mentioned earlier, Matza's (1964) drift theory applies to offenders who drift in and out of delinquency, fluctuating between total freedom and total restraint, drifting from one extreme of behavior to another. While they may accept the norms of society they develop a special set of justifications for their behavior which allows them to justify behavior that violates social norms. These techniques of neutralization (Sykes and Matza 1957) allow them to express guilt over their illegal acts but also to rationalize between those whom they can victimize (e.g. animals, the environment) and those they cannot (other humans), and when and where they should conform and when it may be acceptable to break or subvert the law. As an example, for those offenders whose activities have only recently been the subject of legislation, the legitimacy of the law itself may be questioned, allowing for unlawful activities to be justified. For others whose activities are subject to weak enforcement or purely technical regulatory regimes noncompliance may be a legitimate tactic.

Corporate activity linked to oil exploration in the Niger Delta indicates a range of problems that suggest companies may drift in and out of corporate delinquency (Tombs and Whyte 2015). Problems include oil spills which carry the threat of contamination of the local environment and undermine farming and fishing livelihoods. Steiner identifies that as a consequence of oil production in the Niger Delta the region has suffered:

> extensive habitat degradation, forest clearing, toxic discharges, dredging and filling, and significant alteration by extensive road and pipeline construction from the petroleum industry. (Steiner 2010, 4)

The extent to which such actions and consequences are the result of deliberate or accidental activity is contested. Yet, a green criminological approach concerned with environmental harms and environmental victims (Hall 2013) would contend that a failure to consider and mitigate the harmful effects of corporate action should be classed as crime even where the criminal law has not yet dictated this (White 2008). Hawke identifies that

> historically there has been considerable reluctance to characterize anti-environmental behaviour as criminal, even assuming that it has been straightforward to draw a line below which the sanctions of the law—civil *and* criminal—will apply to such behavior. (1997, 12)

Stallworthy (2008, 22) identifies environmental problems and environmental regulation as primarily being matters of an economic and political nature where competing interests and values and ideological concerns determine the extent of regulation and the nature of sanctions employed where environmental standards are not being complied with. From a criminological perspective, the corporate response to problems within the oil and gas extraction industries indicates that Sykes and Matza's (1957) neutralization techniques are in operation. Given the continued legality of oil extraction and natural resource exploitation and sustainable use, MNCs engaged in lawful activity that is then linked to perceived wrongdoing in a way that arguably challenges their status as legitimate actors by labeling certain actions as "criminal," requires a response. One consequence of this is that the MNEs respond to the labeling either in an increasingly deviant manner (McBarnet 2006, Sykes and Matza 1957) or via the use of neutralization techniques which assert their core values and the underlying legitimacy of their actions while challenging the enforcement or regulatory regime. Thus, techniques such as denial of responsibility, claim of entitlement, denial of the necessity of the law, defense of necessity and condemnation of the condemners are all present, reflecting the research of Sykes and Matza (1957) which identified that individuals involved in offending use these techniques both before and after engaging in illegal or deviant activity.

Case Study: Litigating against Oil Companies for Their Activities in Africa

Oil spill incidents are common in the oil industry in Nigeria, a fertile area of oil exploration. The main sources of oil spill on the Niger Delta are: vandalization of the oil pipelines by the local inhabitants; aging of the pipelines; oil blow outs from the flow stations; cleaning of oil tankers on the high sea and disposal of used oil into the drains by the road side mechanics. By far the most serious source of oil spill is through the vandalization of pipelines either as a result of civil disaffection with the political process or as a criminal activity. The United Nations Environment Programme (UNEP) assessing the problem of oil spills concluded that "oil spills are frequent events in Ogoniland" (UNEP 2011, 167). The oil spills negatively impacted on communities in the Niger Delta, destroyed livelihoods, and endangered the health of local populations. UNEP's environmental assessment concluded that "oil contamination in Ogoniland is widespread and severely impacting many components of the environment." (UNEP 2011, 204). Commenting that the effects of oil pollution are felt by the Ogoni people 365 days of the year UNEP also noted that given a low average life expectancy (at one point under 50 years) in Nigeria, it is a fair assumption that most members of the current Ogoniland community have lived with chronic oil pollution throughout their lives. (UNEP 2011, 204)

However, taking prosecutions against the oil companies within Nigeria has proven problematic for a variety of reasons. UNEP identify that there are considerable difficulties with bringing legal action using domestic legislation in Africa due to the inaccessibility of much legislation. UNEP states

> few texts are available online and many are not easily available even in paper form. In addition, printed copies of legislation, such as the "Laws of the Federation of Nigeria," are extremely expensive and therefore limited to those able to bear the costs. (2011, 142)

As a result there is a lack of transparency in the legal system which undermines confidence both in its efficacy and in the ability to access the system and gain appropriate remedies.

Accordingly, a number of cases have taken place in Europe for activities carried out in Africa by the major oil companies as the following case examples illustrate.

Milieudefensie (Friends of the Earth Netherlands) versus Royal Dutch Shell

Milieudefensie (Friends of the Earth Netherlands) and four Nigerian farmers brought charges against both Shell Nigeria (Shell Petroleum Development Company of Nigeria (SPDC), a subsidiary of Shell) and the Dutch parent company/multinational (Royal Dutch Shell Plc) due to oil pollution. The case is considered unique as the first time that a Dutch multinational has been brought before the court in its own country for environmental damage caused abroad. Examination of the case documents and related press statements published online by the Dutch Court, by Milieudefensie and by Shell provide a means through which the criminological aspects of the case can be explored. Content analysis of the documents reveals the conflicting perspectives of Milieudefensie, Shell, and the Nigerian farmers involved on the nature of: the level of environmental harm; the clean-up requirements for the alleged harm; culpability for any environmental damage arising from the oil company's activities in Nigeria; and the necessity of legislation and the role of the NGO as "regulators" or monitors of corporate environmental wrongdoing.

The case focuses on three oil leaks in the villages of Goi, Aruma, and Ikot Ada Udo which took place between 2004 and 2007. Milieudefensie and the four victims argued that:

a. Shell must repair the damage in the three villages by properly cleaning up the oil;
b. Shell must prevent new leaks from occurring in the future, by properly maintaining its material and protecting it from sabotage;
c. Shell must compensate the four victims for the damages suffered.

The case sought to determine the liability of Shell Headquarters in The Hague for damages allegedly caused by its subsidiary SPDC in Nigeria, establishing liability on the part of corporations for the behavior of their subsidiaries. The cases were heard in the Dutch court, because the claims were not only directed at Shell Nigeria, but also target the parent company. Despite objections from Shell the Dutch district court ruled that it was justified to adjudicate on the lawsuits against all Shell entities in the Netherlands, because the lawsuits were closely connected and EU law provides a means through which EU and overseas cases can be heard together where doing so is deemed to be in the interests of justice.

Green criminology has documented the persistent nature of law-breaking in respect of pollution, disposal of toxic waste, and misuse of environmental resources (Pearce and Tombs 1998). Corporate crime discourse argues that corporations armed with the knowledge of a weak environmental regulatory regime (both nationally and internationally) and the preference of governments to use administrative or civil penalties as tools to deal with corporate environmental offending may creatively adopt noncompliance or partial compliance with environmental regulations within their operating practices. White and Heckenberg argue that "the politics of denial (at both the level of ideology and policy) is propped up by various techniques of denial" (2014, 133). Where prosecutions are taken, market interests are not best served by admissions of guilt or other actions which might hamper sectoral business interests. Thus, denial of culpability becomes a legitimate if not necessary tactic which runs the gamut from denial of injury through to condemnation of the condemners as exhibited in this case. While neutralization techniques are in no way indicative of the respondent's culpability in either criminal or civil cases, they are of criminological interest in assessing attitudes towards the offense, the perceived legitimacy of proceedings and towards the alleged victims. Hawke identifies that

> many environmental regulatory agencies are only gradually developing policies targeting those who are the "directing mind and will" of a polluting company. (1997, 19)

The question of who within a corporation is directly responsible for polluting activity takes on added importance when dealing with subsidiary corporations in developing world countries. Indeed central to this case and Shell's defense was the argument that Royal Dutch Shell (RDS) is not responsible for the activities of its Nigerian Subsidiary SPDC.

In its response to the Summons issued by Friends of the Earth Shell argued that:

> Even though Royal Dutch Shell plc (RDS) regret that this spill occurred, of course, they are not liable for this spill or for the consequences for the reasons that will be set out below. The oil spill was caused by sabotage, the oil flow was stopped and the clean-up and remediation of the consequences of the spill were properly performed.

In addition to denying liability, and contending that the blame lay with third party saboteurs, Shell argued that SPDC took adequate action before, during, and after the spill (para 30 of its response to the summons). In addition, Shell contend that the remediation efforts were blocked by the Oruma community (paras 32 and 35 of the summons response) who denied access to the site thus also invoking denial of the victim as a further neutralization technique. Shell note that the Oruma spill was reported on Sunday June 26, 2005, but that for various reasons

> the Oruma community did not allow Shell to inspect the site of the oil spill until 29 June 2005, and then merely to verify the existence and location of the oil spill and subject to the strict condition that SPDC would not perform any (repair and /or containment) work. Thus the inspection could only comprise an overall identification of the location and scope of the oil spill. . . .
>
> As soon as SPDC managed to verify the existence and location of the oil spill on 29 June 2005—contrary to what Oguru et al. argue—SPDC stopped the oil flow through the pipeline.

Implicit in this explanation and further text within the response to the summons is an explanation of the "victims" contributing to their own harm and arguably mitigating any liability the corporation might have. Arguably the explanation also serves to undermine claims of losses and damage by the alleged victims; if the spill were serious, logic dictates that they would take advantage of the MNEs help on offer to address this. the global reach of MNEs is situated within international markets and systems of production, requiring a system of understanding and addressing environmental harm that incorporates appreciation of its international dimensions (Beirne and South 2007). In this respect where oil companies cause environmental harms in developing world countries, their activities may be viewed as a crime of the powerful irrespective of whether formally recognized as such by the criminal law or whether requiring action under civil law to address (Barak 2015;

Tombs and Whyte 2015; Situ and Emmons 2000). Implicit in the court documents is a view of the corporation as providing a valuable service hampered by the activities of the local community. Shell notes:

> It requires no explanation that the fact that the community refused to grant SPDC access also resulted in delays in the clean-up and remediation work and that these delays and the resulting damage must come at the expense of the community. (Para 56 of Shell's response)

In this respect there is a downplaying of the concerns or needs of the affected community compared with those of the corporation. Schlosberg (2007) identifies environmental justice concerns as being predominantly those of marginalized groups (ethnic minorities and poor communities) unable to exert their environmental rights and gain access to justice. The implied failure of the community to provide access for clean-up operations carries with it the implication that victims have contributed to their own misfortune and thus should be denied the claimed remedy. Shell's account of the reasons for the Oruma community's actions also suggests that the community was less concerned with addressing the immediate problems and potential harm and more with frustrating the actions of the MNC. Perhaps inadvertently, this indicates an "us and them" mentality.

The Hague District Court found that four out of five oil spills which were the subject of the legal action were not the result of poor maintenance by Shell but were caused by sabotage by third parties. The court applied the relevant Nigerian law which specifies that an oil company is in principle not liable for any oil spills resulting from sabotage. This conclusion identifies that the primary fault or harm is not an action of the oil company but results from damage or environmental harm caused by a third party. Applying this principal, the court dismissed four out of the five cases and, in respect of four lawsuits regarding an oil spill near the village of Goi in 2004 and an oil spill near the village of Oruma in 2005, the district court concluded that Shell Nigeria took sufficient measures to prevent sabotage of its submerged oil pipelines. However, in the fifth claim relating to two oil spills in 2006 and 2007 from an abandoned wellhead near the village of Ikot Ada Udo, the district court concluded that Shell Nigeria had violated its "duty of care" under applicable Nigerian law and had committed the "tort of negligence." The district court acknowledged that the 2006 and 2007 spills were also the result of an act of sabotage but noted that this was committed in a very simple way near that village by using a wrench to remove above-ground heads of an oil well abandoned by Shell Nigeria. The court ruled that Shell Nigeria could and should have easily prevented the sabotage by installing a concrete plug prior to 2006, whereas it only did so in 2010 while the lawsuit was pending.

The court therefore concluded that Shell could be held *partly* responsible for the claimed pollution in the Niger Delta. The judgment, while falling some way short of declaring Shell responsible for all of the pollution incidents, identified that Shell should have prevented sabotage at one of its facilities in Nigeria which caused a spill damaging to the environment and local wildlife resources.

The Ogale and Bille People versus Shell

In 2016, London's High Court heard lawsuits filed by the Ogale and Bille people alleging that decades of oil spills have fouled the water and destroyed the lives of thousands of fishermen and farmers in the Niger River Delta, where a Shell subsidiary has operated since the 1950s. Shell again argued that the case should be heard in Nigeria, pointing out it involves its Nigerian subsidiary SPDC, which runs a joint venture with the government, and Nigerian plaintiffs. The Ogale and Bille people sought compensation for damages arising as a result of serious and ongoing pollution and environmental damage caused by oil spills emanating from Shell's oil pipelines and associated infrastructure. They also sought damages for clean-up and remediation costs or alternatively injunctive relief.

In January 2017 the London High Court rejected jurisdiction over the claims against the parent company, finding that the claimants failed to present an arguable claim that the parent company was responsible for the systematic pollution caused by its subsidiary. The court held that, since the case against the parent company had no prospect of success, the claims against the Nigerian subsidiary could also not proceed in English courts thus it held that claimants needed to seek redress in Nigerian courts. The claimants appealed the case arguing that the court decided the merits of the case at a very early stage before full disclosure of documents and oral testimony, which would have provided evidence on the relationship between the parent and the subsidiary thereby influencing the outcome. On February 14, 2018: The Court of Appeal dismissed the appeals. In a split decision, the court ruled that there is no arguable case that RDS could be held legally responsible for the actions of its Nigerian's subsidiary. At time of writing the claimants are believed to plan taking their case to the UK Supreme Court.

The Bodo Community versus Shell

This case was also heard in London and handled by London law firm Leigh Day. It relates to oil spills in Bodo in late 2008. Shell accepted responsibility for the spills but contested the volume of oil spilled which it claimed was about 4,000 barrels, impacting on only 36 hectares of land. By contrast, the ‘claimants’ experts suggested that the amount of the spill was as large as that of the Exxon Valdez Alaskan disaster of 1989. SPDC’s (Shell’s Nigerian subsidiary) pipelines running through Bodo are nearly 50 years old and have not been maintained or inspected properly by SPDC. Both spills continued to pour oil out into the environment for weeks even after SPDC had been alerted to the oil spills. They claimants stated that the Bodo spill caused the largest loss of mangrove habitat by oil pollution in history. The oil spills resulted in massive contamination of the creek, rivers, and waterways in the Bodo area and devastated the local mangroves, fauna, wildlife, and fishing stocks. In July 2011, following a letter of claim from Leigh Day, SPDC admitted liability for the two oil spills in the Niger Delta. An agreement was reached where SPDC formally agreed to accept liability and accepted the jurisdiction of the English courts, which meant that a claim against SPDC could be brought in the High Court in London. Shell originally offered $50,000 before the Bodo people took their case to the UK court. The case was eventually concluded via a landmark agreement from Shell to pay $83.5m in compensation to the Bodo community for damage caused by oil spills in 2008 and 2009 (BBC News 2015).

Corporate Environmental Crime and Oil Exploration

Holtom (2011) has suggested that the crime of ecocide could be applied to severe environmental damage such as major oil spills on the basis of strict liability; i.e., that to convict somebody of the crime all one need do is prove that the incident occurred, irrespective of the intentions of the person or corporation responsible for the event. Criminological analysis of oil extraction in Africa identifies corporations as integral to environmental harm problems, particularly those which impact on nonsustainable habitats and exhibit a failure to address the needs of other species (Benton 1998 and 2007, Nurse 2013). Ecocide remains a contested notion which has not yet been adopted within international criminal law regimes. Yet the principle of responsibility for environmental harm through alleged negligence is an important one explored in this case.

Corporations who break environmental laws and expected standards of environmentally responsible behavior illustrate green criminology’s concern with the failure of justice systems to address environmental harms. Baumüller et al. identified that while oil companies will sometimes take action to address the harmful impacts of their activities, corporate social responsibility activities largely remain piecemeal and short term, community engagement is inadequate and requirements for accountability and transparency are either insufficient or not enforced. (2011, 7)

Despite the existence of various international conventions and legislation, the regulatory approach and criminal justice response to environmental crime is often not a core policing responsibility; is frequently left to NGOs to monitor; or is dealt with via "lesser" options like environmental tribunals and is the responsibility of environment departments like the Department for Environment Food and Rural Affairs in the UK, and the US Department of the Interior rather than criminal justice ones like the Home Office (UK) and Department of Justice (US). The Shell case in the Netherlands is unique in being the first time the Dutch multinational has been brought before the court in its own country for environmental damage caused abroad. It's also the first time Shell has been ordered to pay compensation for damage caused in Nigeria.

The impact of the Shell case is difficult to quantify. Initial responses to the case saw both sides claiming victory with Shell declaring itself satisfied with the verdict and commenting that it would not change the way it conducts its business in Nigeria (UPI 2013). Shell also successfully defended claims against its parent company for the actions of its Nigerian subsidiary. However, Friends of the Earth and the Nigerian Plaintiffs also claimed victory because despite the dismissal of four claims Shell was found liable in a Dutch court for failings in Africa. Given that the plaintiff, the Nigerian defendant and, the environmental claims at the heart of the case were all located outside of the EU, the ruling can be seen as a significant step forward in allowing court action to be taken for corporate environmental crimes and arguably legitimizes such action being taken by NGOs. The cases taken by Leigh Day in London are also of interest in showing how the problems inherent in taking cases in Africa where the government has an interest in the case and in ensuring continued oil revenues. The judgments of the District Court of The Hague can thus be seen as part of the development of international law dealing with corporate harms which allows multinationals to be held accountable in their home jurisdiction for damage that has been caused by or is related to the operations of their foreign subsidiaries. This is significant in part because the use of subsidiaries in countries with (perceived) weak judicial systems is a mechanism through which corporations seek to protect themselves from costly environmental litigation (Kneller and Manderson 2008 and discussed elsewhere in this book). However, in the UK and the US, for example, we have seen multinationals sued on the basis of a so-called "foreign direct liability." A claimant may seek to bring proceedings before an EU or US court rather than locally for a variety of reasons including, for example, dissatisfaction with local proceedings, lack of independence or expertise of the courts, or extensive possibilities for delay. An additional reason for organizations such as Friends of the Earth Netherlands to bring a claim against both the subsidiary and the parent company in the country of the parent company will be to draw attention to the issue of corporate social responsibility in the home market of the multinational. However, the *Okpabi v. Shell* case (the Ogale/Bille communities) illustrates that there are continuing difficulties with such cases. In the Okpapi case the judge disregarded certain evidence on the close relationship between the parent company and its subsidiaries that was available in the public sphere. The burden of proof in proving the relationship to a court's satisfaction is a substantial barrier to claimants bringing foreign direct liability cases in a parent company's home state. Claimants rarely have access to the internal documents of the company revealing its structure, organization, and true relationship to its subsidiary. The issues identified here may be even more pronounced in the case of indigenous peoples addressing "theft" by corporations, as the next chapter illustrates.

Chapter 7

Corporate Environmental Crime, Biopiracy

This chapter examines biopiracy as a form of corporate environmental crime. In particular, the chapter examines the actions of biotechnology corporations involved in the exploitation of natural products with medicinal and healing properties in a manner where doing so exploits the resources of developing nations. This chapter's examination of biopiracy provides for a theoretical explanation of the manner in which indigenous or peasant knowledge of nature (e.g. on medicinal plants or agricultural seeds) is used by others for profit. In one sense biopiracy is a problem of the Global North's continued exploitation of the Global South; thus raising questions about neocolonialism and the appropriation of others' knowledge (Aoki 2017). Smith (2010) identifies how Western (Global North) multinational corporations are dominant in exploiting natural resources often at the expense of the rights of indigenous peoples. Supporters of western corporations' activities call this "bio-prospecting," while opponents often refer to it as biopiracy using the following broad definition of "the practice of commercially exploiting naturally occurring biochemical or genetic material, especially by obtaining patents that restrict its future use, while failing to pay fair compensation to the community from which it originates" (Oxford English Dictionary 2013).

This chapter examines biopiracy in the context of commercial development of naturally occurring biological materials, such as plant substances or genetic cell lines. This takes place in a manner that is arguably criminal involving such activity as land theft, human rights abuses, bribery, and fraud. Accordingly, the chapter argues that biopiracy represents a crime of the powerful where illegal or at least unethical means are employed to pursue a legitimate goal. Green criminology's ecological justice perspective (Benton 1998, White and Heckenberg 2014, Nurse 2015) is also of relevance to assessing how biopiracy's corporate environmental crime issues should be dealt with via justice systems. This chapter critically examines the advantages and disadvantages of dealing with biopiracy as a criminal justice issue rather than a civil law or commercial (business) law issue.

DEFINING BIOPIRACY

The term biopiracy is a somewhat contested term, with its implication of illegal or harmful activity denoted by the "piracy" part of the word and its connotations of theft. Shiva (2007, 307) suggests that the term bioprospecting "was created in response to the problematic relationship between global commercial interests and the biological resources and indigenous knowledge of local communities." Bioprospecting is preferred as the word for describing the discovery of an unknown plant or organism which is then subject to scientific processes to identify unknown beneficial properties (Garcia 2015, 8). These previously unknown properties can then be turned into a new patentable (and trademarked) product. For example, the discovery of caffeine-like properties in a previously unknown plant could lead to the development of a new energy drink. The company producing the drink has developed a new product from a naturally occurring compound and will quite reasonably wish to protect its investment and recover the costs of its scientific and manufacturing processes. However, the plant arguably only exists due to cultivation by local people who are then denied access to a share of any profits from the drink that arguably only exists due to their cultivation of the original compound. Activities by transnational corporations who seek to exploit natural resources thus raise various concerns over ownership and intellectual property (discussed later in this chapter).

Robinson (2010) suggests that "biopiracy" refers either to the unauthorized extraction of biological resources, such as plants with medicinal properties, and associated traditional knowledge from indigenous peoples and local communities, or to the patenting of "inventions" based on such knowledge or resources without compensation. This denotes the reality that biopiracy is somewhat of an umbrella term for a range of activities that can involve exploitation of natural resources and knowledge and the creation of new products. Hamilton (2006) suggests that the term biopiracy originally emerged to challenge various aspects of the intellectual property rights regime in respect of living organisms. Global North citizens are likely aware from even a relatively early age that the protection of ideas and knowledge involves legal systems and complex discussions around ownership and authorship. However, as bioprospecting (and biopiracy) by its very nature invariably involves engaging with naturally occurring flora and fauna generally unfamiliar to Global North citizens, this requires engaging with indigenous and Global South communities that may be unfamiliar with the concepts of intellectual property and complex Global North notions of land or ideas ownership. Thus, biopiracy also raises issues surrounding the extent to which concepts of environmental knowledge are socially constructed and are an aspect of corporate environmental crime. Thus, biodiversity raises a number of issues surrounding power relationships where illegal or at least unethical means are employed to develop new pharmaceuticals and medicines (Ruggiero 2015). Arguably as the commercial development of naturally occurring biological materials in biopiracy, such as plant substances or genetic cell lines, takes place in a manner that is arguably criminal as it involves such activity as land theft, human rights abuses, bribery, and fraud.

Biopiracy discussions also examine corporate use of nature which is potentially unlawful where it is done without permission from and with little or no compensation or recognition to the indigenous people or vulnerable communities themselves who may lay claim to the natural resources involved. However, local people and indigenous peoples who have arguably contributed to the development of natural resources are often marginalized in the development of such projects and in some cases their rights are actively ignored. White and Heckenberg (2014) refer to this as the "corporatization of agriculture" identifying that major corporations have begun to take control of agriculture to the extent that "the basic means of life of humans is being reconstituted and reorganized through global systems of production" (2014, 146).

Assessing the scale of biopiracy is difficult given that much activity will take place outside of the sight of monitoring agencies and official bodies. Given the conflicting definitions and perspectives outlined earlier in this chapter it is also likely that many biopiracy problems will only come to light once a challenge is raised to the exploitation of a natural resource. Thus, a dark figure of biopiracy likely exists as has been suggested in other areas of crime where under-reporting masks the true extent of the activity (Penney 2014, Skogan 1977). However, biopiracy is generally recognized as a global problem and studies suggest that Africa alone could be losing more than US$15 billion from its biodiversity as medicines, cosmetics, agricultural products, and indigenous knowledge surrounding these are being patented illegally by multinational companies. India is also estimated to be losing more than $250 million annually from biopiracy and estimates put the illegal exploitation of the Amazon's resources through biopiracy in Amazonia as costing Brazil $16 million USD per day. This is mostly due to a lack of policy and poor enforcement of what protections they do have (Danley 2011).

LAND THEFT AND BIOPIRACY

Rob White (2012b) identifies that land use is often integral to the survival of indigenous people who have a close relationship with the land and resources derived from sustainable use of natural resources (discussed further later in this chapter). However, White also argues that transnational corporations have increasingly taken over and utilized the planet's natural resources. He contends that "in some places, the appropriation of formerly communal or traditional lands is at the point of a gun, as companies hire thugs to remove and bulldoze people's home and villages" (2012b, 205). White argues that two core problems exist in relation to land grabbing:

1. Lands are being converted from food production to biofuel production, thereby reducing the amount of food available and leading to escalating prices for crops such as soya and corn.
2. Formerly communal lands are being forcibly seized by companies and/ or governments and transferred into private hands. The "ownership" as well as the use of the land is being re-jigged in favor of private interests and private profits.

Bioprospecting (in the context of being the worldwide search for plants with special properties, such as for medicinal use) that is unregulated and inappropriate can be considered a form of over-exploitation which has the potential to degrade ecosystems and increase biodiversity loss, as well as impacting on the rights of the communities and nation-states from which the resources are taken (see for example, Mgbeoji 2006). This form of bio-piracy involves taking from the land, and claiming ownership over what the land produces, without regard to the significant knowledge, traditions, and contributions of traditional land holders. Biopiracy also raises concerns in respect of flex crops (a crop that has multiple characteristics and uses) and genetically modified organisms (GMOs). The four key flex crops are maize, palm oil, soya beans, and sugar cane but others exist and a crop such as fast-growing trees can be sold, for example, for timber products, biofuel, and carbon offsets. Accordingly, biopiracy offers a means for transnational corporations to develop flex crops through the process of genetic modification, loosely defined as:

- deletion, multiplication, modification, or moving of genes within a living organism; or
- transfer of genes from one organism to another; or

- modification of existing genes or construction of novel genes and their incorporation in an organism; or
- utilization of subsequent generations or offspring of organisms modified in any of the above ways (White and Heckenberg 2014, 147)

GM technologies have achieved some notoriety in respect of the application of the technology to food products and claims that GM crops are vital in order to feed the world. However, GMOs are also used to provide modified strains of plants and vegetation that can be developed into pharmaceuticals and this is often the core focus of biopiracy. Once a product has been modified into a new form, considerations under patent law arise (discussed later in this chapter) where corporations claim ownership and intellectual property rights over new products that can then be exploited within global markets. This is a multi-million (if not billion) dollar industry because once ownership is asserted and a product is patented, transnational corporations can take legal action against anybody infringing their ownership and intellectual copyright in a product, including the indigenous people from the area in which the original plant was sourced.

As example, Richard Lloyd Parry writing in *The Independent* in 2001 outlined the story of the Bintangor tree, which grows in swampy ground in the Malaysian part of Borneo. Parry explained how American scientists had identified that the Bintangor tree contained a drug called Calanolide A, which could be extracted from the tree's latex and reduces the levels of the Aids virus in the blood and also works against tuberculosis. If successfully developed in a way that allows it to be sold commercially, the drug derived from the Bintangor tree could be worth as much as £250 million a year, but the native Dyak people who still live in the area will see nothing from the exploitation of the tree despite their cultivation of the tree and its habitat over several generations which has allowed the tree to reach its current state. Lloyd Parry raises the prospect that much scientific research is in reality biological copyright infringement perpetrated upon native people—not so much bio-prospecting as bio-piracy. The issues are legally, ethically, and politically complex. Aoki (1998) blames neoliberal markets, arguing that the principle of free trade means that western multinational corporations are in a dominant position which allows them to exploit developing nations and their vulnerable communities. However, in some cases, indigenous people and local farmers have developed the strains of natural products over generations, thus they arguably have some intellectual property rights over natural resources and so for a transnational corporation to come in and make a profit off the back of indigenous peoples' labor without paying due compensation arguably amounts to theft.

Legal Protection for Indigenous Peoples

Certain cultures have practices involving use of nature and even animal harm (Nurse 2013) that represent a form of cultural self-expression at odds with accepted Global North notions of environmentalism of animal use and exploitation as inherently criminal or evil, reflecting different cultural notions concerning the acceptability of animal killing (Preece 1999). Indigenous peoples may, therefore, have developed cultural practices arguably at odds with contemporary environmental protection legislation and environmental protection paradigms that seek to limit or eliminate certain forms of natural resource exploitation. Thus, potentially contemporary environmental protection legislation risks threatening the cultural expression and identity of indigenous peoples where their traditional practices might be criminalized as a consequence of changes in environmental and wildlife protection laws. Contemporary environmental protection perspectives, for example, generally include prohibitions on unsustainable use of animals and unnecessary suffering caused to animals in food production. Killing of animals for food is also tightly regulated (Croall 2007) such that much killing of animals outside of the regulated activity of animal processing operations risks giving rise to legal problems in the taking and use of animals. Use of rare or threatened plants for medicinal purposes might also be regulated and some plants are protected by mechanisms such as the Convention on International Trade in Endangered Species of Wild Fauna and Flora (CITES) which protects some 30,000 species of plants against over-exploitation through international trade. National endangered species protection laws that implement CITES or domestic conservation and nature protection laws may also include nation specific regulations on the possession and use of indigenous plants. However, human rights law explicitly recognizes the "difference" of indigenous practices via its incorporation and classification of the rights of indigenous peoples into a framework of exemptions from certain legislative provisions. Specifically, human rights law provides land rights and rights of cultural preservation that sometimes recognizes that indigenous peoples should be exempt from the confines of national environmental or animal law where it is considered necessary to do so in order to give effect to cultural self-preservation and expression.

Indigenous peoples are broadly recognized as distinct ethnic groups by international and regional regulatory bodies. They are given a legal status in international law that acknowledges both historic and present threats and the assimilation and alienation of their traditional way of life. The International Labour Organisation's (ILO) 1953 guidelines (still in force today) describe indigenous peoples as:

descendants of the original aboriginal population living in a given country at the time of settlement or conquest (or successive waves of conquest) by some of the ancestors of the non-indigenous groups in whose hand political and economic power at present lies. In general, these descendants tend to live more in conformity with the social, economic and cultural institutions which existed before colonization or conquest . . . than with the culture of the nation to which they belong; they do not fully share in the national economy and culture owing to barriers of language, customs, creed, prejudice, and often out-of-date and unjust systems of worker-employer relationship and other social and political factors. (ILO 1953, para 25–26)

The International Covenant on Civil and Political Rights of 1966 also states that:

In those States in which ethnic, religious or linguistic minorities exist, persons belonging to such minorities shall not be denied the right, in community with the other members of their group, to enjoy their own culture, to protect and practice their own religion or to use their own language. (Article 27)

Further protection for indigenous peoples and clarification of their rights was provided by the United Nations Declaration on Indigenous Peoples (UNDRIP) which was adopted by the UN General Assembly on Thursday, September 13, 2007, by a majority of 144 states in favor, 4 votes against (Australia, Canada, New Zealand, and the United States) and 11 abstentions (Azerbaijan, Bangladesh, Bhutan, Burundi, Colombia, Georgia, Kenya, Nigeria, Russian Federation, Samoa, and Ukraine). The four countries originally voting against UNDRIP subsequently reversed their position and by 2017 were all in support of the declaration. UNDRIP is arguably the most comprehensive contemporary international instrument on the rights of indigenous peoples. The UN argues that "it establishes a universal framework of minimum standards for the survival, dignity and well-being of the indigenous peoples of the world and it elaborates on existing human rights standards and fundamental freedoms as they apply to the specific situation of indigenous peoples" (United Nations 2018). The basis of the declaration is to affirm that indigenous peoples are equal to all other peoples, while recognizing the right of all peoples to be different, to consider themselves different, and to be respected as such. In this context, the declaration recognizes "the urgent need to respect and promote the inherent rights of indigenous peoples which derive from their political, economic and social structures and from their cultures, spiritual traditions, histories and philosophies, especially their rights to their lands, territories and resources" (Annex to the Declaration, United Nations, 2018). Accordingly, Article 5 of the declaration states that "indigenous peoples have the right to maintain and strengthen their distinct political, legal, economic, social and cultural institutions, while retaining their right to participate fully, if they so choose, in the political, economic, social and cultural life of the State." Article 8 provides that states shall provide for effective mechanisms for prevention and redress for (among other things):

a. Any action which has the aim or effect of depriving [indigenous peoples] of their integrity as distinct peoples, or of their cultural values, or ethnic identities;
b. Any action which has the aim or effect of dispossessing [indigenous peoples] of their lands, territories, or resources;

Several articles of UNDRIP also set out the framework for forms of access to environmental justice including Articles 24, 25, and 26 which arguably protect the right of indigenous peoples to exploit natural resources (including wildlife) located within their community and to have their indigenous knowledge recognized and protected, as follows:

• Article 24—Indigenous peoples have the right to their traditional medicines and health practices, including the right to the protection of vital medicinal plants, animals and minerals.
• Article 25—Indigenous peoples have the right to maintain and strengthen their distinctive spiritual and material relationship with the lands, territories, waters and coastal seas and other resources which they have traditionally owned or otherwise occupied or used, and to uphold their responsibilities to future generations in this regard.
• Article 26—Indigenous peoples have the right to own, develop, control, and use the lands and territories, including the total environment of the lands, air, waters, coastal seas, sea-ice, flora, and fauna and other resources which they have traditionally owned or otherwise occupied or used. This includes the right to the full recognition of their laws, traditions and customs, land-tenure systems and institutions for the development and management of resources, and the right to effective measures by states to prevent any interference with, alienation of, or encroachment upon these rights. (United Nations 2018)

Accordingly, UNDRIP provides a framework for a form of environmental justice for indigenous peoples and indicates to states the importance of protecting their rights. In addition to the general provisions in international law such as the International Covenant on Civil and Political Rights and UNDRIP which puts states under an obligation to positively protect minority rights, specific provisions exist in national laws to provide aboriginal subsistence rights. Such rights are the main route through which aboriginal people may achieve food security and thus the animal killing which takes place in exercising those rights constitute legal activities that would otherwise be unlawful. Harvesting of rare plants arguably also falls within the provisions of Article 24 and might be permitted where it would otherwise be unlawful. However, such activities are usually strictly controlled mainly through the use of quotas which determine the number of animals that can be killed and permits which specify who is authorized to carry out activities. Control and monitoring by external authorities and through legal or regulatory systems raises questions about both the mechanisms through which cultural identity is controlled. Cultural self-expression is arguably also evidence in the form of traditional knowledge although there is no clear or universally accepted definition of what constitutes traditional knowledge. Accordingly, traditional knowledge can be defined as any knowledge developed by or within indigenous communities and can also be defined as any form of tradition-based intellectual activity (Garcia 2015). Knowledge can be classed as tradition-based in any environment where there is a circulation of knowledge within a community where knowledge is handed down to each successive generation. Such knowledge likely also needs to evolve and adapt to suit changing circumstances and developments, particularly where communities have increased contact with or are influenced by other aspects of contemporary society. Thus, traditional knowledge which forms part of the self-expression of a community can include a wide range of activities incorporating everything from the cultivation of plants and creation of medicines through to recipes and nutritional supplements or knowledge for the preservation and propagation of plants. This knowledge may be exploited by biopiracy companies, sometimes without the knowledge of the indigenous peoples, thus legal mechanisms may become important to protect indigenous groups from this form of corporate environmental crime or to provide a remedy when such crime occurs.

Biopiracy and the Law

As the preceding text illustrates, biopiracy raises a number of legal issues surrounding ownership of biogenetic material and the rights to exploit this. While a full assessment of the legal issues and resultant case law is beyond the scope of this book, some basic principles can be outlined within this chapter's discussion. International law has sought to provide some background protection for biodiversity within the Convention on Biological Diversity (CBD) an international treaty written in Rio de Janeiro in June 1992. The CBD aims to conserve biodiversity on an international scale by promoting sustainable use and benefit-sharing. The CBD also seeks to ensure that access to a genetic resource is divided on mutually agreed terms and is subject to prior informed consent of the group providing access to the resource. Thus, in theory indigenous groups who will often provide access to biogenetic material and arguably have an interest in the exploitation of such material should be protected. While in one sense nobody *owns* nature or natural resources, the cultivation of natural resources by indigenous communities arguably provides them with some claim towards compensation or a share of the profits for products that arguably would not exist but for their knowledge and involvement. However, what constitutes appropriate compensation for the use of genetic resources is not defined within the CBD and specific regulations are left to the decision of the countries who ratified the convention. Thus, legal control and ownership of plants and traditional (indigenous) knowledge of the uses of plants (TKUP) is problematic particularly at the international level, because of the conflicting interests of states or groups of states and the manner in which they will implement anti-biopiracy measures within national law.

The patent system provides a means through which ownership of compounds derived from bioprospecting can be asserted. Greenacre (2002, 34) explains that "patents play an integral role in the industrial development and production of knowledge, particularly in the post-industrial 'knowledge economies' of the North." Arguably patent regimes have to straddle several different and conflicting objectives. From a purist perspective, patent regimes exist to stimulate development, innovation, and originality by providing inventors and others with rights that ideally ensure that they can obtain a financial return "for their investment of time, money and effort" (Greenacre 2002, 34). This goal must also be balanced against the competing need "to ensure that the technological, economic and social benefits of new knowledge are able to permeate as widely as possible through society" (Greenacre 2002, 34). Accordingly, patent regimes provide limited rights that arguably only extend for a short period of time and amount to protection of the original idea or innovation that then needs to be quickly exploited. Arguably this system favors those with the time and resources to create, innovate, and then manufacture or develop and inevitably in areas such as bioprospecting, major corporations have become involved.

International patent standards are enforced through the 1883 Paris Convention for the Protection of Industrial Property. However, the extent to which traditional knowledge and the rights of indigenous peoples are protected under current international patent standards is questionable as "anyone can patent traditional knowledge without providing any financial compensation to the actual inventors" (Garcia 2015, 18). The TRIPS agreement (mentioned earlier) arguably aims to provide protection to intellectual property rights owners and creators, rewarding their innovativeness and creates intellectual property standards. However, it too fails to protect traditional knowledge by allowing states to determine aspects of their own patent law.

Garcia (2015, 14) also notes that "because traditional knowledge is still generally transferred by oral tradition, it is not found in printed publications that patent examiners look to during prior art searches." Thus, knowledge that falls outside of existing documentation and recognition risks falling outside of consideration when patents are applied for, effectively allowing corporations to claim their exploitation of natural resources as new and innovative knowledge that the patent system arguably is intended to protect. In this respect, the patent system and Global North legal mechanisms arguably favor multinational corporations to the detriment of indigenous communities and other actors who lack knowledge of such legal mechanisms or the resources to engage with patent systems. Subbiah (2004) suggests that traditional knowledge faces considerable difficulties in being recognized under patent law. There are challenges, for example, in establishing the exact date at which knowledge became formalized and accepted. Evidentiary barriers also arise during the application process for a patent where a failure to establish when any knowledge breakthrough took place means that traditional knowledge cannot qualify for legal protection. The wording of patent law that might include phrases such as "identifiable inventor" are also problematic in relation to traditional knowledge. Indigenous communities do not necessarily document the creation of knowledge in the same manner as Global North communities that are steeped in the language and concepts of legal protection and documenting dates of discovery and authorship. Gebru (2019) identifies that a core requirement of patentability is that patent applicants provide background and contextual information about their invention to the patent office. Since patent applications must also be written in the language of the patent law system (Garcia 2015, 18) this arguably disadvantages indigenous communities unfamiliar with patent law and such legal application processes. Thus, indigenous communities are at a distinct disadvantage when pitted against the resources and legal expertise of multinational biotechnology corporations. Even where communities are able to engage the services of expert outside counsel; they may still find themselves at a disadvantage against a major corporation. The patent system is a product of international law and institutions and is arguably Eurocentric in nature. The system favors transnational corporations and international agricultural research institutions as they affect legal ownership and control of plants. Within the system, non-Western forms of knowledge are systemically marginalized and devalued as "folk knowledge" and are characterized as being suitable only as objects of anthropological curiosity (Mgbeoji 2006).

Some states have begun to introduce biopiracy laws that protect against theft of naturally occurring resources. For example, India's Biological Diversity Act 2002 contains a clause (4) that states:

No person shall, without the previous approval of the National Biodiversity Authority, transfer the results of any research relating to any biological resources occurring in, or obtained from, India for monetary consideration or otherwise to any person who is not a citizen of India or citizen of India who is non-resident as defined in clause (30) of section 2 of the Income-tax Act, 1961 or a body corporate or organization which Is not registered or incorporated in India or which has any non-Indian participation in its share capital or management. makes biopiracy a crime

The act contains clauses aimed at making biopiracy a crime (see the case study later in this chapter) as part of the country's response to its obligations under the 1992 Rio Convention. Nijar (2017) also indicates that Malaysian biopiracy law means that "a permit will be required to access our biological resources for research and development; or to access traditional knowledge of indigenous peoples associated with these resources. If it is for a commercial purpose, then there must be a benefit-sharing agreement with the resource provider—invariably indigenous and local communities." Other countries have begun to follow suit with biopiracy laws and attempts have been made to prosecute biopiracy offenses in some states. For example, it was widely reported in 2012 that Brazil had fined thirty-five firms US$44 million for biopiracy (Andrade 2012). The decision to issue the fines followed official complaints filed by the Genetic Heritage Department of the Brazilian Ministry of Environment to the Brazilian Institute of Environment and Renewable Natural Resources (Ibama) the agency in charge of protecting biodiversity. Andrade (2012) reported that thirty-five different companies were responsible for 220 violations of Brazilian national law on biodiversity, and most of the fines were levied on Brazil-based cosmetic and pharmaceutical multinational corporations. Some of the companies were fined for not sharing financial benefits from the exploitation of Brazil's biodiversity, and others for falsely claiming that they did share the benefits, according to Ibama. Brazil's national law on biodiversity stipulates that benefit-sharing resulting from the exploration of biodiversity can include: the sharing of profits or payment of royalties; technology transfer; and the training of people in the region from which a resource has been taken. In 2018 American firm Sambazon were investigated by Brazilian authorities for allegedly using the genetic material of Brazilian acai fruit without permission (Boadle 2018). While there are several such illustrative cases, prosecuting biopiracy is problematic because it involves clearly identifying an offense for which there is no common definition. Most countries have legislation protecting natural resources however not all countries have legislation which assigns intellectual property rights over natural resources meaning that permission must be sought from a rights owner before a natural resource can be modified or exploited. In some cases, it also unclear who actually "owns" the plant or crop which is the subject of biopiracy unless a state has passed a specific law protecting its biodiversity and making its exploitation unlawful. However, where this has been achieved, there is scope for a prosecution as the following case study illustrates.

Case Study: Monsanto in India

In India, Monsanto and its Indian partners have faced prosecution for biopiracy for violating the country's biodiversity laws over a genetically modified version of eggplant in what became known as the Bt Brinjal case (Tencer 2011). The National Biodiversity Board (NBA) and the Karnataka Biodiversity Board filed a case for criminal prosecution of thirteen individuals, including some top management officials of Mahyco or Maharashtra Hybrid Seeds Co. Limited (partly owned by Monsanto) for biopiracy.

Abdelgawad (2012, 136) "identifies that India is one the ten megadiverse countries of the world accounting for 7.8 of the global recorded species." As indicated earlier in this chapter, India's Biological Diversity Act 2002 contains provisions to protect biodiversity and also sets up a statutory regulatory body, the National Biodiversity Authority of India (NBA). Sudha (2014, 49) identified that the NBA and other authorities complained in 2012 that the Monsanto subsidary along with others had unlawfully accessed and modified "at least 10 varieties of brinjal in Karnataka and Tamil Nadu" without the mandatory approvals and then laid illegal proprietary claim to the genetically modified seeds of the local eggplant. Accordingly, they were accused of biopiracy under India's Biodiversity Act 2002 because the law dictates that when biodiversity is being accessed *in any manner* (my emphasis) for commercial, research, and other uses, "local communities who have protected local varieties and cultivars for generations must be consulted and if they consent benefits must accrue to them per the internationally applicable Access and Benefit Sharing Protocol" (Sudha 2014, 49). In essence the case is about genetic modification of India's biological resources without permission. The case originated in a biopiracy complaint made by Environment Support Group, a Bangalore-based NGO in 2010. However, the authorities took no formal action for two years even after investigating and concluding that there was a clear case of biopiracy involved. It was only when Environment Support Group, seeing inaction by the government, filed a public interest litigation complaint in the Karnataka High Court in 2012 seeking directions to compel the regulatory agencies to move against existing complaints of biopiracy, strengthen the regulatory processes to prevent any further acts of biopiracy, and also ensure that the Biological Diversity Act was implemented in its letter and spirit, that the authorities finally filed charges against the accused in November 2012.

Biopiracy as Corporate Environmental Crime

Cases such as the Indian Bt Brinja one are relatively rare, although various countries are now beginning to view biopiracy as something which requires them to take action. The issue to be determined is how best to address biopiracy concerns, through natural resources legislation, criminal legislation, civil law, or business legislation. Despite the existence of international agreements on biological diversity, it is still largely left to the individual state to decide how it will implement biodiversity protection in its national law and how best to regulate sharing benefit from the resources of biodiversity exploitation. Thus, the risk remains that in developing countries dependent on the economic input of transnational corporations; biodiversity regulation could remain relatively weak or favor corporations over indigenous people.

Biopiracy once again illustrates the exercise of neutralization techniques by corporations in the appeal to higher loyalties (economic interests over environmental concerns) and the denial of harm being caused to nature or indigenous communities (Wyatt and Brisman 2017). It also illustrates how a regulatory approach needs to extend beyond the narrow confines of criminal law enforcement to consider other aspects of the environmental harm involved.

Chapter 8

Corporate Environmental Crime and Climate Justice

Undoubtedly climate change is one of the most significant threats facing mankind and represents a major form of environmental harm, placing it firmly within the remit of an environmental harm-based green criminology (Hall 2014). Yet arguably, criminology has only recently paid attention to the issue despite scientific concern being expressed about global warming over several years. This chapter examines the enforcement and regulation of corporate polluting activities linked to climate change. Antipollution legislation generally allows regulators such as the US Environmental Protection Agency (EPA) to take action where a corporation fails to adhere to pollution or emission limits. Environmental protection laws often provide regulators with tools that allow them to require remedial action, such that corporations may need to modify their processes to reduce environmental harm. Tempus (2014) identifies environmental action through the courts as one route through which climate change might be addressed and by which climate justice could be achieved. But the effectiveness of climate change litigation is questionable and court action arguably fails to directly address breaches of greenhouse gas regulations although regulatory action which imposes noncriminal sanctions will likely be the mechanism through which such actions are resolved. This chapter discusses climate justice through two case studies; one involving state failure to deal with pollution issues and the second a discussion of the Volkswagen emissions case.

PERSPECTIVES ON CLIMATE CHANGE AND CLIMATE JUSTICE

Discussions of climate change largely center around its effects in the form of global warming and changed weather patterns. White (2018a, 50) identifies that "narrow sectoral interests embedded in present socioeconomic dynamics are driving global warming as well as responses to regulating or taxing the emissions that contribute to it." Climate change is a consequence of a range of activities, some lawful and some unlawful but with the majority of these situated within corporate activity. White and Heckenberg (2014) provide the following definitions of climate change and global warming:

> *Global warming* describes the rising of the earth's temperature over a relatively short time span. *Climate change* [emphasis in original] describes the interrelated effects of this rise in temperature: from changing sea levels and changing ocean currents, through to the impacts of temperature change on local environments that affect the endemic flora and fauna in varying ways (for instance the death of coral due to temperature rises in sea water, or the changed migration patterns of birds). (2014, 1)

These definitions clarify the far-reaching effects of global warming and climate change which identify them as causing significant environmental harm. Arguably climate change could be defined as ecocide according to a definition that characterizes this as "the extensive destruction, damage to or loss of ecosystem(s) of a given territory, whether by human agency or by other causes, to such an extent that peaceful enjoyment by the inhabitants of that territory has been severely diminished" (Higgins 2010, 63). Were the crime of ecocide to be added to the definitions of international crime contained within the Rome Statute of the International Criminal Court, arguably some climate change causing activities would become actionable as crimes under international law. Williams (2011, 500) identifies that "the effects of rising global temperatures are likely to be experienced across every aspect of human life and will vary dependent on the extent of the temperature increase." Field et al. (2014) identify that human interference with climate systems and the resultant climate changes poses risks for both human and natural systems. They identify that: glaciers continue to shrink worldwide as a result of climate change and that melting snow and ice are altering hydrological systems impacting negatively on water resources' quality and quantity; while only a few species extinctions can be directly attributed to climate change, many terrestrial, freshwater, and marine species have altered their geographical ranges, seasonal habits, and migration patterns; and climate change has negatively affected wheat and maize yields for several regions and is having negative impact on crops (Field et al. 2014, 4–6).

These issues should characterize climate change as worthy of consideration from an academic perspective as being concerned with the negative impacts on human health and in respect of action that causes social harm. However, White (2018b, 9) suggests that the (relative) silence within criminology in respect of research into climate change "is itself a form of denialism—involving as it does passive denial of topicality and importance." Schlosberg and Collins (2014) suggest that generally discussions of climate justice in the academic literature focus on ideal conceptions and normative arguments of justice theory, or on the pragmatic policy of the more elite environmental NGOs. However, green criminology examines climate change within critical notions of climate justice that focus on impacts of climate change, vulnerabilities, and the litigation and enforcement efforts of NGOs. It is perhaps understandable that climate change would not automatically draw the attention of criminologists, particularly given the reality that much climate change is as a result of lawful activity, or at least the behavior of legal actors (mainly corporations) albeit actors causing significant environmental harm. The lack of a clear offender or specific criminal offense of "climate change" would also place climate change outside the remit of mainstream criminology. Criminology has also been somewhat slow to consider corporate and state crimes again understandable given that not all jurisdictions provide for corporations to be treated as criminal actors (Nurse 2014).

However, climate change clearly permeates contemporary policy discourse and most contemporary governments recognize that climate change represents a problem that must be addressed (White and Heckenberg 2014, 103) although there may not be consensus on precisely how to achieve this. While there are international agreements on climate change and individual states have passed their own legislation dealing with aspects of climate change (discussed later in this chapter), as with many other areas of environmental harm the enforcement of legislation and the development of appropriate policy are larger problems than the specifics of legislation. Effective enforcement of environmental laws and policy requires a regulatory or criminal justice regime able to appropriately deal with offenses and enforce standards.

However, despite a general scientific consensus of climate change as the result of human action and thus also meeting Lynch and Stretesky's (2014) criteria of being harmful human action which should be the subject of green criminological enquiry, the question remains whether climate change constitutes a crime? Notwithstanding the existence of some climate change deniers who contend that human action is not *directly* responsible for global warming (discussed later in this chapter) much climate change is likely the result of lawful activities. Legitimate business activities are the cause of some harmful impacts on the environment and greenhouse gas emissions are frequently a by-product of lawful operations, thus business' climate change causing activities are not crime in the strict socio-legal sense (Situ and Emmons 2000). Even where climate change is the result of regulatory breaches such as exceeding or ignoring pollution controls and other violations of environmental protections and clean air statues, it may not constitute crime, particularly where climate change is an incidental consequence of the regulatory breach. Such offenses are often regulatory or administrative in nature and do not fall within the remit of the criminal law. Kramer (2012, 1) goes so far as to suggest that "any consideration of environmental crime and its victims should include an analysis of anthropocentric global warming and associated climate change. Outside of a nuclear war, there is no other form of environmental crime that can produce a wider range of victims." He further explains that climate change has been variously described as "an ecological catastrophe, an existential threat and an apocalyptic event" (ibid.) thus from an ecocentric environmental harm perspective, climate change would undoubtedly constitute a green crime.

Climate Change Denial

While there is a general consensus among the scientific community that climate change is a real human-caused phenomenon (White 2018a) there remain some pockets of climate change denial. Such denial exists in the form of those who contest either the reality of climate change or the reality of climate change as having a *direct* human cause. Kramer argues that there has been political failure to act to regulate or mitigate emissions which cause climate change and a "socially organized denial of climate change that shapes that failure" (2012, 1). The consequences of this denial has resulted in "crimes of omission by individual states and the international political community" (ibid.) which has failed to effectively consider climate change as an international crime.

A range of corporate and state actors engaged in climate change denial interact to deny that global warming is caused by human activities, to block efforts to mitigate harmful greenhouse gas emissions, to exclude or prevent ecologically sound or just adaptations to climate change from the political arena; and also to adopt responses to climate change that have the effect of excluding marginalized communities and those likely to suffer most from climate change's harmful effects (White & Heckenberg 2014, 112). Dunlap (2013) provides a somewhat rational explanation for climate change denial noting that the complex nature of anthropocentric global warming makes it difficult for the layperson to understand its causes, to fully appreciate its impacts, and to grapple with the necessity of taking action that could alleviate its impacts. In addition, policy makers may underestimate the severity of the problem and may be unconvinced about what action to take or deny the necessity of particular causes of action. Denial of climate change may, therefore, constitute a rational response to a problem that appears beyond an individual's ability to solve.

Antonio and Brulle (2011) suggest that climate change denial might also be situated in ideological positions. Their contention reflects the notion that American politics operates within two polarized positions: *market liberalism* that stresses strong property rights and unfettered capitalism, and *social liberalism* that favors modest state intervention, redistribution, and welfare provision. Thus, in one sense acceptance of climate change and measures that would limit the structures of capitalism and even end the treadmill of production is "anti American" (Antonio and Brulle 2011, 195). Accordingly, those imbued with the spirit of market liberalism may strongly contest climate change policies on ideological grounds. From a criminological perspective their neutralization techniques once again link us back to Sykes and Matza (1957) and a whole range of neutralizations and justifications from denial of injury through to an appeal to higher loyalties (the continuation of the capitalist way of life). McCright and Dunlap (2011) identify that in the US, conservative white males are significantly more likely than other Americans to endorse denialist views on climate change; even more so in the case of those conservative white males who self-report understanding global warming very well. Via an analysis of ten Gallup opinion surveys from 2001 to 2010 focusing on five indicators of climate change denial, McCright and Dunlap (2011) concluded that the views of conservative white males contribute significantly to the high level of climate change denial within the United States. In part, they identify that conservative think tanks, media, and corporations have a vested interest in disputing climate change, given the likely consequences of emissions controls and curbs on business activities, and that conservative white males are receptive to such climate change denial views. Arguably this is reflected in what McRight and Dunlap (2011) refer to as the "climate change denial machine," which consists of a coordinated campaign of climate change denial. The machine may be effective (from a criminological perspective) because it allows individuals to form perceptions about risk shaped by their cultural worldviews such as hierarchism, egalitarianism, individualism, and adherence to market principles (Kahan et al. 2007). Thus, corporations and politicians that wish to resist changes to the operation of markets and production processes are able to deploy Sykes and Matza's (1957) techniques of neutralization as tools to exercise their own sociocultural perspectives on climate change denial. Kahan et al. (2007) identify that individuals are likely to adopt shared beliefs according to socioeconomic cultural and intellectual groups to which they belong or identify with "often resisting revision of such beliefs when they are confronted with contrary information from perceived out-groups" (McCright and Dunlap 2011, 3). Kahan et al. refer to this as "identity-protective cognition" which serves as a protective mechanism for the status and self-esteem that individuals receive from group membership (2007, 470). Criminologically neutralization techniques serve a similar function by allowing offenders to: appeal to higher loyalties such as membership of a deviant group or group which finds itself being stigmatized; deny the legitimacy or enforcement action or to challenge the motives of an enforcer; rely on tradition; or to claim that the alleged crime is victimless and not deserving of official attention (Sykes and Matza 1957). Perspectives on climate change can, thus, be challenged in a variety of ways using various explanations to do so.

Climate change denial is also socially constructed as arguably it is experienced in different ways according to a range of factors such as class, socioeconomic status, and geography. Thus, politicians and commentators in the Global North who are largely protected from the impacts of climate change may be freer to deny climate change than those in the Global South who are more likely to experience its effects. The lack of a direct personal impact is, thus, a potential factor as the effects of climate change as a global phenomenon may be disproportionately felt by Global South countries in the form of failed crops or the negative impacts of adverse weather patterns. Western communities may well be affected by changes in temperature or increased extreme weather events; but are generally either equipped to deal with these or are served by emergency services capable of preventing large scale loss of life. Insurance and other services are also able to aid in the rebuilding process where negative impacts have been felt. Thus, the effects of climate change and global warming might be seen as transient or temporary with the more severe impacts being felt by "other" or future communities. Where people receive conflicting information from scientists, politicians, and the media, a risk exists that they will either align themselves with the scientific and policy perspective that best matches their existing viewpoint and cultural beliefs or will be disincentivized to act due to uncertainty.

Williams (2011) identifies the global nature and impact of climate change as requiring "an international solution, one that reconciles the interests of different states and achieves a widespread agreement on an appropriate and effective plan of action" (2011, 503). One mechanism in place to pursue such climate justice at an international level is the United Nations Framework Convention on Climate Change which entered into force on March 21, 2004, and at time of writing has been ratified by 197 countries (Parties to the Convention) which include all UN member states and the supranational European Union.

Article 1(2) of the Convention defines climate change as:

a change of climate which is attributed directly or indirectly to human activity that alters the composition of the global atmosphere and which is in addition to natural climate variability observed over comparable time periods.

Article 2 of the Convention specifies that:

The ultimate objective of this Convention and any related legal instruments that the Conference of the Parties may adopt is to achieve, in accordance with the relevant provisions of the Convention, stabilization of greenhouse gas concentrations in the atmosphere at a level that would prevent dangerous anthropogenic interference with the climate system. Such a level should be achieved within a time frame sufficient to allow ecosystems to adapt naturally to climate change, to ensure that food production is not threatened and to enable economic development to proceed in a sustainable manner

Article 3 of the Convention specifies:

1. The Parties should protect the climate system for the benefit of present and future generations of humankind, on the basis of equity and in accordance with their common but differentiated responsibilities and respective capabilities. Accordingly, the developed country Parties should take the lead in combating climate change and the adverse effects thereof.
2. The specific needs and special circumstances of developing country Parties, especially those that are particularly vulnerable to the adverse effects of climate change, and of those Parties, especially developing country Parties, that would have to bear a disproportionate or abnormal burden under the Convention, should be given full consideration.
3. The Parties should take precautionary measures to anticipate, prevent or minimize the causes of climate change and mitigate its adverse effects. Where there are threats of serious or irreversible damage, lack of full scientific certainty should not be used as a reason for postponing such measures, taking into account that policies and measures to deal with climate change should be cost-effective so as to ensure global benefits at the lowest possible cost

Taken together, these conditions, accepted by states when ratifying the treaty, amount to an obligation to prevent climate change irrespective of any doubts about the scientific case for climate change or the necessity of taking action based on scientific assessment. The Convention uses the language of the precautionary principle (Gullett 1997) to specify that action is required to deal with climate change before it happens ("anticipate, prevent") as well as to take action where harmful activities are taking place ("minimize the causes of climate change and mitigate its adverse effects"). Employing the precautionary principle means adopting a "risk based" regulatory approach that arguably requires proactive rather than reactive legislation, i.e., legislative and regulatory response that prevent something from happening rather than responding after the event (Fazio and Strell 2014).

Measures such as the US Clean Air Act 1970 and the UK's Environmental Protection Act 1990, while not explicitly or solely climate change legislation also create regulatory and enforcement frameworks to deal with emissions. Arguably climate change adaptation fails to deal with existing harms caused by climate change and the impending threats to ecosystems. However, from a criminological perspective, adaptation and mitigation can be integrated into justice systems through regulatory and criminal justice measures that act as social controls. For example, emissions controls can have the effect of punishing those who drive fuel inefficient vehicles via higher road taxes (where applicable). Excessive pollution, particularly that consisting of harmful emissions that contribute to climate change can be the subject of regulatory or criminal sanctions such that corporate activity that contributes to climate change becomes a crime or subject to regulatory control aimed at changing behavior. Arguably a range of environmental legislation already serves this function such that while specific "climate change" offenses may not exist, polluting activities linked to climate are, in some cases, already environmental crimes.

Climate Justice through Litigation

Provisions in domestic (national) law relating to damage to the environment or pollution already exist that provide for some pollution actions which cause climate change to be addressed. While practical enforcement in laws like the Clean Air Act 1970 and the Environmental Protection Act 1990 may be predominantly directed at low-level emissions such as fumes or smoke that exceed permit levels, they provide a means through which enforcers might take action to address harms that have a cumulative effect and where a corporation fails to adhere to pollution or emission limits. Legislation such as the clean air acts generally provide regulators with tools that allow them to require remedial action, such that corporations may need to modify their processes to reduce environmental harm. Environmental statutes may contain criminal and civil sanctions with discretion provided to regulators over which sanctioning mechanism to use and over the form that regulatory enforcement will take.

Contemporary climate change litigation is arguably a growth area, in respect of both campaigners seeking to use litigation to enforce climate change rules, and business seeking to reduce the burden of climate change-related legislation on corporate activity. As an example of the former, in *Massachusetts v the Environmental Protection Agency* 549 U.S. 497 (2007) a group of private organizations petitioned the EPA requesting that the EPA regulate emissions of carbon dioxide and other gases that contribute to global warming from new motor vehicles. The case hinged on an interpretation of the US Clean Air Act which defines "air pollutant" to include "any air pollution agent . . ., including any physical, chemical . . . substance . . .

emitted into . . . the ambient air" §7602(g). The Act requires that Congress via the administrative and regulatory functions of EPA "shall by regulation prescribe . . . standards applicable to the emission of any air pollutant from any class . . . of new motor vehicles . . . which in [the EPA Administrator's] judgment cause[s], or contribute[s] to, air pollution [and that can] reasonably be anticipated to endanger public health or welfare" (§202(a)(1) of the Clean Air Act). The EPA denied the petition arguing that the Clean Air Act did not authorize it to regulate greenhouse gas emissions. The EPA also argued that even if this was a correct interpretation of the Act, it had discretion to defer a decision until more research could be done on "the causes, extent and significance of climate change and the potential options for addressing it." The case was ultimately decided in the US Supreme Court which concluded that greenhouse gases (GHGs) which are widely viewed as contributing to climate change, constitute "air pollutants" within the meaning of the US Clean Air Act. Meltz (2013, 2) identifies that as a result, the Court concluded that "the U.S. Environmental Protection Agency (EPA) had improperly denied a petition seeking CAA regulation of GHG emissions from new motor vehicles by saying the agency lacked authority over such emissions." The consequence of this was that the EPA would be required to determine whether or not emissions of greenhouse gases from new motor vehicles cause or contribute to air pollution which may reasonably be anticipated to endanger public health or welfare (EPA 2013). Subsequent to this case, the EPA issued a series of greenhouse gas-related rules including: an Endangerment Finding, in which the EPA determined that greenhouse gases may "reasonably be anticipated to endanger public health or welfare"; and the EPA issued the "Tailpipe Rule" setting emission standards for cars and light trucks.

Markell and Ruhl (2012, 21) identify "a rapidly building wave of litigation" in the US, identifying that since the *Massachussets* case "EPA and other state and local agencies have put climate change law on the books in the form of regulations, permit issuances and denials, and other discrete decisions" (ibid.). Thus, separate from regulatory action aimed at polluting bodies and industry, litigation that seeks to enforce existing legislation and take action against state failures and the state-corporate crime arguably inherent in corporate actions that cause climate change (White 2018b) provides for contemporary climate change action. The Natural Resources Defense Council[1] collates data on litigation against clean air act provisions and a brief sample of cases from its database identifies where industry-related challenges seek to prevent increased clean air rules. While it is beyond the scope of this book to produce a complete analysis of the cases, the following brief examples illustrate some aspects of contemporary climate change litigation.

In *Arkema Inc. v. U.S. EPA, 618 F.3d 1* (D.C. Cir. 2010) Protection the EPA lost to an industry challenge to the EPA's cap-and-trade program for ozone depleting substances. Under the Clean Air the EPAs cap-and-trade program involves setting overall caps on production and consumption of various HCFCs for each year, as well as determining EPA-administered baseline allowances of HCFCs for each participating company. Companies are then permitted to transfer their allowances, subject to certain statutory and regulatory restrictions. The D.C. Circuit Court vacated portions of EPA's cap-and-trade program for reducing ozone-depleting substances and determined that that EPA had illegally invalidated credit transfers. The lawsuit concerned EPA regulations designed to meet U.S. commitments under the Montreal Protocol, which requires member countries to phase out production and consumption of a range of ozone-depleting substances, including hydrochlorofluorocarbons (HCFCs), a potent greenhouse gas. The EPA (in 2003) had set rules for HCFC production and consumption between 2004 and 2009 that allowed companies to transfer HCFC allowances both between and within companies for one year or permanently through baseline credit transfers. However, in December 2009, the EPA issued a rule governing 2010–14 credits that determined that the Clean Air Act barred permanent baseline transfers. The lawsuit alleged that the EPA's 2009 rule had the effect of illegally invalidating baseline emissions transfers within companies. The D.C. Circuit held that the rule was illegally retroactive because it altered transactions approved under the 2003 rule that were intended to be permanent.

Portland Cement Association v. U.S. EPA, 665 F.3d 177 (D.C. Cir. 2011) involved National Emission Standards for Hazardous Air Pollutants (NESHAP). The case represents a partial victory for EPA over challenges from industry and environmental groups. The court upheld EPA's NSPS rule-making but granted an industry group's petitioner for review of the NESHAP rule. The court also dismissed environmental petitioners' challenge for lack of jurisdiction

Texas v. U.S. EPA, 726 F.3d 180 (D.C. Cir. 2013) is a complex case involving several areas of climate change law. The case is based in the Clean Air Act provisions that are arguably structured around the principle of "cooperative federalism" (Kastorf 2014). This means that in the US, air pollution control is considered the primary responsibility of states and local governments. However, federal leadership is considered necessary to ensure cooperation and integration between federal, state, regional, and local programs that can address air pollution problems. The EPA is the body that approves state intervention plans (SIPs) the state measures to address air pollution and the EPA can require a state to revise its SIP if the EPA considers the state plan to be inadequate. The Texas case represented a challenge to the EPAs attempt to try and force revisions after Texas (and Wyoming) failed to prepare SIPs implementing EPA's greenhouse gas rules. After the decision in *Massachusetts* the EPA took the view that greenhouse gas emissions from motor vehicles could be considered as a danger to public health and welfare by contributing to climate change. The EPA concluded that this determination automatically triggered PSD permitting requirements for stationary sources of greenhouse gases, thereby requiring states to revise their SIPs. Texas (and Wyoming) along with industry petitioners, challenged the EPA's implementation of the new permitting requirements. EPA asserted that the petitioners lacked standing because they were not harmed by the rules. According to EPA, the Clean Air Act unambiguously prohibits construction of a major greenhouse gas emitting facility without a PSD permit, regardless of whether the applicable SIP had been updated. Because the states could not issue permits for greenhouse gas emitting facilities until they updated their SIPs, the FIP provided the only means of obtaining such permits and its existence therefore benefitted petitioners. The Court agreed with the EPA and Judge Rogers, writing for the majority, explained that section 165(a) of the Clean Air Act bars construction of a "major emitting facility" without a permit that includes emissions limitations for regulated pollutants. The judgment also explains that Clean Air Act section 167 *requires* the EPA [my emphasis] to take measures to prevent the construction of facilities not in compliance with the Clean Air Act. The court concluded that these provisions, read together, created "self-executing" permitting requirements. This conclusion, in turn, deprived petitioners of standing because their injury stemmed from automatic operation of the CAA, not from EPA's rules enabling the issuance of permits, which, if anything, benefited petitioners. Judge Kavanaugh dissented, asserting that a relevant EPA regulation gave states three years to revise their SIPs and that section 165 applies only through the relevant SIP. The decision arguably allows the EPA to continue restricting states' flexibility where it views state action as delaying implementation of the Clean Air Act or potentially hampering federal enforcement efforts. While the EPA may not always succeed in such cases, it has been provided with some judicial support for its actions to address state failures in relation to climate change and pollution plans.

While these are admittedly selective, illustrative cases, Peeples (2015) identifies that "several state and international [climate change] cases remain in the pipeline" concerning governments' failure to protect current and future citizens from the effects of climate change. While it is beyond this book's scope to analyze climate change litigation in depth, there are examples of cases that relate to challenges to governmental inertia over climate change as well as to regulator's decisions either in favor of restricting omissions or in failing to rigorously enforce climate change laws. Such issues are increasingly being considered by the courts and these climate change cases invariably develop our understanding of the obligations on government and business in respect of climate change while also clarifying issues of climate change law and the enforceability of climate change restrictions. The following case example

from the UK shows how NGOs/activists have engaged with national government failure over air pollution that is arguably linked to corporate activity.

Case Study One: Client Earth versus the UK Government and the Battle over Clean Air

This case study examines litigation in the UK concerning the UK Government's
failure to take action over air pollution. In April 2015 campaigning NGO
ClientEarth won a five-year legal battle with the government over illegal
levels of air pollution in the UK when the UK Supreme Court ordered the
government to take action over high levels of illegal air pollution. The case
came out of admitted and continuing failure by the United Kingdom since
2010 to secure compliance (in certain zones) with the limits for nitrogen
dioxide levels set by European law, under Directive 2008/50/EC. Again, in
November 2016 ClientEarth were victorious when the UK High Court agreed
that the Environment Secretary had failed to take measures that would bring
the UK into compliance with European law "as soon as possible" and said
that ministers knew that over optimistic pollution modelling was being used.
This case illustrates how environmental activism to uphold environmental
law contrasts with government complacency and inaction. It highlights the
role of NGOs as monitors of environmental compliance and demonstrates
how NGO action, particularly action in the courts, can serve to highlight and
remedy government failures in environmental protection that might otherwise
go unnoticed.

The 2008 ambient air quality directive (2008/50/EC) contains the following overall objective:

> In order to protect human health and the environment as a whole, it is particu-
> larly important to combat emissions of pollutants at source and to identify and
> implement the most effective emission reduction measures at local, national
> and [European] Therefore emissions of harmful pollutants should be avoided,
> prevented or reduced and appropriate objectives set for ambient air quality tak-
> ing into account relevant World Health Organisation standards, guidelines and
> programmes. (2008/50/EC, Para 2)

Accordingly, the directive sets legally binding limits for concentrations in
outdoor air of major air pollutants that impact public health (e.g. nitrogen
dioxide [$NO2$]). By virtue of its (then) membership of the EU, the UK
Government was required to comply with the law and thus was required to
meet "limit values" which specify the legal limitations that can be placed
on pollutants. The UK Government was also required to produce a national
air quality strategy setting out how it would comply with EU air quality

requirements. However, the arguments of NGOs and the scientific and monitoring evidence suggest that the UK has consistently failed to meet its targets and NGOs and the media have constructed a narrative of UK air quality as being problematic and harmful to citizens' health (Carrington 2016; Ares and Smith 2017). In principle, a legal mechanism exists that would result in action being taken against the UK Government for the failures in air quality by way of referral to the EU institutions. However, in the absence of effective enforcement action being taken and given the lack of improvements in air quality over a period of time, NGOs became involved in pursuing a resolution as this case study illustrates.

Article 23 of Directive 2008/50/EC specifies that where levels of pollutants in ambient air exceed the set limits a Member State must adopt an air quality plan. In 2010, 40 out of 43 UK "zones" were in breach of one or more of the nitrogen dioxide limit values. The UK Government had adopted a plan in accordance with Article 23 but did not notify the European Commission with a plan for achieving the limits by 2015 as it was required to do by Article 22 of the directive. NGO ClientEarth requested the UK Government to confirm how it would comply with limits in 16 "zones" by 2015. Government failure resulted in litigation and the UK Supreme Court judgment (May 2013) included a declaration that the UK was in breach of its obligations under Article 13 of Directive 2008/50/EC. The matter was then referred to the Court of Justice of the European Union (CJEU) for a ruling on a technical point regarding forcing the UK Government to comply with EU law. The CJEU instructed the UK Court to adopt "any necessary measure" on the UK Government to establish plans for air quality. The CJEU also clarified that: "Natural or legal persons" directly concerned by limit values must be able to require the authorities to establish an air quality plan that demonstrates how limits will be achieved. The CJEU identifies that national courts should interpret their national laws in a way that are compatible with EU environmental directives, and when such interpretation is not possible, they must disregard national rules that are incompatible with the directives. Given the UK's membership of the EU at the time of this case, the court reaffirmed the supremacy of EU law which means that individuals (EU member state nationals) should be able to take legal action in national courts

The UK Government's Draft Air Quality Plan was ordered to be produced by April 24, 2017. The government attempted to delay until after the General Election,[2] but ClientEarth successfully obtained a High Court order to require the plans to be produced. ClientEarth's contention was that the published plan failed to articulate specific measures for devolved nations, including Wales and Northern Ireland, and so is unlawful. Both parties were back in court on July 5, 2017. Unfortunately, the UK's High Court ruled that there was "nothing unlawful" in the government's draft air quality plan but Mr.

Justice Garnham suggested that final plans could well be open to legal challenge if they do not deal with some of the concerns laid out by ClientEarth. Subsequently, the parties were back in court in February 2018. In *R (on the application of ClientEarth) No 3* [2018] EWHC315, the court concluded that the Department for Environment, Food and Rural Affairs' 2017 air quality plan was unlawful in that, in its application to 45 local authority areas, it did not contain measures sufficient to ensure substantive compliance with Directive (EC) 2008/50 and the Air Quality Standards Regulations 2010, SI 2010/1001. The Administrative Court further held that the plan did not include the information required by Annex XV to the Directive and Schedule 8 to the Regulations in respect of those same areas.

Ostensibly Case Study One is about action taken against the state in respect of air quality and associated climate justice issues. However, linked to this case is the challenges governments face in dealing with air quality issues when linked to the demands of neoliberal markets and corporate activity. Pollution from cars constitutes a major cause of air quality problems in urban areas (Fenger 1999; Cropper et al. 2014). In both the UK and US reports suggest that the car industry lobby has fought against clean air rules. Carrington (2017) goes so far as to suggest that "conniving" car manufacturers and their lobbying efforts "were the key factors in producing the diesel-fuelled air pollution crisis the UK is struggling with today." The second case study directly examines the behavior of a major motor manufacturing corporation.

Case Study Two Volkswagen and the US Clean Air Act

In 2015, the EPA confirmed that major automotive manufacturer Volkswagen had intentionally equipped its diesel cars with software designed to evade emissions standards aimed at smog reduction (Krall and Peng 2015). The EPA indicated that Volkswagen had installed the "defeat device" in four-cylinder Volkswagen and Audi vehicles from model years 2009 to 2015, including the Jetta, Beetle, and Golf from those model years as well as the 2014–2015 Passat. The vehicles were said to be emitting up to 40 times the official limit of nitrogen oxides (NOx) and EPA calculations suggested that the affected vehicles may have been contributing excess NOx into the air for up to 7 years (Krall and Peng 2015).

The EPA claimed that Volkswagen's actions violated the Clean Air Act, which requires that automakers certify to the EPA that their vehicles will meet federal emissions standards for controlling air pollution. As part of its enforcement response, the EPA filed a civil complaint under Sections 204 and 205 of the Clean Air Act on January 4, 2016. The complaint sought injunctive relief and the assessment of civil penalties. A civil complaint does not preclude the government from seeking other legal remedies. In decisions handed down in December 2017 Volkswagen AG (VW) pleaded guilty to three criminal felony counts, and agreed to pay a $2.8 billion criminal penalty, as a result of the company's long-running scheme to sell approximately 590,000 diesel vehicles in the U.S. by using a defeat device to cheat on emissions tests mandated by the EPA and the California Air Resources Board, and by lying and obstructing justice to further the scheme. In separate *civil* resolutions of environmental, customs, and financial claims, VW agreed to pay $1.5 billion. This includes the EPA's claim for civil penalties against Volkswagen for vehicle importation and sale and customs fraud. Crête (2016) implies that the emissions scandal indicates a failure in corporate governance (discussed earlier in this book) and "significant misbehaviour by a major corporation" given that the action undertaken by Volkswagen was a deliberate attempt to circumvent regulations.[3]

Corporate Environmental Crime and Climate Justice: Some Preliminary Conclusions

White (2018b, 9) identifies climate change as "the most important international issue facing humanity today" while noting that it has only recently become the subject of criminological inquiry. In his call for a climate change criminology (2018b) White calls for more attention to be paid to climate change consistent with the notion that it is a significant cause of environmental harms and marginalization of vulnerable communities directly affected by the consequences of climate change and global warming (Nurse 2015, Lynch and Stretesky 2014). Where activities that cause global warming contravene environmental protection regulations or where state failure to address climate change contravenes international agreements and customary international law climate change constitutes corporate environmental crime (according to this book's definition).

From a green criminological perspective climate change illustrates Lynch and Stretesky's (2014, 24) view that "the assumption that the environmental changes we are witnessing today are evolutionary, natural, and largely independent of human action permeates the general manner in which humans think about the environmental and environmental problems." Lynch and Stretesky (ibid.) identify that it is only recently that there has been broad acceptance that humans are the primary cause of environmental problems and that it is only through direct human action that such problems can be addressed. Yet despite the existence of both international and domestic legal mechanisms through which climate change might be addressed, there remains a lack of willingness on the part of politicians and regulators to directly address climate change as a significant problem via existing, or better and more stringent, legal regimes and the criminalization that White and Heckenberg (2014) suggest may be necessary. This idea is central to this book's theme of Corporate Environmental Crime and Criminal justice. Williams (2011, 503) identifies justice system failure in this area as a climate justice deficit, arguing that ineffectual climate change law contributes to sites of social and economic insecurity. Indeed Williams goes so far as to state that "it is becoming increasingly apparent that many of the legal, financial, and social structures created in response to climate change are doing little to ease the burden of insecurity, in fact in many cases they are further promoting insecurity and inequity" (2011, 510). Wealthy industrialized nations who bear significant responsibility for harmful greenhouse gas emissions are reluctant to criminalize and prosecute the actions of otherwise legal actors (mostly corporations) who contribute to economic growth, provide jobs, and pay taxes and whose continued existence serves the interests of policymakers. Yet as other chapters of this book and the cases discussed in this chapter identify, it is often in enforcement of legal regimes that problems occur. In many areas of environmental harm, particularly those that engage with corporate environmental crime, well-meaning legislation exists on paper that is poorly enforced in practice.

Brisman (2014, 29) identifies that "green criminology can help uncover the etiology of environmental crime" which includes uncovering some of the mysteries of environmental crime and harm including climate change. White and Heckenberg (2014, 115) argue that while the obvious and scientific-based answer to climate change is to minimize harmful emissions, there is also a need to criminalize carbon emissions and to forcibly shut down "dirty industries" whose activities contribute to climate change and resultant global warming. However, other regulatory and legislative mechanisms exist or have potential to address corporate environmental harms as the next chapter illustrates.

Daimler has subsequently been reported to have agreed a $1.5 billion (€1.2 billion) payout to US authorities and to have agreed to pay out $700 million dollars as part of a class-action lawsuit brought by owners of polluting vehicles fitted with cheat devices in the US (BBC News, 2020).

NOTES

1. See for example https://www.nrdc.org/sites/default/files/CAA-rules-and-litigation-table.pdf

2. The [then] UK Prime Minister Theresa May called a General Election to take place on June 8, 2017. The Prime Minister's stated intention was to increase her parliamentary majority which would arguably aid efforts to challenge the supremacy of the EU and EU law and provide an enhanced mandate for a "hard Brexit"; facilitating

a clear break from the EU. However, the gambit failed, and the government majority was actually decreased as the opposition parties made gains.

3. Since the Volkswagen case, KBA, the German road vehicle authority, found that Daimler, the parent company of Mercedes, had used illegal software to alter diesel emission in its diesel vehicles. It ordered the German motor giant to recall affected vehicles. In September 2019, Daimler AG was fined €870 million for negligently failing to supervise the production of these vehicles.

Chapter 9

Corporate Environmental Harm and Human Rights

While human rights principles normally apply to the state, a lack of clarity exists on the extent to which human rights norms apply to private business. Earlier chapters of this book set out how CSR codes incorporate some consideration of human rights to the activities of private business. The UN created its Guiding Principles on Business and Human Rights, setting out criteria that should apply to business in remedying harm and providing access to redress through both state and nonstate means. This chapter examines the application of human rights norms to the actions of private business and assesses how the UN principles apply in respect of environmental harm, examining the availability and effectiveness of remedies including how the principles adopted by the UN are enforced by the courts whether directly or indirectly. In doing so, it examines the extent to which private business can be bound by human rights norms as well as the extent to which rights can be asserted by citizens when seeking redress.

The UN itself identifies failure to enforce laws in respect of business and human rights as a significant failure in state legal practice (UNOHCHR 2011, 5). In respect of the environment, access to justice is a key area where "in the last 20 years non-governmental organisations (NGOs) and community groups have begun to play an increasingly significant and diversified role in environmental policy-making" (Vanhala 2013, 309). Environmental litigation by NGOs has the benefit of clarifying the law, providing for remedies in respect of environmental harm and identifying weaknesses in public policy. Litigation by individuals may be the only way to secure a remedy, particularly in respect of harms caused by private business. Yet the availability of remedies in the context of corporate environmental crime depends on the extent to which states have implemented policies, legislation, regulations, and enforcement measures which are effective in addressing business involvement in practices which subvert human rights norms (UNOHCHR 2011, 8–9). This chapter examines this area in detail with a view to establishing any difference between the theoretical conception of a business and human rights framework and the practical reality of whether rights and remedies are effective.

BUSINESS AND HUMAN RIGHTS

Human rights principles frequently operate at the level of the state and public authorities such that, for example, the UK's Human Rights Act 1998 is primarily concerned with the behavior of emanations of the state and the extent to which these impact on the rights of citizens (Stone 2010, 45–46). Bernaz (2017, 1–12) identifies that a conservative reading of the current treaty-based human rights framework suggests that "corporations, even multinational corporations, are not subjects of international human rights law and are therefore under no legal obligation to abide by human rights treaties." Thus, human rights infringements by corporations risk being outside the scope of human rights redress mechanisms. However, a contemporary notion of corporate accountability might hold that corporations through their CSR auditing, policies, and other corporate governance structures are now obliged to consider the harm their operations might cause to the communities in which they operate. Indeed Bernaz (2017, 2) identifies that "the business and human rights field looks into violations of the whole spectrum of human rights, civil and political, as well as economic, social and cultural rights" by private business.

Yet as chapter 4 illustrates, a range of approaches to CER exist within the broad CSR framework such that corporations audit and report on the impact of their activities on environments and local communities in varied ways (Spence 2011). However, despite its voluntary nature, increasingly CSR and regulatory compliance demands may impose obligations on business to observe human rights and to make recompense where a breach of rights has occurred, particularly where CSR overlaps with legal requirements. In this regard, the UN's Ruggie Principles (discussed later) are an important component in ensuring business compliance with human rights and providing for a remedy where problems occur. Contemporary legislation may also impose obligations on private business actors that amount to a practical requirement to observe human rights. Such legislation (and public policy) may carry with it the potential for remedies to be pursued or sanctions imposed where business actions infringe on human rights whether directly or indirectly. In a broader context, environmental legislation may well provide for a remedy for harm caused to citizens' rights in a manner that captures the actions of corporations and allows for citizen redress. This chapter examines how human rights norms arguably can have horizontal effect; applying to the relationships between private individuals (including between individuals and companies).

Thus, it is directly concerned with how citizens can obtain redress for human rights abuses caused by corporate environmental crime.

Integral to assessing the application of human rights norms to private business is analysis of the acceptance of human rights norms by business and the means through which such norms are enforceable in environmental cases. McPhail and Adams (2016) explore how respect for human rights is emerging and being operationalized in the discourse of 30 Fortune 500 companies in the mining, pharmaceutical, and chemical industries. Their analysis explores the scope of rights for which corporations are accountable and, more specifically, the degree of responsibility a company assumes for enacting these rights. McPhail and Adams suggest that corporate constructions of human rights are broad: from labor rights, through social and political rights, to the right to health and a clean environment (2016, 650) consistent with Bernaz's (2017) conception on an expansive human rights and business discourse. McPhail and Adams suggest that a corporate discourse now exists that is one of promoting, realizing, and upholding rights that also constructs the corporation as an autonomous source of power beyond the state. Where this is the case, mechanisms must exist to hold corporations to account and it is here that the Ruggie Principles come into play.

Business and Human Rights: The UN Principles

Bernaz (2017, 6) identifies that within contemporary CSR discourse; active consideration of human rights has taken hold despite business actors largely being outside of human rights compliance mechanisms. Potoski and Prakash (2004, 152) suggest that one trend in CER and environmental governance is the proliferation of voluntary compliance mechanisms such as ISO 14001 and the UN's Global Compact. These measures outline indicative standards of behavior and environmental compliance and specify the expectations on business (and states). A second governance trend is government and enforcer experimentation with regulatory relief (or compliance incentive) programs where environmental protection agencies and regulators "offer businesses incentives for complying with regulations, including greater flexibility in how they meet regulations, technical assistance, and sometimes even forgiving violations and eschewing punishments and sanctions" (Potoski and Prakash 2004, 152). Smith (2010, 369) also identifies that the United Nations Global Compact which contains measures aimed at encouraging business to respect human rights, also contains principles relating to the environment including:

- Principle 7—businesses should support a precautionary approach to environmental challenges;

- Principle 8—states should undertake initiatives to promote greater environmental responsibility; and
- Principle 9—encourage the development and diffusion of environmentally friendly technologies.

The Global Compact thus recognizes the importance of environmental rights and the negative effects for communities when these are infringed. At EU level, the European Commission defines CSR as requiring that "enterprises should have in place a process to integrate social, environmental, ethical, human rights and consumer concerns into their business operations and core strategy in close collaboration with their stakeholders" (EU Commission 2011, 6). The EU identifies that effective CSR concerns actions "over and above their legal obligations towards society and the environment" (EU Commission 2011, 3) such that corporations operate in a climate of respect and protection for rights and one in which they participate in remediating any environmental harms they cause. This environment is one envisaged by the UN Principles as discussed below.

The UN policy framework proposed by John Ruggie, Special Representative of the Secretary General, has three core pillars in respect of business and human rights. First, the UN policy framework suggests that the state has an obligation to protect against human rights abuses by third parties, including business, by putting in implementation of appropriate policies, regulation, and adjudication. Secondly, the framework states that corporations have a responsibility to respect human rights, to act with due diligence and to avoid infringing the rights of others. Finally, the framework states that victims of human rights infringements should be afforded greater access to an effective remedy.

The UN identifies that as a minimum, the responsibility of business enterprises to respect human rights refers to those contained "in the International Bill of Human Rights (consisting of the Universal Declaration of Human Rights and the main instruments through which it has been codified: the International Covenant on Civil and Political Rights and the International Covenant on Economic, Social and Cultural Rights) coupled with the principles concerning fundamental rights in the eight International Labour Organization (ILO) core conventions as set out in the Declaration on Fundamental Principles and Rights at Work" (UNOHCHR 2011, 14). However, while in principle the UN guidelines have been implemented and various legislative redress mechanisms exist, in practice there may be barriers to achieving effective redress. Central to assessing this is an exploration of the extent to which a right to a healthy environment exists and can be enforced.

Clapham (2006, 79) suggests that given that it must be acknowledged that sometimes individuals have rights and duties under human rights law "we have to admit that legal persons may also possess the international legal personality necessary to enjoy some of those rights, and conversely to be prosecuted for violations of the relevant international duties." However, crucial to the UN Principles is the idea of the state applying human rights norms through its own (domestic) legislation and governance structures. Within its operational principles on regulatory and policy functions, the UN Principles articulate that states should "enforce laws that are aimed at, or have the effect of, requiring business enterprises to respect human rights" (UNOHCHR 2011, 4). This is not a static requirement; the UN makes clear that states should monitor the adequacy of any such laws and address gaps. States should also provide guidance to business on how to respect human rights within their operations and should "where appropriate require, business enterprises to communicate how they address their human rights impacts" (UNOHCHR 2011, 4). Thus, the UN Principles envisage that business compliance with human rights should become a legal requirement, with legislation periodically assessed for its effectiveness and with a reporting component that "can range from informal engagement with affected stakeholders to formal public reporting" (UNOHCHR 2011, 6). The UN Principles also make clear that business enterprises should have in place "a human rights due diligence process to identify, prevent, mitigate and account for how they address their impact on human rights" (UNOHCHR 2011, 16).

In respect of remedies and remediation, the UN Principles state that "where business enterprises identify that they have caused or contributed to adverse impacts, they should provide for or cooperate in their remediation through legitimate processes" (UNOHCHR 2011, 24). The foundational principle on remedies is framed as follows:

> As part of their duty to protect against business-related human rights abuse, States must take appropriate steps to ensure, through judicial, administrative, legislative or other appropriate means, that when such abuses occur within their territory and/or jurisdiction those affected have access to effective remedy. (UNOHCHR 2011, 27)

The UN observes that "unless States take appropriate steps to investigate, punish and redress business-related human rights abuses when they do occur, the State duty to protect can be rendered weak or even meaningless." Thus, access to justice requires that there should be a range of remedies available to those whose rights have been infringed. Remedies can range from a simple apology through to restitution, rehabilitative, compensation, or punitive sanction or injunctive relief that prevents environmental harm from occurring (or reoccurring). In its guidance on the Principles, the UN notes that "access to effective remedy has both procedural and substantive aspects" (UNOHCHR

2011, 27). Thus, the remedy must in some way "counteract or make good any human rights harms that have occurred" which may involve recompense where this is not possible e.g., in the case of irreversible environmental damage linked to a breach of rights (UNOHCHR 2011, 27). The UN refers to both judicial and nonjudicial remedy mechanisms noting that ensuring access to effective remedy for business-related human rights abuses "requires also that States facilitate public awareness and understanding for these mechanisms, how they can be accessed, and any support (financial or expert) for doing so" (UNOHCHR 2011, 28). In respect of state-based judicial mechanisms, the UN specifies that states should take appropriate steps to ensure the effectiveness of domestic judicial mechanisms. This includes "considering ways to reduce legal, practical and other relevant barriers that could lead to a denial of access to remedy" (UNOHCHR 2011, 28). Thus, this chapter explores issues around the cost of any remedy and the ease with which it can be accessed by any marginalized groups as well as by more affluent citizens able to bring litigation or pursue other remedies. Cost in particular, is noted by the UN as a potential procedural barrier and the UN indicates a need for costs in such cases to be reduced to reasonable levels "through Government support, 'market-based' mechanisms (such as litigation insurance and legal fee structures), or other means" (UNOHCHR 2011, 29).

The UN also recommends that provision should be made for state-based non-judicial grievance mechanisms such as mediation-based adjudicative processes (e.g. Ombudsmen) or other schemes.[1] Consideration should also be given to non-state based grievance mechanisms.

The Right to a Healthy Environment

While often not specifically enshrined in public law, rights relating to the environment are spread across a number of instruments as chapter 2 illustrates. These include: the Universal Declaration on Human Rights; the International Covenant on Economic Social and Cultural Rights; and the UN Convention on the Rights of the Child. Environmental human rights are also articulated within various case law and national legislation which provide for the following broad environmental rights: right to ecologically sustainable development; right to an adequate standard of living including access to safe food and water; rights of children to live in an environment suitable for physical and mental development; right to participation in environmental decision-making; and right of access to education and information including information on the links between health and the environment

Human Rights conventions generally impose obligations on states to positively uphold rights and/or to ensure that they are interfered with only so far as is necessary, and that any interference is done in accordance with the law and is proportionate. Thus, human rights conventions and domestic human rights law potentially provide for a means to achieve environmental protection where human rights and the right to live in a healthy environment are at issue. The European Convention on Human Rights (ECHR), for example, does not specifically provide for a right to live in a healthy environment but manages to achieve this goal by engaging several of its individual rights. Case law before the European Court of Human Rights (ECtHR) has engaged Article 2 (right to life) Article 8 (respect for privacy and family life) Protocol 1, Article 1 (the right to peaceful enjoyment of possessions and property) and even Article 6 (the right to a fair hearing) in order to develop the idea of a right to a healthy environmental and to clarify the extent to which this is a principle that public authorities (e.g. the state and local government) are required to uphold as the following case examples illustrate.

In respect of Article 2 (the right to life), in *Oneryildiz v. Turkey, 48939/99 [2004] ECHR 657 (30 November 2004)* the right to life linked to a healthy environment was explicitly considered in the first ECtHR case involving loss of life linked to environmental harm. The case concerned a 1993 methane explosion that killed nine members of the applicant's family. The argument in the case was that the explosion was foreseeable yet no measures had been taken to prevent this from occurring. This was despite the existence of an expert report dating back to 1991 which identified the risk of methane explosions and identified that no measures had been taken to prevent a possible explosion of methane gas from a tip near where the applicant lived. The applicant's complaint that Article 2 of the ECHR had been breached because the accident had occurred as a result of negligence on the part of the relevant authorities was upheld. The ECtHR concluded that there had been a violation of the right to protection of life enshrined in Article 2 in its procedural aspect; violation of the right to peaceful enjoyment of possessions as protected by Article 1 of the Protocol No. 1; and violation of the right to a domestic remedy.

Article 2 was also engaged in *Budayeva and Others vs. Russia,* Application, 15339/02, 21166/02, 20058/02, 11673/02 and 15343/02 *[2008] (20 March 2008)* which involved a claim that the Russian government had failed to fulfill its Article 2 obligations to protect the right to life. *Budayeva* also identified a public authority failure to ensure a safe environment, this time in respect of a mudslide which caused eight deaths. This was considered to be a breach of Article 2 ECHR, because the authorities failed to implement land-planning and emergency relief policies despite the fact that the area of Tyrnauz where the incident occurred was known to be vulnerable to mudslides. In this case local authority failure to act exposed residents to a known "mortal risk" in respect of which the authorities had an obligation to take action to prevent loss of life. Failure to take such action was considered to be an infringement of the Article 2 right to life while the lack of any state investigation or examination of the accident was considered by the ECtHR to also constitute a violation of Article 2 ECHR.

These and other cases illustrate that the right to a healthy environment is often interlinked with other human rights mechanisms and thus need not be explicitly written into environmental laws or a country's constitution in order to be enforced. While some states have done so, effectively making the right to a healthy environment a public law matter that may be directly enforceable (Smith 2010, Fenwick 2007) other mechanisms can create a right to a healthy environment that can be relied upon in practice. The UNECE Convention on Access to Information, Public Participation in Decision-making and Access to Justice in Environmental Matters (Aarhus Convention), for example, provides for the right of access to environmental justice in a manner that creates a conception of environmental justice and regulatory control based around providing citizens with distinct access to information about the environment. Within the Aarhus Convention there are also mechanisms that allow citizens to raise concerns about alleged breaches of environmental rights found within the Convention.[2] In this respect, the Aarhus Convention can be an important consideration in practical implementation of the UN Principles in respect of identifying and remedying environmental harm. The Aarhus Convention is based on three core pillars: the right to know; the right to participate; and the right of access to environmental justice.

Aarhus explicitly recognizes every person's right to live in a healthy environment in its preamble affirming that "every person has the right to live in an environment adequate to his or her health and well-being, and the duty, both individually and in association with others, to protect and improve the environment for the benefit of present and future generations." Article 1 of the convention states that

> In order to contribute to the protection of the right of every person of present and future generations to live in an environment adequate to his or her health and well-being, each Party shall guarantee the rights of access to information, public participation in decision-making, and access to justice in environmental matters in accordance with the provisions of this Convention.

Thus, the Aarhus Convention provides a framework for the enforcement of a distinct environmental right and an obligation on states both to monitor threats to that right and to provide for access to a remedy where that right is infringed. The Aarhus Convention also provides a means for NGOs to pursue claims in respect of environmental harm, recognizing that individuals sometimes require assistance to exercise their rights. Articles 9.3 and 9.4 of the Aarhus Convention specify as follows:

9.3 . . . members of the public [should] have access to administrative or judicial procedures to challenge acts and omissions by private persons and public authorities which contravene provisions of its national law relating to the environment.

9.4 . . . the procedures referred to in paragraphs 1, 2 and 3 above shall provide adequate and effective remedies, including injunctive relief as appropriate, and be fair, equitable, timely and not prohibitively expensive. Decisions under this article shall be given or recorded in writing. Decisions of courts, and whenever possible of other bodies, shall be publicly accessible.

Accordingly, one conception on environmental rights linked to the UN principles to "respect, protect and remedy" (UNOHCHR 2011) is that of right to effective judicial remedies against private companies for environmental harm. Aarhus requires that the public must be informed of activity or specific projects which could adversely affect the environment (the right to know) in order that they might exercise rights to question or challenge an activity. The UN Principles suggest that any remedy must be effective and accessible and, as mentioned earlier, suggest that a range of judicial and nonjudicial measures may be appropriate (UNOHCHR 2011, 27–28). Vanhala (2013, 311) notes that the Aarhus Convention "grants rights to members of the public, including environmental organizations, to challenge the legality of decisions by public authorities that are contrary to the provisions of national laws relating to the environment." However, the extent to which such provisions are implemented depends on such things as the extent to which the UN Principles are enshrined in public policy and the manner in which the courts apply human rights principles to business actors. This chapter suggests that the intended remedies may not always be easily available.

IMPLEMENTING THE UN PRINCIPLES

Arguably, the United Nations 2011 Guiding Principles on Human Rights (UNOHCHR, 2011) allow citizens to seek redress in respect of environmental harms caused by private business. Analysis of how the UN principles apply and are implemented into law and policy and whether in practice citizens requires consideration of the texts and case law of the ECHR and the UK's Human Rights Act 1998 (among other legislation such as The EU Environmental Liability Directive which enshrines the "polluter pays" principle into EU Environmental law). Vanhala (2013, 309) identifies "increasing levels of representation of NGOs and community groups in policy-relevant venues where they had previously been absent." She notes the engagement of actors in the environmental movement where they "have sought to enforce challenge and influence policy in judicial arenas."

The UN's "Ruggie Principles" create an appropriate international framework for applying human rights to the activities of private commercial entities. However, it is arguably essential that such rights are appropriately reflected in both legislation and national policy and are also effectively enforced and developed through case law that determines how private law mechanisms can uphold private business' obligations towards rights. The UK Government's policy document on implementing the Ruggie Principles was updated in May 2016. The policy document *Good Business Implementing the UN Guiding Principles on Business and Human Rights* (HM Government 2016) states that the UK was the first country to produce a National Action Plan to implement the UN Principles. The updated 2016 policy guidance stresses that the UK Government considers that:

> Respect for human rights should be at the heart of a company's core operations, it is not the same as philanthropy or social investment. The responsibility of businesses to respect human rights exists independently of States' abilities and/or willingness to fulfil their own human rights obligations. Different businesses will need to take different approaches to embedding this approach. Implementation will be progressive and will need to be compatible with the resource limitations of small and medium-sized enterprises. Companies also need to act in accordance with local law, which may sometimes be a constraint on acting in compliance with human rights. In such situations, the Government expects companies to seek ways to honor the principles of internationally recognized human rights. (HM Government 2016, 15)

The government's policy sets out a number of ways in which it encourages and facilitates business compliance with human rights. Specifically, it notes that a range of judicial mechanisms exist to address human rights abuses by business including: employment tribunals; avenues to pursue civil law claims in relation to human rights abuses by business enterprises; criminal law provisions, including those contained within the Bribery Act 2010, Modern Slavery Act 2015, Serous Crime Act 2007, Corporate Manslaughter and Corporate Homicide Act 2007 and Gangmasters (Licensing) Act 2004.

However, analysis of the government policy document identifies it as largely being aspirational and facilitative and a question remains as to the extent to which the principles outlined in the document are applied in practice. It is unclear, for example, whether the private law remedies integral to the government's approach is sufficiently accessible, effective, or easy to use.

Collins (2012) explores the question of the incompatibility of human rights with private law. He identifies that "private law has traditionally shunned any explicit reference to the discourse of human rights because it originated in the one-sided claims of public law and therefore seemed unsuitable to the need for a balancing of the competing interests and rights of two formally equal parties" (Collins 2012, 4). However, Kinley and Chambers (2006) illuminate this debate in respect of their analysis of earlier (2003) UN norms on human rights for corporations. They argue that the substance of human rights principles provides for universal standards against which business behavior can be judged. This chapter's analysis seeks to determine the extent to which this is the case in practice, particularly in respect of the availability of a remedy to those affected by environmental harm caused by private business.

The UN identifies the need for access to an *effective* remedy (my emphasis). This principle is at issue in *Austin & Others and Miller Argent* (South Wales) [2011] EWCA Civ 928 discussed later in this chapter. *Austin and Others* concerned an appeal against refusal of a Group Litigation Order (GLO) where over 500 parties wished to pursue a claim in nuisance caused by open cast mining operations conducted by the defendants. The extent to which the Aarhus Convention should apply is relevant to the costs in this case which arguably has bearing on the feasibility of pursuing a remedy.[3] *Austin and Others* arguably illustrates the problems for individuals seeking to secure redress for the problems caused by private companies and the availability of access to justice in line with Aarhus Convention principles. Vanhala (2013: 314) identifies that issues of standing to pursue a case are raised in some case law but noting that in *Mary Buchan Forbes v Aberdeenshire Council and Trump International Golf Links* [2010] CSOH the judge cited the Aarhus Convention and the need to interpret standing issues in line with the objective of giving the public wide access to justice. Thus, the courts may liberally interpret the extent to which citizens have sufficient interest in or are affected by private business actions. Yet Vanhala (2013) also notes costs as a potential issue in pursuing cases, as *Austin and Others* illustrates, indicating that access to justice carries potential risk of loss.

The UN Principles impose a duty on states to protect human rights. The UN specifies that while states "are not per se responsible for human rights breaches by private actors," states may "breach their international human rights law obligations where such abuse can be attributed to them, or where they fail to take appropriate steps to prevent, investigate, punish and redress private actors' abuse" (UNOHCHR 2011, 3). Accordingly, states have an obligation both to promote the UN Principles and to put in place mechanisms to ensure that private business actors and citizens understand the human rights principles applying to business. The legal and policy framework under which business operates within a given state should also be clear. One mechanism for providing guidance and establishing the framework under which the UN Principles operate is the publication of a national action plan for implementing the Principles. At time of writing (July 2019), the EU website identifies seven EU countries as having national action plans on Business and Human Rights in place (European Commission 2017a). The countries listed are: the UK; the Netherlands; Italy; Denmark; Finland; Lithuania; and Sweden.[4]

PRIVATE BUSINESS AND ENVIRONMENTAL HARM

White (2008, 90–91) identifies a broad range of private actor activities as causing environmental harm. These include: corporate colonization of nature; transborder movement and dumping of waste products; diminished quality and quantity of water resources and the influence of transnational corporations in controlling water resources; generation of toxic waste, environmental degradation on indigenous people's land; and inequalities in the distribution of environmental risk, especially as this relates to poor and vulnerable communities. White's conception is a broad one and does not specifically relate to specific environmental rights. However, Principal 22 of the UN Guiding Principles identifies that as part of their responsibility to respect communities and their rights "businesses have a responsibility to cooperate in remediation where they identify that they have caused or contributed to adverse human rights impacts"' (Thomson 2017, 56). In the context of this book's discussion, an adverse human rights impact can include negative impact on the right to live in a healthy environment (broadly defined). But it can also engage with a specific right such as the ECHR rights to life (Article 2), right to private and family life (Article 8), and the right to peaceful enjoyment of property provided for in some national legislation.

For example, the UN Special Rapporteur on the implications for human rights of the environmentally sound management and disposal of hazardous substances noted air pollution, fracking, the long-term disposal of high-level radioactive waste, legacy landfills, and other issues as being at issue during his official visit to the United Kingdom in January 2017. These issues implicate individuals' right to life, the right to the enjoyment of the highest attainable standard of physical and mental health, equal participation in political and public affairs, the right to access information, and the right to an effective remedy, as well as the special protections provided to children under the Convention on the Rights of the Child. Thus, private business actors engaged in a range of activities risk causing environmental harm of a kind that the UN Principles envisage goes against the idea of business observance of human rights and the state's obligations to protect those rights. Judicial and court-based remedies are available for such environmental harm although the UN Principles suggest that these should not be the only remedies available.

Case Study: Access to Environmental Justice Austin & Others and Miller Argent (South Wales) [2011] EWCA Civ 928

This case relates to a dispute about open cast mining operations which allegedly caused nuisance by dust and noise to local residents. Work to mine 10m tonnes of coal over 17 years from Ffos-y-Fran in Wales began in 2007. Miller Argent (South Wales) Ltd initially received planning permission following a public inquiry, only for the planning permission to be overruled by the High Court. However, the Welsh government, which supported mining at Ffos-y-Fran, won the right to appeal and an appeal judge allowed the mining operation to go ahead. Local residents opposed the mining operation claiming that it had a devastating environmental impact but also that it impacted directly on residents. Alyson Austin (2015) claimed that "the dust from the mine soils our washing and coats every flat surface. Merthyr already has sky-high rates of lung disease."

Austin sought to pursue a private nuisance action against Miller Argent (South Wales) Ltd in respect of Miller Argent's noncompliance with planning permission conditions. Austin and other residents complained that since November 2007, Miller Argent had carried on its opencast operations (including mining, coal haulage, blasting, waste removal, stripping, formation etc.) in such a manner as to cause or permit both noise and dust to be emitted from the site in such a way as to cause detriment to the use and enjoyment of residents (the claimants') homes. Austin and the other residents complained that this amounted to a material interference with the use and enjoyment of their homes and has been a nuisance. They also indicated that Miller Argent's activities amounted to an interference with their Article 8 ECHR right to private and family life.

In particular it was alleged that Miller Argent carried out its operations with sufficient regularity, frequency, duration, and at a level of intensity to cause a nuisance to the claimants, in particular by way of:

i. noise emitted from the site by its various operations including mining, blasting, coal haulage, waste removal stripping and replacement of soils, and the formation and removal of baffle mounds;
ii. dust to be emitted from aforesaid mining operations such as to fall on the homes, in the gardens, on cars and on other property of the claimants; and
iii. fumes, odors and other air pollution to be emitted as a result of its operations, in the gardens, on cars, and on other property of the claimants.

The planning permission and section 106 agreement contained certain dust suppression and noise mitigation measures.[5] However the claimants alleged that these measures, to the extent that they were employed, had "been ineffective to prevent both noise and dust nuisance to the claimants' homes on a regular basis." On that basis Austin and her fellow claimants sought damages and an injunction to prevent continuance of the nuisance.

As Mrs. Austin could not afford the costs of legal proceedings she made a pre-action application to the High Court for costs protection in a proposed claim in private nuisance. This application argued that the proceedings would be an environmental claim and were thus required to be "fair, equitable, timely and not prohibitively expensive under Article 9(4) of the Aarhus Convention 1998." However, the High Court dismissed the application in August 2013 although permission to appeal was granted on the basis that the matter was one of "significant public importance." The Court of Appeal agreed with Mrs. Austin that private nuisance proceedings were capable of falling within the scope of the Aarhus Convention but introduced a restriction on the application of the convention by requiring that there is a "significant public environmental benefit" to any claim. The judge refused Austin a protective costs order (PCO) and she appealed. The Court of Appeal, Civil Division, in dismissing the appeal, held that article 9.3 of the Aarhus Convention could apply to private nuisance actions. However, having regard to the limited public benefit which the appellant's action would achieve, it did not fall within the scope of the convention, art 9.3.

Subsequently in 2010, around 500 other local residents applied for a GLO aiming to bring an action against the coal mining company and alleging that they too were suffering from dust and/or noise from the opencast coal mine. The High Court dismissed the GLO application on the basis that it was "premature" due primarily to the uncertainty as to how many potential claimants could afford to bring any proceedings. The Court of Appeal dismissed an appeal against that ruling.

Austin and Others v Miller Argent (South Wales) Ltd is arguably a landmark case concerning the Aarhus Convention's requirements on the cost of litigation in environmental matters as applied to private nuisance claims. The case clarifies that private nuisance actions were in principle capable of constituting procedures which fall within the scope of article 9.3 of the Aarhus Convention. The Court of Appeal recognized that it was unrealistic for those suffering pollution to have to rely upon public authorities to remedy environmental harm and to achieve the Aarhus Convention's objectives. In this regard, the judgments confirm that the focus of the Aarhus Convention is on *participation* in environmental decision-making and that there is merit in recognizing the valuable function individual litigants can play in helping to ensure that high environmental standards are kept. This may be the case even if in the process they are also pursuing and seeking to uphold a private interest. The court also indicated that the range of alternative procedures that might be available is not sufficient to constitute compliance with the convention. However, Elias LJ, giving the judgment of the court said that the court would only be obliged to grant a protected costs order ("PCO") if it was satisfied that the proceedings would otherwise be prohibitively expensive and the claimant was able to rely upon provisions in either the Aarhus Convention, which was concerned with protecting the environment, or in Directive 2011/92/EU of the European Parliament and of the council of December 13, 2011, on the assessment of the effects of certain public and private projects on the environment (2012)OJ L p 261, which implemented it (at least in part). The court concluded that there has to be a significant public interest in the action to justify conferring special costs protection on a claimant. The article 9.4 obligation which afforded procedural costs protection was no more than a factor to take into account when deciding whether to grant a protected costs order, it was not an obligation.[6]

The reality in UK law is that every uninsured person who embarks upon litigation, must accept some degree of cost risks while Aarhus and the UN Principles would argue that any costs incurred should not be prohibitively expensive. While UK public policy would argue that there is a need to maintain proper discipline over litigation, to incentivize reasonable litigation behavior and to reduce the financial burden upon those who are vindicated, Aarhus seeks to provide *effective* access to justice and public participation in environmental protection. However, the Aarhus Convention does not require that environmental litigation should be "cost free," merely that it should be not prohibitively expensive, a factor that the Austin case upholds.

However, potentially high costs remain a factor in possibly deterring claimants from pursuing cases concerning environmental rights.

Remedying Environmental Harm using Human Rights Principles

As indicated earlier, the UN framework and guiding principles identifies that remedies for harm caused by business should be via both judicial and nonjudicial mechanisms. In environmental cases the extent and nature of environmental harm may mean that a remedy can never truly put affected communities and the environment back on the position they would have been in had the environmental harm not occurred. Instead, the remedy may need to provide recognition of the environmental harm that has been caused and seek to provide some form of redress. The guiding principles refer to "apologies, restitution, rehabilitation, financial or nonfinancial compensation, punitive sanctions, and the prevention of future harm" (Thomson 2017, 59). The case study discussed earlier in this chapter refers to judicial sanctions achieved through litigation. Austin sought damages (restitution and compensation) and the prevention of future harm by way of an injunction intended to cease or prevent further nuisance being caused by the activities.

While national action plans implementing the Ruggie Principles theoretically provide for the use of criminal sanctions against corporations, civil action arguably remains the dominant mechanism through which citizens may seek a remedy. Where damages or compensation might offset environmental harm or infringement of environmental rights, civil action offers scope for dispute resolution through recognition of harm and provision of a remedy. However, *Austin* identifies the potential difficulties faced by a group of litigants seeking to make a claim against a corporation. Arguably nonjudicial remedies are preferable in some cases. The broad range of remedies provided for by the UN's guiding principles envisage, for example that informal resolution or mediation between private actors and aggrieved citizens has a part to play and that where a company has caused or contributed to adverse impacts it should provide redress to victims. The national action plans produced by EU states also take this into account. However, as the Swedish action plan illustrates "no ready made model exists for how a company should best organize its own grievance redress mechanism. It is for each company to assess what is appropriate on the basis of its specific circumstances" (Ministry for Foreign Affairs 2015, 17). Accordingly, there is variation between different industries (and size of company within an industry) and between different countries concerning the extent to which resolution by direct communication with a company is available.

Enforcement action by statutory authorities and environmental regulators can also provide a remedy without the need for court action. However, the UN Special Rapporteur for human rights of the environmentally sound management and disposal of hazardous substances identified that the impact of austerity measures initiated in 2010 has meant a radical lack of resources and reduction in public grants for the main environmental regulators across the United Kingdom. The Special Rapporteur noted that between May 2015 and May 2016, the Department for Environment, Food and Rural Affairs and its agencies agreed to 500 voluntary exit packages, while the environment department, which is operating with a third of its core staff compared with just 10 years ago, must further trim its budget by 15 percent by 2019 or 2020. Coupled with increased responsibilities for environmental matters given to the devolved authorities, the decreasing financial, technical, and human resources due to austerity arguably created serious governance gaps. Regulators may thus need to exercise discretion over which cases they take and how they exercise their functions in taking enforcement action against private business. This can impinge on the effectiveness of remedies.

The Effectiveness of Remedies

The reality of remedies is such that court remedies potentially remain the most effective in resolving human rights breaches. However, the UN Special Rapporteur on the implications for human rights of the environmentally sound management and disposal of hazardous substances and wastes human rights identified that seeking remedy in the United Kingdom can be extremely challenging for victims. The Special Rapporteur heard substantial evidence on the range of obstacles that obstruct access to remedies for victims of human rights abuses by companies related to exposures to toxic substances. Court procedures have made it increasingly difficult to obtain access to corporate documents. In addition to severe difficulties in accessing information and the challenge of establishing legal causation, cuts in legal aid, limits on the recovery of legal costs, and increases in court and tribunal fees in England and Wales have made it even more difficult for victims of pollution and contamination to seek remedy. Furthermore, austerity measures have driven many local councils to withdraw funding from welfare rights services and law centers, often to be replaced by only a helpline or website. Victims abroad face even greater hurdles, confronted with the burden of proving that their claim falls within the jurisdiction of the United Kingdom (UN Human Rights Council 2017, 22–23)

Conclusions: The UN Principles and Private Business

The UN Principles provide a theoretical framework for business to comply with human rights norms. Within these principles, the state has a duty to protect against human rights abuse within their territory and/or jurisdiction by third parties, including private business actors. The duty requires taking actions to "prevent, investigate, punish and redress such abuse through effective policies, legislation, regulations and adjudication" (UNOHRC 2011, 3). However, state action is not always truly effective in the context of punishing and addressing abuses of human rights. In a policy sense, state action risks amounting to facilitating the use of existing law and remedies rather than *direct* action that would impose legal binding human rights standards on private business and provide for sanctions to be imposed. Thus, in practice, the provision of an effective remedy relies on the extent to which citizens are able to access judicial and nonjudicial mechanisms and assert their rights in certain areas, particularly the right to a healthy environment provided to EU citizens via the Aarhus Convention.

This discussion highlights the importance of remedy mechanisms that go beyond the purely punitive approach of the criminal law. The Aarhus Convention is valuable in the context of implementing the Ruggie Principles because it enshrines the right to live in a healthy environment within EU environmental law discourse. It also provides for access to justice by requiring that, within the framework of its national legislation, each party to the convention shall ensure that members of the public who have sufficient interest in an issue or who claim impairment of a right (where the administrative procedural law of a party requires this as a precondition) shall have access to a review procedure before a court of law and/or another independent and impartial body established by law. This provides for "Aarhus claims" in relation to environmental rights and decisions that impact negatively on the environment, this includes consideration of the acts of private business. Thus, mechanisms exist for applying the UN Principles on human rights to the activities of private business in respect of corporate environmental harm. In the UK, a governmental framework exists that, while aspirational, seeks to achieve this. More importantly, legislation such as the Aarhus Convention and the ECHR provide a means through which the right to a healthy environment can arguably be recognized as a human right. Thus, human rights instruments can provide for environmental rights to be directly enforced by environmental victims, where state failure to ensure a healthy environment has resulted in negative consequences including loss of life, loss of home, or adverse negative impact on living arrangements and the right to peaceful enjoyment of property. Accordingly, when looking at environmental governance and the extent to which human rights principles apply to the activities of private business it becomes necessary to examine a range of instruments on the governance spectrum, ranging from coercive legislative instruments to governance approaches that engage the agency and knowledge of resource users and require states to positively implement different forms of environmental protection.

NOTES

1. While the use of environmental Ombudsmen is not widespread, public-sector Ombudsmen with a remit to consider human rights failures potentially offer a means through which some conflicts involving infringement of rights might be resolved through the adjudicative means identified in the UN Principles.

2. Article 15 of the Convention also provides for a compliance mechanism via a committee that reviews allegations of noncompliance of the Convention by member states. Instances of noncompliance can be prompted by a communication from a member of the public although the Compliance Committee is not a judicial body.

3. Other cases such as *Hunter & ors v Canary Wharf Ltd* [1997] UKHL 14 and *Morgan and Baker v Hinton Organics (Wessex) Limited and CAJE* [2009] EWCA

Civ 107 illuminate issues around nuisance, the latter in respect of the extent to which Article 9.3 of the Aarhus Convention applies to private nuisance.

4. Analysis of the seven plans identifies that they are largely facilitative in nature. Generally, the plans make reference to existing legislation within each state and the state's compliance with international measures such as OECD and ILO guidelines and a general commitment to promoting good standards of CSR

5. A *section 106 agreement* (Town and Country Planning Act 1990) is an agreement between a developer and a local planning authority that specifies measures that the developer must take to reduce the impact of their development on the community.

6. The judgment is arguably consistent with the UK's Civil Procedure Rules 1998, SI 1998/3132, r 45.41–44 which requires costs protection in environmental judicial review claims to ensure that those proceedings are not prohibitively expensive.

Chapter 10

Remedying Corporate Environmental Crime

As the preceding chapters have identified, corporate environmental crime is a complex phenomenon. The harm caused by corporations is varied as are the behaviors involved in corporate environmental crime. Activities can be accidental or deliberate and the harm can be relatively minor such as a slight increase in odors or smoke that can be easily rectified, but it can also involve serious impacts and extensive damage to communities and even result in loss of life.

Green criminology identifies that corporate environmental crimes "often eclipse the scope and reach of the criminal law" (Sollund 2012, 3) as many environmentally harmful activities fall outside of the strict definition of crime as acts prohibited by the criminal law (Situ and Emmons 2000). Instead, they amount to regulatory noncompliance or technical breach outside the remit of mainstream policing agencies. Ideologically, this raises questions about how best to deal with noncompliance by ostensibly legal actors where a lack of regulatory control fails to encourage environmentally responsible behavior (White and Heckenberg 2014).

The default reaction to many offenses is based on a law enforcement perspective; use of the criminal law and mainstream policing agencies. This book identifies that this approach is not always effective or desirable and that in practical terms a purely punitive approach fails to address the nature of environmental harm. White (2007) identifies inequality as a significant aspect of environmental justice, particularly the manner in which ethnic minority and indigenous communities suffer at the hands of western forces. Where this is the case, standard criminal justice practices may be inadequate to deal with the harm that has been caused and so the "polluter pays" principle has been developed as a means of ensuring that as part of any "punishment" corporations are required to remedy the harm that they cause. By making goods and services reflect their total cost including the cost of all the resources used, the principle required polluters to integrate (or internalize) the cost of use or degradation of environmental resources. However, environmental damage is not solely an issue of cost and increasingly legislators, regulators, and the courts apply the basic principles of restorative justice which include the "repair of harm" principle and mediation or contact between victim and offender as tools to remedy or mitigate corporate environmental damage. This can involve the use of market-based punishments applied by regulators to incorporate restorative principles as a tool for changing business behavior. The ideal for effective environmental restorative justice is that offenders are held to account for what they have done and realize the harm that they have caused. This chapter contains a case study of regulatory action taken against the major utilities (water) companies in the United Kingdom, through which regulators have attempted to implement the polluter pays principle enshrined in law. It summarizes the book's core argument that corporate environmental offending is inevitable given the operation of neoliberal markets and the failure of regulatory systems to prevent and address corporate environmental harm. It also articulates the book's argument that regulatory and enforcement responses need to be tailored to the nature of environmental crimes and harms.

PRINCIPLES OF JUSTICE AND CORPORATE ENVIRONMENTAL CRIME

The reality is that laws and approaches to environmental crime vary across jurisdictions (White 2007, 184) with the problems of environmental harm being compounded by much environmental damage being committed by corporations. In many countries environmental crime falls within the jurisdiction of the enforcement arm of the state environment department, rather than being integrated into mainstream criminal justice. Thus, Western conceptions of environmentalism, the need to protect the planet and criminalize environmentally damaging actions are not universally shared and the concept of corporate criminal environmental activity is relatively new. Unlike traditional crimes, environmental crimes (and environmental harms) frequently have long-lasting and irreversible effects. Lynch and Stretesky argue "there is little doubt that humans produce an extraordinary amount of pollution and harm the world in numerous ways by damaging the environment" (2014, 8). Many environmental damage incidents such as major chemical or oil spills or widespread deforestation may also have severe and irreversible consequences beyond the initial event. Where this is the case; the criminal justice system, predicated on notions of punishing offenders rather than repairing harm, may be inadequate to deal with the consequences of environmental damage and alternative justice approaches may be required. Successful restorative justice also avoids the escalation of legal justice and its associated costs and delays (Marshall 1999) by engaging both offender and victim in finding a resolution to environmental crime problems. Applied to environmental damage, restorative justice also provides for legal enforcement of CER by requiring corporations to understand and mitigate their harms, offering hope of behavioral change.

Marshall (1996, 37) describes restorative justice as "a process whereby all the parties with a stake in a particular offense come together to resolve collectively how to deal with the aftermath of the offense and its implications for the future." In discussing the implementation of restorative justice in criminal justice cases, attention often rests on the meeting between offender and victim and as a result the public perception of restorative justice is mostly based on this issue, the opportunity for a victim/offender meeting to achieve understanding of the impact and consequence of their actions. This is in part because the focus in criminal justice is for victims to obtain answers and for offenders to face up to their crimes and begin the process of rehabilitation, thereby achieving the criminal justice system aim of reducing crime by preventing reoffending.

Potentially it is in the area of achieving reparation for environmental harms that restorative justice can best be applied to environmental cases. In environmental cases, the core restorative aims of securing healing and making amends can be achieved as long as enforcers and designated regulators have the power to make binding awards and pursue negotiated settlements for complaints. Where legislation provides that regulators can decide not to take enforcement action if they can achieve compliance through negotiation and settlement with potential offenders; this option could be used by applying restorative principles. Thus, the focus of enforcement and regulatory action is on identifying what harm has occurred and identifying an appropriate means to address it. Specialist environmental courts or tribunals might also be used in order to apply specialist environmental knowledge to the resolution of problems.

Macrory and Woods (2003) have made the case for specialist environmental tribunals to consider environmental harm cases, consistent with consideration by other scholars that the case for dedicated green courts incorporates a need for specialist expertise not just in judicial consideration of cases but also as regards "valuation of the harm degree of seriousness, extent and nature of victimization and remedies" (White and Heckenberg 2014, 262). White (2013, 270) identifies consistency in sentencing as being a special concern of the New South Wales Land and Environment Court which has also established a data base which provides sentencing information including judgments, recent law and other publications. Other environmental courts such as Vermont's Environmental Division also provide an online database of opinions. Specialist environmental courts thus offer the benefit of evolving procedural norms suited to their jurisdiction and secure more effective jurisprudence through development of judicial and prosecutorial expertise given that judges will have greater exposure to a homogenous legal policy regime and consistent consideration of specialist evidence and legal argument. Thus, in theory, specialist environmental courts will bring uniformity, consistency, and predictability in developing the appropriate evidentiary base and robust decision-making. White (2013) also comments that specialist environmental courts offer the hope of lower costs for enforcement agencies as well as the use of an array of alternative dispute resolution procedures including mediation. Arguably there are two conceptions on the specialist green court; one is the regulatory or dispute resolution environmental tribunal indicated by Macrory (2011) and which exists in several jurisdictions to deal with appeals and regulatory breaches and appeals against planning or land use decisions as a problem-solving court. The second is a specialist environmental court which arguably acts as a specialist criminal court considering a range of civil and criminal environmental offenses. The former is more common within the environmental court model although Macrory and Woods' 2003 conception makes specific reference to trade in endangered species, the overlapping of civil and criminal remedies, and sustainable development questions to which the latter model might be suited.

ENVIRONMENTAL HARM AND REGULATORY JUSTICE

Intervention on environmental crime involves a range of different activities involving complex legislative and regulatory measures combining international laws (treaties conventions and customary law) together with nationals laws, regulations, voluntary, and statutory schemes and codes of practice. Whereas accepted definitions of crime are generally concerned with punishment by the state through the criminal law (Barnett, 2011) environmental offending operates within a regulatory framework which, as previous chapters indicate, is more one of facilitation than punitive. White and Heckenberg (2014, 217) identify that it is rare for the state to solely exercise its coercive powers in relation to environmental regulation. Instead, a variety of measures are used to deal with environmental damage and environmental offending. The nature of the offense determines which agency has jurisdiction, and a cocktail of civil, administrative, and criminal measures might be used, determined also by the content of legislation/regulation and public policy perspectives being employed. Environmental crime also involves both state and non-state actors, particularly in areas where failures of state action or the transnational nature of crimes dictates that international NGOs may be best placed to monitor and "enforce" environmental crime problems, or where the cross border nature of crimes means that it otherwise falls outside the remit (or interest) of nation states.

Thus, at a micro level, local authority environmental health or planning departments administer planning and environmental protection legislation to ensure that development complies with land use rules. Where this is not the case they are empowered to take enforcement action which sometimes involves the use of criminal penalties to secure compliance. At a macro level, statutory environmental regulators may enforce laws against companies harming the environment or states may take enforcement action against each other in international courts for breaches of international law. NGOs may also monitor and seek enforcement action where transnational problems occur and states appear unable or unwilling to act.

As various scholars have observed, environmental enforcement broadly falls outside the remit of mainstream policing bodies and instead falls to environmental regulators, often employing a mixture of civil and criminal law to achieve their goals (Nurse 2015, White and Heckenberg 2014, Stallworthy 2008). Situ and Emmons (2000) identify the EPA and Department of Justice as the main enforcers of environmental law in the US (The Fish & Wildlife Service deals with wildlife issues) with the EPA (discussed in earlier chapters) currently the main investigator and regulator. Specialist environmental agencies such as the US Fish and Wildlife, the EPA (US), and English Nature (UK) can provide both regulatory and criminal enforcement options. However, limitations are often placed on these agencies by virtue of their enacting legislation and tightly defined jurisdiction (Stallworthy, 2008), determined by both political and practical considerations. In respect of corporate activity the principle is one of allowing corporations to continue operating and encouraging changes in behavior rather than adopting a punitive tone that could result in corporations being put out of business. This arguably only occurs in extreme cases of persistent and serious wrongdoing. Across jurisdictions, a range of problems have been identified within environmental law enforcement as follows:

1. Lack of resources
2. Inconsistency of legislation
3. Inconsistency in sentencing
4. Lack of police priority and inconsistency in policing approaches

Investigatory and prosecutions philosophy is also a significant factor. White and Heckenberg (2014, 218) identify that environmental protection agencies generally have a role to deal with pollution and waste offenses, parks and fisheries departments deal with "green" issues such as conservation, animal welfare, and land use, whereas specialist animal welfare or animal control agencies may deal with animal abuse and domestic animal issues. The manner in which offenses are dealt with and enforcement priorities determined is largely a matter of law, policy, resources, and priorities. Situ and Emmons (2000) identify that investigations and enforcement action is either proactive or reactive although the reality of environmental crime enforcement activity is that reactive enforcement approaches dominate. This is partly because the nature of offending is that it is not routinely under the eye of a public likely to report it to regulators, but also that unlike mainstream policing where the purpose of enforcement activity is prevention and detection, regulated environmental activity assumes that the underlying corporate activity is lawful. Braithwaite and Pettit (1990) suggest that the regulatory compliance system that dominates polluting and waste industries is one of systematic negotiation albeit criminal enforcement remains an option. However as with mainstream crime, problems in the enforcement regime and in the consistency of approach by enforcers undermine its effectiveness (Nurse 2015).

The reality of environmental enforcement is that it is subject to a range of factors determining whether an offense is detected and prosecuted or punished. Akella and Cannon (2004, 10) identify the following as the varied links in the enforcement chain:

- *Probability of detection*—corresponds to incentives given to enforcers, public knowledge of offenses, availability of equipment, and technical knowledge and skill of personnel
- *Probability of arrest*—relates to public knowledge and awareness of a crime, police and other enforcer pay and reward structure, availability of equipment, quality of evidence
- *Probability of prosecution*—rewards for prosecutors, capacity of the justice system, civil or criminal nature of the offense, social attitudes towards crime
- *Probability of conviction*—corresponds to rewards for judges and magistrates, capacity of the justice system, nature of the crime, social attitudes towards the crime, and quality of evidence

Implicit in these various activities is the role of discretion among investigating and prosecuting agencies and how discretion is exercised can be subject to policy drivers that change over time. Also of importance is the uncertainty of the detection, apprehension, and punishment model that dominates the environmental enforcement landscape. Akella and Allan argue that "investments in patrols, intelligence-led enforcement and multiagency enforcement task forces will be ineffective in deterring wildlife crime, and essentially wasted if cases are not successfully prosecuted" (2012, 11). Similarly in pollution and waste offenses lack of effective enforcement and the exercise of discretion not to pursue cases can be a factor.

However, it should be noted that in some cases regulatory enforcement and criminal enforcement can combine to address environmental problems. The following case study illustrates this.

Case Study—Ofwat versus Southern Water

Water Utilities companies in the United Kingdom are regulated. The Water Industry Act 1991 regulates the supply of water and the provision of sewerage services in England Wales. Provisions in the act are intended to ensure that those providing sewerage services are fit and proper people to do so and can provide services appropriately. A regulatory mechanism for water services exists that includes a regulator (Ofwat) established when the sewerage system was privatized in 1989. Ofwat's duties include: further the consumer objective to protect the interests of consumers, wherever appropriate by promoting effective competition, ensuring secure that water companies properly carry out their statutory functions and can finance the proper carrying out of their statutory functions. Ofwat has some oversight over the pricing structure for water services.

In June 2019, regulator Ofwat announced its intention to issue water utilities company Southern Water with a financial penalty amounting to £37.7 million reduced to £3 million for breaches of its license conditions and its statutory duties. The case arose following failings relating to the management, operation, and performance of wastewater treatment works run by Southern Water.

REGULATOR OFWAT IDENTIFIES IRREGULARITIES

In November 2017, whilst Southern Water was collating material for Ofwat, it discovered serious irregularities in the way the sampling of final effluent at its wastewater treatment works was being and had been carried out. It commenced an internal investigation of its own which found widespread and deliberate measures that were taken by employees, including at senior management levels, to prevent samples of wastewater from being taken at treatment works to check compliance with environmental permit conditions. This meant that the true performance of its treatment works was hidden and incorrect data was reported to Ofwat and to the Environment Agency.

Southern Water's failure to operate its wastewater treatments works properly has meant that there have been unpermitted and premature spills of wastewater from those treatment works—where wastewater has not gone through all of the processes it is supposed to before being released into the environment (Ofwat, 2019: 1).

Ofwat's investigation found that Southern Water breached its license conditions and statutory obligations as follows:

- Condition F of its license in relation to the adequacy of its resources and systems of planning and internal control to enable it to properly carry out its regulated activities, particularly in relation to its obligations under section 94(1)(b) of the Water Industry Act 1991; and
- Section 94(1)(b) of the Water Industry Act 1991 in relation to Southern Water's duty to make provision for dealing effectually, by means of sewage disposal works or otherwise, with the contents of the sewers in its sewerage system.

Ofwat's investigation concluded that Southern Water failed to operate a number of wastewater treatments works properly, including by not making the necessary investment which led to equipment failures and spills of wastewater into the environment. The regulator also found that Southern Water manipulated its wastewater sampling process which resulted in it misreporting information about the performance of a number of sewage treatment sites. This meant the company avoided penalties under Ofwat's price review incentive regime.[1] Ofwat's investigation also identified that problems had existed at several of Southern Water's wastewater treatment works, some over a long period of time. The regulator concluded that some Southern Water facilities failed to perform effectively "either through lack of timely investment by the company or inadequate maintenance of those assets" Oftwat 2019, 3). The regulator also concluded that "there had been the widespread use and adoption of improper practices within Southern Water, including at senior management levels, to present a false picture of compliance" (ibid.).

This regulatory analysis concluded that there were failings of corporate culture and governance within the company. Ofwat stated that "Southern Water's Board did not take the steps that we would expect a diligent and reasonable company to take; firstly to put in place and check that there were adequate systems and processes to ensure that wastewater treatment works were being operated in a compliant manner, and secondly steps to ensure it had sight of and could identify problems at an early stage in order to take action to prevent these" (ibid.).

The penalties imposed also reflect the fact that Southern Water had deliberately misreported data to Ofwat and as a consequence of this had avoided penalties that could have been imposed.

The penalties imposed by Ofwat are not criminal in nature but relate to regulatory obligations that fall within Ofwat's jurisdiction. The Environment Agency as the environmental regulator with criminal powers of enforcement also considered whether permit failures or the acts of Southern Water or its employees were criminal in nature and pursued a major criminal investigation into Southern Water's activities. In July 2021 Southern Water was handed a £90 million fine after pleading guilty to 6, 971 illegal discharges of sewage between 2010 and 2015, breaching environmental law. In his sentencing remarks in the case, Mr. Justice Johnson stated:

> When the Environment Agency sought to investigate these offenses it met a level of obstruction that it says was unprecedented in its experience of a company of this size. On multiple occasions, employees refused to permit Environment Agency officers to take away documentation that it wished to seize under its statutory powers, refused to allow them to walk around sites unaccompanied, citing "health and safety", and refused to answer questions, despite the Agency's powers to require answers. (Paragraph 11 of the judgment)

The judge also commented on the rationale for the high fine stating:

> The sentence to be imposed for these offenses is a fine. The history shows that fines of hundreds of thousands or low millions of pounds have not had any effect on the Defendant's offending behavior. It is necessary to set a fine which will bring home to the management of this and other companies the need to comply with laws that are designed to protect the environment. (Paragraph 12 of the judgment)

Factors increasing the severity of the fine included previous convictions, underreporting of spills, and motivation for the offending which the judge concluded was to increase the company's income and disregarding its wider compliance obligations (paragraph 46 of the judgment).

Remedying Corporate Environmental Crime: Some Conclusions

As the discussion throughout this book has shown, environmental crime is a complex area where much offending is dealt with outside of criminal justice norms. Thus, examining the need to consider how courts and other justice systems need to evolve to deal with environmental offending and disputes is a focus of this book. Environmental harm cases represent a challenge for "traditional" justice systems and for regulators. As Lord Woolf identified as long ago as 1992, jurists are not always familiar with the scope and technicality of environmental cases. The implications of such incidents also represent a challenge to punishment-based criminal justice systems. A purely punitive approach does not address the often long-lasting harm caused by environmental offenses. When committed by corporations who by necessity need to continue operations, a penal response risks focusing punishment on the individual offender rather than addressing issues within the corporation such as a deliberate culture of non-compliance. Accordingly, this book concludes that justice and regulatory systems need to consider actions aimed at directly addressing environmental harm even where offender punishment takes place. Market-based sanctions imposed by regulators and civil sanctions that provide redress for affected communities and the environment should be provided for alongside other approaches.

However, the Ofwat case discussed in this chapter also identifies some of the challenges for regulatory justice. The regulator's role is not one that is intended to be punitive operating within a coercive notion of justice. Instead, as earlier chapters have indicated, it is intended to be supportive and to facilitate business compliance. Thus, any penalties imposed need to be "reasonable," at best offering a persuasive change in behavior rather than employing a strict punishment approach. As various chapters of this book and the examples used indicate, there are questions about the efficacy of such an approach. Braithwaite (2004) argues for "reintegrative shaming," disapproval of the crime act within a continuum of respect for the offender, as a means of preventing crime through forgiveness. Thus, restorative penalties and application of the polluter pays principle serves to assist the offender. Braithwaite (2004) identifies restorative conferences as a means through which offender and victim discuss the consequences of a crime and draw out the feelings of those who have been harmed. But in accordance with Foucault's conception that power exists only when it is put into action, one aspect of restorative justice is to give power back to the victim (Dreyfus and Rabinow 1982). This is potentially problematic in environmental cases where the rights of the environment as crime victim may not be formally recognized and where regulators arguably hold little power over the major corporations that have considerable resources to deal with any regulatory problems. Ofwat's actions represent a market-based response aimed at addressing the profits that Southern Water unfairly gained by failing to comply with regulations. But arguably this was not sufficient and criminal investigation was also a factor in addressing the company's actions. Yet even the Environment Agency's criminal investigation met with obstruction and the judge in that case identified that previous fines had failed to address the company's wrongdoing or change its behavior.

The case studies discussed in this book represent a small sample of corporate environmental activity. Yet the analysis carried out for this book indicates that environmental harm caused by corporations is widespread and as green criminologists have identified requires a shift away from anthropocentric, punishment-based justice approaches in order to effectively address corporate environmental harm.

NOTE

1. In essence this regime means that where sampling data shows certain levels of pollution or evidence of spills, the company is required to pay a penalty determined in accordance with the regulator's scheme. By manipulating the data and misreporting its performance, Southern Water managed to avoid paying penalties over a period of time.

Bibliography

Abdelgawad, Walid. 2012. "The *Bt* Brinjal Case: The First Legal Action Against Monsanto and Its Indian Collaborators for Biopiracy." *Biotechnology Law Report*, 31(2): 136.

Akella, Anita, S., and Cannon, James. 2004. *Strengthening the Weakest Links: Strategies for Improving the Enforcement of Environmental Laws*. Washington, DC: Conservation International Centre.

Akella, Anita, S., and Allan, Crawford. 2012. *Dismantling Wildlife Crime*. Washington: World Wildlife Fund.

Alcock, R. and Conde, C. 2005. "Socially and Environmentally Responsible Business Practices: An Australian Perspective." *Corporate Governance Law Review*, 2005, 329.

Amnesty International. 2009. *Nigeria: Petroleum, Pollution, and Poverty in the Niger Delta*. London: Amnesty International Publications.

Amnesty International and CEHRD. 2011. *The True "Tragedy" Delays and Failures in Tackling Oil Spills in the Niger Delta*. London: Amnesty International Publications.

Andrade, Rodrigo. 2012. "Brazil Fines 35 Firms US$44 Million for Biopiracy." *Sci Dev Net*. Available at: https://www.scidev.net/global/news/brazil-fines-35-firms-us-44-million-for-biopiracy/

Antonio, Robert, and Brulle, Robert. 2011. "The Unbearable Lightness of Politics: Climate Change Denial and Political Polarization." *The Sociological Quarterly* 52: 195–202.

Aoki, Keith. 1998. "Neocolonialism, Anticommons Property, and Biopiracy in the (Not-so-Brave) New World Order of International Intellectual Property Protection." *Indiana Journal of Global Legal Studies* Vol. 6: Iss. 1, Article 2.

Aoki, Keith. 2017. "Neocolonialism, Anticommons Property, and Biopiracy in the (Not-so-Brave) New World Order of International Intellectual Property Protection" in Alexandra George (ed.) *Globalization and Intellectual Property*. London: Routledge.

Ares, Elena, and Smith, Louise. 2017. *Air Pollution: Meeting Nitrogen Dioxide Targets* (Parliamentary Briefing Paper, No. 8179). London: House of Commons.

Attfield, Robin. 2016. *Environmental Ethics*. Cambridge: Polity Press.

Austin, A. 2015. "Can you imagine what it's like to live next to an opencast coal mine?", Friends of the Earth. Online at: https://www.foe.co.uk/green-blog/can-you-imagine-what-its-like-live-next-opencast-coal-mine. [Accessed 1 October 2017]

Baker, Mallen. 2012. *The Global Reporting Initiative is Growing Up.* http://www.mallenbaker.net/csr/index.php [Accessed 20 June 2018]

Baker, S. 2007. "Sustainable Development as Symbolic Commitment: Declaratory Politics and the Seductive Appeal of Ecological Modernisation in the European Union." *Environmental Politics*, 16(2), 297–317.

Barak, G. (ed.) 2015. *The Routledge International Handbook of the Crimes of the Powerful*. Abingdon: Routledge.

Barnett, Hilaire. 2011. *Constitutional & Administrative Law* (Ninth Edition). Abingdon: Routledge.

Barrett, Stoyan, and White, Rob. 2017. "Disrupting Environmental Crime at the Local Level: An Operational Perspective," *Palgrave Communications*, 3(2): 1–8.

Bassey, N. 2008. *Gas Flaring: Assaulting Communities, Jeopardizing the World. National Environmental Consultation Hosted by the Environmental Rights Action in Conjunction with the Federal Ministry of Environment at Reiz Hotel, Abuja*, 1–11. Available at: http://www.eraction.org/publications/presentations/gas-flaring-ncc-abuja.pdf

Baumol, William J. 1990. "Entrepreneurship: Productive, Unproductive and Destructive." *Journal of Political Economy* vol. 98, no. 5, pp. 893–921.

Baumüller, Heike, Donnelly, Elizabeth, Vines, Alex, and Weimer, Markus. 2011. "The Effects of Oil Companies' Activities on the Environment, Health and Development in Sub-Saharan Africa." Brussels: The European Parliament.

Baxi, Upendra. 2010. "Writing about Impunity and Environment: The Silver Jubilee of the Bhopal Catastrophe." *Journal of Human Rights and the Environment* Vol. 1(1): 23–44.

BBC News. 2015. *Shell Agrees $84m Deal over Niger Delta Oil Spill.* Available at: https://www.bbc.co.uk/news/world-30699787

BBC News. 2020. *Daimler to Pay $1.5bn over Emissions Cheat Claims in US.* Available at: https://www.bbc.co.uk/news/business-54153126

Becker, Gary Stanley. 1968. "Crime and Punishment: An Economic Approach." *Journal of Political Economy*, 76(2): 169–217.

Becker-Olsen, Karen, Cudmore, Andrew, and Hill, Ronald P. 2006. "The impact of perceived corporate social responsibility on consumer behaviour." *Journal of Business Research* Vol. 59(1): 46–53.

Beebeejaun, Y. 2013. "The Politics of Fracking: A Public Policy Dilemma?" *Political Insight*, 4(3), pp. 18–21. doi: 10.1111/2041-9066.12032.

Beirne, Peirs, and South, Nigel. 2007. "Introduction: approaching green criminology," in Beirne, P. and South, N. *Issues in Green Criminology*, Cullompton: Willan.

Beirne, Peirs and South, Nigel. (eds) 2007. *Issues in Green Criminology: Confronting Harms Against Environments, Humanity and Other Animals*. Devon: Willan.

Bell, Stuart, McGillivray, Donald, and Pedersen, Ole. 2013. *Environmental Law*, 8th Edition, Oxford: Oxford University Press.

Benton, Ted. 1998. "Rights and Justice on a Shared Planet: More Rights or New Relations?" *Theoretical Criminology*, 2(2), 149–75.

Benton, Ted. 2007. "Ecology, Community and Justice: The Meaning of Green," in Beirne, P., and South, N. *Issues in Green Criminology*. Cullompton: Willan.

Berman, Harold. 2012. "The Alien Tort Claims Act and the Law of Nations." *Emory International Law Review*. Retrieved from: http://papers.ssrn.com/sol3/papers.cfm?abstract_id=666146

Bernaz, Nadia. 2017. *Business and Human Rights: History Law and Policy—Bridging the Accountability Gap*. London and New York: Routledge.

Biela, J. 2014. *Accountability: On the Measurement of an Elusive Concept*. In 5th Biennial Conference of the ECPR Standing Group on Regulatory Governance. Barcelona.

Black, Julia. 2005. "The Emergence of Risk-Based Regulation and the New Public Risk Management in the United Kingdom." *Public Law 510–546.*

Block, Alan, and Scarpitti, Frank R. 1985. *Poisoning for Profit: The Mafia and Toxic Waste in America*. New York: William Morrow.

Bodansky, D. 1995. "Customary (And Not So Customary) International Environmental Law," *Indiana Journal of Global Legal Studies*, 3(1): 105–119

Bovens, Mark. 2007. "Analyzing and Assessing Accountability: A Conceptual Framework." *European Law Journal*, 13, 447–468.

Bowen, Francis. 2014. *After Greenwashing: Symbolic Corporate Environmentalism and Society*. Cambridge: Cambridge University Press.

Braithwaite, John. 2004. "Restorative Justice: Theories and Worries," *Visiting Experts Papers*, 123rd International Senior Seminar, Resource Material Series No. 63, pp. 47–56. Tokyo: United Nations Asia and Far East Institute for the Prevention of Crime and the Treatment of Offenders. Available at: https://www.unafei.or.jp/publications/pdf/RS_No63/No63_10VE_Braithwaite2.pdf

Braithwaite, John, and Pettit, Philip. 1990. *Not Just Deserts: A Republican Theory of Criminal Justice*. Oxford: Oxford University Press.

Brennan, A., and Lo, Y. 2008. "The Early Development of Environmental Ethics." *Stanford Encyclopedia of Philosophy*. Available at: http://plato.stanford.edu/

Brisman, Avi. 2014. "Of Theory and Meaning in Green Criminology." *International Journal for Crime, Justice and Social Democracy* Volume 3(2): 21–34.

Brown, M. P., Bush, B., Rhee, G., Shane, L., John F. Brown, J.F., and Wagner, R.E. 1988. "PCB Dechlorination in Hudson River Sediment." *Science*, vol. 240 (4859): 1674–1676. DOI: 10.1126/science.3132740

Brown, Mark P., Werner, Mary B., Sloan, Ronald J., and Simpson, Karl W. 1985. "Polychlorinated Biphenyls in the Hudson River." *Environmental Science & Technology* 19(8): 656–661. DOI: 10.1021/es00138a001.

Bruno, K., Karliner, J., and Brotsky, C. 1999. *Greenhouse Gangsters vs. Climate Justice*. San Francisco, CA: Transnational Resource and Action Centre.

Bullard, R.D. (ed) 1994. *Unequal Protection: Environmental Justice and Communities of Color*, San Fracisco, CA: Sierra Club Books.

Bullard, R.D. 2000. *Dumping in Dixie: Race, Class, And Environmental Quality*, Third Edition, New York: Routledge.

Carrabine, Eamonn. 2017. *Crime and Social Theory*. London: Palgrave.

Carrington, Damian. 2016. "MPs: UK Air Pollution Is a 'Public Health Emergency,'", *The Guardian* (Online). Available at: https://www.theguardian.com/environment/2016/apr/27/uk-air-pollution-public-health-emergency-crisis-diesel-cars [Accessed 20 April 2018]

Carrington, Damian. 2017. "How Conniving Carmakers Caused the Diesel Air Pollution Crisis," *The Guardian*. Online at: https://www.theguardian.com/environment/2017/apr/07/how-conniving-carmakers-caused-the-diesel-air-pollution-crisis [Accessed 12 July 2019]

Casertano, Stefano. 2013. *Our Land, Our Oil!: Natural Resources, Local Nationalism, and Violent Secession*. Berlin: Springer.

Cass, V. (1996). "Toxic tragedy: Illegal hazardous waste dumping in Mexico." In S. Edwards, T. Edwards, & C. Fields (Eds.), *Environmental Crime and Criminality: Theoretical and Practical Issues*. New York: Garland.

Cetindamar, Dilek. 2007. "Corporate Social Responsibility Practices and Environmentally Responsible Behavior: The Case of The United Nations Global Compact." *Journal of Business Ethics* 76(2): 163–176. https://doi.org/10.1007/s10551-006-9265-4.

Clapham, Andrew. 2006. *Human Rights Obligations of Non-State Actors*. Oxford: Oxford University Press.

Claudio, Luz. 2002. "The Hudson: A River Runs Through an Environmental Controversy." *Environmental Health Perspectives* Vol. 10(4): 184–187.

Cohen, Mark. 1992. "Environmental Crime and Punishment: Legal/Economic Theory and Empirical Evidence on Enforcement of Federal Environmental Statutes." *Journal of Criminal Law & Criminology* 82(4): 1054–1108.

Cohen, A. J., Ross Anderson, H., Ostro, B., Pandey, K. D., Krzyzanowski, M., Künzli, N., Gutschmidt, K., Pope, A., Romieu, I., Samet, J. M., & Smith, K. 2005. "The Global Burden of Disease Due to Outdoor Air Pollution." *Journal of Toxicology and Environmental Health*, 68(13–14), 1301–1307. https://doi.org/10.1080/15287390590936166

Cole, L., and Foster, S. 2001. *From the Ground Up: Environmental Racism and the Rise of the Environmental Justice Movement*. New York: New York University Press.

Collins, Hugh. 2012. On the (In)compatibility of Human Rights and Private Law. LSE Law, Society and Economy Working Papers 7/2012. Online at: https://www.lse.ac.uk/collections/law/wps/WPS2012-07_Collins.pdf [Accessed 7 December 2016]

Connelly, James and Smith, Graham 1999. *Politics and the Environment: From Theory to Practice*. London: Routledge.

Cornish, D.B., and Clarke, R.V. (eds) 2014. T*he Reasoning Criminal: Rational Choice Perspectives on Offending*. New Brunswick, New Jersey: Transation Publishers

Cownie, F. 2004. *Legal Academics*. Oxford: Hart Publishing.

Cox, R. 1997. "Democracy in Hard Times: Economic Globalization and the Limits of Liberal Democracy," in Anthony McGrew (ed.), *The Transformation of Democracy? Democratic Politics in the New World Order*. Milton Keynes: The Open University.

Cray, C. 2001. "Toxics on the Hudson: The Saga of GE, PCBs, and the Hudson River." *Multinational Monitor* Vol. 22(7/8): 9–18.

Croall, Hazel. 2007. "Food Crime," in Beirne, P., and South, N. *Issues in Green Criminology*. Cullompton: Willan.

Cropper, M.L., Jiang, Y., Alberini, A. et al. 2014. "Getting Cars Off the Road: The Cost-Effectiveness of an Episodic Pollution Control Program," Environmental and Resource Economics, 57(1): 117–143. https://doi.org/10.1007/s10640-013-9669-4

Crowhurst, G. 2006. "The Commercial Impact of Environmental Law." *Business Law Review*. 27(4), 92–97.

Crowther, D. and Aras, G. 2008. *Corporate Social Responsibility*. Copenhagen: Ventus Publishing.

Curry, P. 2011. *Ecological Ethics: An Introduction*. Cambridge: Polity Press.

Danley, V. 2011. "Biopiracy in the Brazilian Amazon: Learning Form International and Comparative Law Successes and Shortcomings to Help Promote Biodiversity Conservation in Brazil." *Florida A&M University Law Review* 7: 292–328.

Dauvergne, P. 2008. *The Shadows of Consumption: Consequences for the Global Environment*. Cambridge, MA: MIT Press.

Dreyfus, Hubert, and Rabinow, Paul. 1982. *Michel Foucault: Beyond Structuralism and Hermeneutics*. Chicago: University of Chicago Press.

Dunlap, Riley E. 2013. "Climate Change Skepticism and Denial: An Introduction." *American Behavioral Scientist*, 57(6), 691–698. https://doi.org/10.1177/0002764213477097

Dunlap, Riley E., and McCright, A. 2011. "Organized Climate Change Denial" in. John Dryzek, Richard Norgaard, and David Schlosberg (eds) *The Oxford Handbook of Climate Change and Society*, Oxford: Oxford University Press.

Eliason, S.L. 2003. "Illegal Hunting and Angling: The Neutralization of Wildlife Law Violations," *Society & Animals* Vol. 11, No. 3, Washington: Society & Animals Forum Inc.

Environmental Protection Agency. 2019. Hudson River PCBs Superfund Site Fact Sheet, April 2019. Available at: https://www.epa.gov/sites/production/files/2019-04/documents/upper_hudson_river_fact_sheet_-five_year_review-april_2019_final.pdf [Accessed 8 July 2019]

Environment Texas/Sierra Club. 2009. *Environmental Groups and Shell Oil Company Propose Landmark Settlement of Clean Air Act Lawsuit*. Texas: Environment Texas/Sierra Club (Press release 23 April 2009).

EU Commission. 2011. *Communication from the Commission to the European Parliament, the Council, the European Economic and Social Committee and the Committee of the Regions: A Renewed EU Strategy 2011–14 for Corporate Social Responsibility*. Brussels: European Commission.

European Commission. 2017a. Corporate Social Responsibility in Practice. Online at: http://ec.europa.eu/growth/industry/corporate-social-responsibility/in-practice_en [Accessed 1 October 2017]

European Commission. 2017b. The Aarhus Convention. Online at: http://ec.europa. eu/environment/aarhus/ [Accessed 1 July 2017\

European Environment Agency. 2016. Premature Deaths Attributable to Air Pollution. Online at: https://www.eea.europa.eu/media/newsreleases/many-europeans-still-exposed-to-air-pollution-2015/premature-deaths-attributable-to-air-pollution [Accessed 12 November 2018]

Eyben, Rosaling. 2011. *Supporting Pathways of Women's Empowerment: A Brief Guide for International Development Organisations.* Brighton: Institute of Development Studies.

Fagan, N. and Thompson, L. 2009. "Corporate Responsibility and Group Redress Mechanisms." *Business Law International* vol. 10, no. 1, pp. 51–60.

Farinelli, F., Bottini, M., Akkoyunlu, S., and Aerni, P. (2011). "Green Entrepreneurship: The Missing Link Towards a Greener Economy." *ATDF Journal*, 8(3/4), 42–48.

Fazio, C., and Strell, E. 2014. "Precautionary Principle: a Rational Approach to Climate Change." *New York Law Journal*, Available at: https://www.clm.com/publication.cfm?ID=506 [Accessed 1 July 2019]

Fenger, J. 1999. "Urban Air Quality." *Atmospheric Environment*, 33(29): 4877–4900.

Fenwick, Helen. 2007. *Civil Liberties and Human Rights* (Fourth Edition). Abingdon: Routledge-Cavendish.

Field, C.B., V.R. Barros, D. J. Dokken, K.J. Mach, M.D. Mastrandrea, T.E. Bilir, M. Chatterjee, K.L. Ebi, Y.O. Estrada, R.C. Genova, B. Girma, E.S. Kissel, A.N. Levy, S. MacCracken, P.R. Mastrandrea, and L.L. White (eds.) 2014."Summary for Policymakers" In: *Climate Change 2014: Impacts, Adaptation, and Vulnerability. Part A:Global and Sectoral Aspects Contribution of Working Group II to the Fifth Assessment Report of the Intergovernmental Panel on Climate Change*, Cambridge/New York: Cambridge University Press.

Finkel, M. and Hays, J. 2013. "The Implications of Unconventional Drilling for Natural Gas: A Global Public Health Concern." *Public Health* 127(10): 889–893.

Fisher, D. and Freudenberg, W. 2001. "Ecological Modernization and Its Critics: Assessing the Past and Looking Toward the Future." *Society and Natural Resources* 14: 701–709.

Friedman, Milton. 1970. "The Social Responsibility of Business is to Increase its Profits." *The New York Times Magazine*, 13 September 1970.

Gallicano, Tiffany. 2011. "A Critical Exploration of Greenwashing Claims." *Public Relations Journal* 5(3), 1–21.

Garcia, Javier. 2015. "Fighting Biopiracy: The Legislative Protection of Traditional Knowledge." *Berkeley La Raza Law Journal*, Vol. 18: 5–28.

Gebru, Aman. 2019. "Patents, Disclosure, and Biopiracy." 96 *Denver Law Review* 535 (2019); Cardozo Legal Studies Research Paper No. 560. Available at SSRN: https://ssrn.com/abstract=3188311 or http://dx.doi.org/10.2139/ssrn.3188311

Gibbs, C. and Simpson, S. 2008. "Measuring Corporate Environmental Crime Rates: Progress and Problems." *Crime Law and Social Change* 51(1): 87–107.

Goldstein, Bernard, Osofsky, Howard, and Litchveld, Maureen Y. 2011. "The Gulf Oil Spill." *New England Journal of Medicine*, 364: 1334–1348.

Goodey, J. 1997. "Boys Don't Cry: Masculinities, Fear of Crime and Fearlessness." *British Journal of Criminology*, 37(3), 401–418.

Gordley, J. 1998. "Is Comparative Law a Distinct Discipline." *American Journal of Comparative Law*, 46(4), pp. 607–9.

Gottschalk, P. and Smith, R. 2011. "Criminal Entrepreneurship, White-Collar Criminality, and Neutralization Theory." *Journal of Enterprising Communities: People and Places in the Global Economy,* 5(4), 300–308.

Gould, K.A., Pellow, D.N., and Schnaiberg, A. 2008. *The Treadmill of Production: Injustice and Unsustainability in the Global Economy*, Abingdon: Routledge.

Gouldson, A., Morton, A., and Pollard, S. 2009. "Better Environmental Regulation— Contributions from Risk-Based Decision-Making." *Science of the Total Environment*, 407(19), 5283–5288.

Government of Lithuania. 2015. *Regarding the Implementation of the United Nations Guiding Principles on Business and Human Rights by HRC Resolution 17/14*, Lithuania: Ministry of Justice.

Greenacre, Simon. 2002. "Terra Nullius of the Mind: Indigenous Knowledges, Biopiracy and Patent Law." *Polemic* 12(2): 33–39.

Greider, T. and Garkovich, L. 1994. "Landscapes: The Social Construction of Nature and the Environment." *Rural Sociology* 59: 1–24. doi:10.1111/j.1549-0831.1994. tb00519.x

Groombridge, N. 1998. "Masculinities and Crimes against the Environment." *Theoretical Criminology*, 2(2), 249–267.

Gullett, Warwick. 1997. "Environmental Protection and the Precautionary Principle: A Response to Scientific Uncertainty in Environmental Management." *Environmental and Planning Law Journal*, 14(1): 52–69.

Gunningham, N. and Sinclair, D. 2007. *Multiple OHS Inspection Tools: Balancing Deterrence and Compliance in the Mining Sector.* Canberra: Australian National University.

Hall, M. 2013. "Victims of Environmental Harm." In R. Walters, D. Westerhuis, and T. Wyatt (eds.), *Emerging Issues in Green Criminology: Exploring Power, Justice and Harm*. Basingstoke: Palgrave Macmillan.

Hall, Matthew. 2014. The Roles and Use of Law in Green Criminology. *International Journal for Crime Justice and Social Democracy*, 3(2): 97–110.

Hall, M. 2015. *Exploring Green Crime: Introducing the Legal, Social & Criminological Contexts of Environmental Harm*. London: Palgrave.

Hall, M., Maher, J., Nurse, A., Potter, G., South, N., and Wyatt, T. 2017. "Introduction: Green Criminology in the 21st Century" in Matthew Hall, Jennifer Maher, Angus Nurse, Gary Potter, Nigel South and Tanya Wyatt (eds) *Greening Criminology in the 21st Century*, Abingdon: Routledge.

Hamann, R. and Kapelus, P. 2004. "Corporate Social Responsibility in Mining in Southern Africa: Fair Accountability or Just Greenwash?", *Development,* 47(3): 85–92. https://doi.org/10.1057/palgrave.development.110005.

Hamilton. C. 2006. "Biodiversity, Biopiracy and Benefits: What Allegations of Biopiracy Tell us About Intellectual Property." *Developing World Bioethics,* 6: 158–173. doi:10.1111/j.1471-8847.2006.00168.x

Hamilton, C. (ed) 2015. *The Anthropocene and the Global Environmental Crisis: Rethinking Modernity in a New Epoch.* Abingdon: Routledge.

Hampton, Philip. 2005. *Reducing Administrative Burdens—Effective Inspection and Enforcement.* London: HM Treasury. Available at: https://web.archive.org/web/20090704105121/http://www.hm-treasury.gov.uk/d/bud05hamptonv1.pdf [Accessed 7 July 2019]

Hanlon, B. 2017. "Protecting the Environment: At What Cost?" London: Victoria Square Chambers. Online at: http://www.victoriasquarechambers.co.uk/protecting-the-environment-at-what-cost/ [Accessed 5 October 2017]

Harris, D.R. 2013. "The Development of Socio-legal Studies in the United Kingdom." *Legal Studies,* 3, pp.315–333.

Harris, F. 2011. "Brands Corporate Social Responsibility and Reputation Management." In A. Voiculescu and H. Yanacopulos (Eds), *The Business of Human Rights: An Evolving Agenda for Corporate Responsibility*, London, Zed Books/The Open University.

Hatchard, J. 2011. "Combatting Transnational Corporate Corruption: Enhancing Human Rights and Good Governance." In A. Voiculescu and H. Yanacopulos (Eds), *The Business of Human Rights: An Evolving Agenda for Corporate Responsibility.* London, Zed Books/The Open University.

Hawke, N. 1997. "Corporate Environmental Crime and Director's Liability." *London Journal of Canadian Law*, 13(1): 12–24.

Heckenberg, Diane. 2010. "The Global Transference of Toxic Harms" in White, R. (ed) *Global Environmental Harm: Criminological Perspectives.* Devon: Willan Publishing, 37–61.

Higgins, Polly. 2010. *Eradicating Ecocide: Exposing the Corporate and Political Practices Destroying the Planet and Proposing the Laws Needed to Eradicate Ecocide.* London: Shepheard-Walwyn Publishers.

Hinteregger, Monika. 2008. *Environmental Liability and Ecological Damage in European Law*. Cambridge: Cambridge University Press.

HM Government 2016. *Good Business Implementing the UN Guiding Principles on Business and Human Rights*. London: Stationery Office. Online at: https://www.gov.uk/government/uploads/system/uploads/attachment_data/file/522805/Good_Business_Implementing_the_UN_Guiding_Principles_on_Business_and_Human_Rights_updated_May_2016.pdf [Accessed 13 December 2016]

Ho, C.M. 2006. Biopiracy and Beyond: A Consideration of Socio-Cultural Conflicts with Global Patent Policies, 39 U. Mich. J. L. Reform 433 (2006).

Hobsbawn, Eric J. 1969. *Industry and Empire from 1750 to the Present Day*. Harmondsworth: Penguin.

Hobson, I., Jr. 2006. "The Unseen World of Transnational Corporations' Powers." *Neumann Business Review*, 1: 23–31. https://www.neumann.edu/academics/divisions/business/journal/Review_SP06/

Hodges, Christopher. 2008. *The Reform of Class and Representative Actions in European Legal Systems: A New Framework for Collective Redress in Europe.* Oxford: Hart Publishing.

Holcomb, Jeanne. 2008. "Environmentalism and the Internet: Corporate Greenwashers and Environmental Groups," *Contemporary Justice Review*, 11:3, 203–211, DOI: 10.1080/10282580802295328.

Holtom, Robert. 2011. "Shell Case Echoes Call to Eradicate Ecocide." United Nations University. http://ourworld.unu.edu/en/shell-case-echoes-call-to-eradicate-ecocide (30 May 2015).

Hosein, Hanson. 1993. "Unsettling: Bhopal and the Resolution of International Disputes Involving an Environmental Disaster." *Boston College International and Comparative Law Review*, Vol XVI(2): 285–319.

House of Commons Environmental Audit Committee. 2005. *Corporate Environmental Crime*, HC136, London: The Stationery Office Limited.

ILO. 1953. *Indigenous Peoples: Living and Working Conditions of Aboriginal Populations in Independent Countries, Studies and Reports, Series 35.* Geneva: International Labour Office.

Jamison, A., Raynolds, M., Holroyd, P., Veldman, E. and Tremblett, K., 2005. *Defining Corporate Environmental Responsibility: Canadian ENGO Perspectives.* Canada: The Pembina Institute/Pollution Probe.

Kahan, D.M., Braman, D., Gastil, J., Slovic, P., Mertz, C.K., 2007. "Culture and Identity-Protective Cognition: Explaining the White-Male Efect in Risk Perception." *Journal of Empirical Legal Studies* 4: 465–505.

Kastorf, Kurt. G. 2014. "Cooperative Federalism: Is There a Trend towards Uniform National Standards under the Clean Air Act?" American Bar Association. Available at: https://www.americanbar.org/groups/environment_energy_resources/publications/trends/2013-14/may-june-2014/cooperative_federalism_there_trend_towards_uniform_national_standards_under_clean_air_act/ [Accessed 12 July 2019]

Keeler, J.T.S. 2016. "The Politics of Shale Gas and Anti-fracking Movements in France and the UK." In: Wang Y., Hefley W. (eds) The Global Impact of Unconventional Shale Gas Development. Natural Resource Management and Policy, vol 39. Springer, Cham Cohort Studies, *American Journal of Epidemiology*, Volume 153, Issue 11, 1 June 2001, Pages 1050–1055, https://doi.org/10.1093/aje/153.11.1050

Kell, Georg. 2013. "12 Years Later: Reflections on the Growth of the UN Global Compact." *Business & Society*, 52(1), pp. 31–52. doi: 10.1177/0007650312460466.

Kercher, K. 2007. "Corporate Social Responsibility: Impact of globalisation and international business." *Bond University Corporate Governance eJournal*, Available at: http://epublications.bond.edu.au/cgi/viewcontent.cgi?article=1003&context=cgej [Accessed 4 April 2013]

Kiely, K. 2014. *Five Major Health Threats from Fracking-Related Air Pollution.* New York: NRDC. Available at: https://www.nrdc.org/media/2014/141216 [Accessed 1 July 2019]

Kinley, David and Chambers, Rachael. 2006. "The UN Human Rights Norms for Corporations: The Private Implications of Public International Law." *Human Rights Law Review* 6 (3): 447–497. doi: 10.1093/hrlr/ngl020.

Kneller, R. and Manderson, E. 2008. *Environmental Regulations, Outward FDI and Heterogeneous Firms: Are Countries Used as Pollution Havens?* Nottingham: University of Nottingham.

Koppell, J.G. 2005. "Pathologies of Accountability: ICANN and the Challenge of Multiple Accountabilities Disorder." *Public Administration Review*, 65: 94–108. doi:10.1111/j.1540-6210.2005.00434.x

Kriebel, D., Tickner, J., Epstein, P., Lemons, J., Levins, R., Loechler, E. L., Quinn, M., Rudel, R., Schettler, T., and Stoto, M. 2001. "The Precautionary Principle in Environmental Science", *Environmental Health Perspectives*, Vol. 109 (9): 871–876.

Künzli, N., Medina, S., Kaiser, R., Quénel, P., Horak, F., Studnicka, M. 2001. "Assessment of Deaths Attributable to Air Pollution: Should We Use Risk Estimates based on Time Series or on Cohort Studies?" *American Journal of Epidemiology*, Volume 153, Issue 11, 1 June 2001, Pages 1050–1055, https://doi.org/10.1093/aje/153.11.1050

Laufer, W.S. 2003. "Social Accountability and Corporate Greenwashing," *Journal of Business Ethics*, 43(3): 253–261

Laville, S. 2017. "UK Withdrawal Bill 'Rips the Heart out of Rnvironmental Law,' Say Campaigners," *The Guardian*. Available at: https://www.theguardian.com/environment/2017/oct/17/uk-withdrawal-bill-rips-the-heart-out-of-environmental-law-say-campaigners [Accessed 1 July 2019]

Law Commission. 2012. *Wildlife Law: A Consultation Paper.* London: Law Commission.

Lea, J., and Young, J. 1993. *What Is To Be Done About Law & Order?* London: Pluto Press.

Lee, M. 2017. *EU Environmental Law, Governance and Decision-Making (Modern Studies in European Law).* Oxford: Hart Publishing. https://doi.org/10.1177/1362480603007002414

Leigh Day & Co Solicitors 2005. "Columbian Farms Start Claim against BP for Pipeline That Has Ruined Lives." Retrieved from www.leighday.co.uk

Long, M.A., Stretesky, P.B., Lynch, M., and Fenwick, E. 2012. "Crime in the Coal Industry: Implications for Green Criminology and Treadmill of Production," *Organization and Environment*, 25(3) 328–346.

Lynch, Michael J. 1990. "The Greening of Criminology: A Perspective on the 1990s," *The Critical Criminologist*, 2: 1–5.

Lynch, Michael, J. 2014. Treadmill of Production Theory. Available at: https://green-criminology.org/glossary/treadmill-of-production-theory/ [Accessed 1 July 2019]

Lynch, Michael J., Long, Michael A., Barrett, Kimberly L., and Stretesky, Paul B. 2013. "Is it a Crime to Produce Ecological Disorganization? Why Green

Criminology and Political Economy Matter in the Analysis of Global Ecological Harms," *The British Journal of Criminology*, Volume 53, Issue 6, November 2013, Pages 997–1016, https://doi.org/10.1093/bjc/azt051

Lynch, Michael and Stretesky, Paul. 2003. "The Meaning of Green: Contrasting Criminological Perspectives." *Theoretical Criminology*, 7 (2), 217–238.

Lynch, Michael and Stretesky, Paul. 2014. *Exploring Green Criminology: Toward a Green Criminology Revolution.* Farnham: Ashgate.

Macrory, R. 2006. *Regulatory Justice: Making Sanctions Effective.* London: Cabinet Office. Available at: https://webarchive.nationalarchives.gov.uk/20121205164501/http://www.bis.gov.uk/files/file44593.pdf [Accessed 8 July 2019]

Macrory, Richard. 2011. *Consistency and effectiveness: Strengthening the New Environment Tribunal.* London: UCL Centre for Law and the Environment.

Macrory R. and Woods, M. 2003. *Modernizing Environmental Justice: Regulation and the Role of an Environmental Tribunal,* Centre for Law and the Environment, University College, London.

Maguire, M., Morgan, R., and Reiner, R. (eds). 1994. *The Oxford Handbook of Criminology.* Oxford: Oxford University Press.

Manderson, E. and Kneller, R. 2012. "Environmental Regulations, Outward FDI and Heterogeneous Firms: Are Countries Used as Pollution Havens?" *Environmental and Resource Economics,* 51(3): 317–352. https://doi.org/10.1007/s10640-011-9500-z

Mansuri, G. and Rao, V. 2013. *Localizing Development: Does Participation Work?* Policy Research Report, Washington, DC: World Bank.

Markell D. and Ruhl, J.B. 2012. "An Empirical Assessment of Climate Change In The Courts: A New Jurisprudence Or Business As Usual?" *Florida Law Review* 64(1): 15–72.

Marquis, C., and Toffel, M. 2012. "When Do Firms Greenwash? Corporate Visibility, Civil Society Scrutiny, and Environmental Disclosure," Cambridge, MA: Harvard Environmental Economics Program, 2012, Working Paper 11-115. Available at: https://heep.hks.harvard.edu/publications/when-do-firms-greenwash-corporate-visibility-civil-society-scrutiny-and [Accessed 8 July 2019]

Marshall, M. 2011. "How Fracking Caused Earthquakes in the UK," *New Scientist.* Online at: https://www.newscientist.com/article/dn21120-how-fracking-caused-earthquakes-in-the-uk/ [Accessed 13 November 2018]

Marshall, T. 1996. "The Evolution of Restorative Justice in Britain." *European Journal on Criminal Policy and Research*, 4(4): 21–43.

Marshall, T.F. 1999. *Restorative Justice: An Overview.* London, Home Office.

Matten, D. 2003. "Symbolic Politics in Environmental Regulation: Corporate Strategic Responses." *Business Strategy and the Environment*, 12(4): 215–226.

Matza, D. 1964. *Delinquency and Drift.* New Jersey: Transaction.

Mazurkiewicz, P. 2002. *Corporate Environmental Responsibility: Is a Common CSR Framework Possible?* Decomm-SDO, World Bank.

McBarnet, Doreen. 2006. "After Enron Will 'Whiter Than White Collar Crime' Still Wash?", *British Journal of Criminology*, 46,1091–1109.

McPhail, K. and Adams, C. 2016. "Corporate Respect for Human Rights: Meaning, Scope, and the Shifting Oder of Discourse." *Accounting, Auditing & Accountability Journal*, Vol. 29 Iss: 4, pp.650–67.

Meltz, Robert. 2013. *Federal Agency Actions Following the Supreme Court's Climate Change Decision in* Massachusetts v. EPA*: A Chronology*. Washington: Congressional Research Service.

Merton, R. K. 1968. *Social Theory and Social Structure*. New York: Free Press.

Mgbeoji, I. 2006. *Global* Biopiracy*: Patents, Plants, and Indigenous Knowledge*. Ithaca, NY: Cornell University Press.

Ministry for Foreign Affairs. 2015. *Action Plan for Business and Human Rights. Stockholm: Ministry for Foreign Affairs*. Available at: https://www.government. se/4a84f5/contentassets/822dc47952124734b60daf1865e39343/action-plan-for-business-and-human-rights.pdf

Mohai, P., Pellow, D. and Roberts, J.T. 2009. "Environmental Justice." *Annual Review of Environment and Resources*, 34:1: 405–430.

Moore, P., T. Greiber, and S. Baig. 2010. *Strengthening Voices for Better Choices: Forest Governance and Law Enforcement: Findings from the Field*. Gland, Switzerland: IUCN, Forest Conservation Programme.

Mouawad, J. 2009. "Shell Settles Air Pollution Accusations." *New York Times*.

Mufson, S. 2012. "BP Settles Criminal Charges for $4 Billion in Spill; Supervisors Indicted on Manslaughter." *Washington Post*. Available at: https://www.washingtonpost.com/business/economy/bp-to-pay-billions-in-gulf-oil-spill-settlement/2012/11/15/ba0b783a-2f2e-11e2-9f50-0308e1e75445_story.html [Accessed 20 February 2020]

Myrup, M. 2012. "Industrialising Greenland: Government and Transnational Corporations Versus Civil Society?" in Ellefsen, R., Sollund, R. and Larsen, G. *Eco-global Crimes: Contemporary Problems and Future Challenges*. Farnham: Ashgate.

Nelken, D. 1994. "White-Collar Crime," in M. Maguire, R. Morgan, and R. Reiner (eds.), *The Oxford Handbook of Criminology*. Oxford: Oxford University Press.

Neumayer, E. 2001. "Pollution Havens: An Analysis of Policy Options for Dealing with an Elusive Phenomenon." *The Journal of Environment & Development*, *10*(2), 147–177. https://doi.org/10.1177/107049650101000203

Newburn, T. 2017. *Criminology* (3rd Edition). London: Routledge.

Nieuwoudt, S. 2007. "How to Turn the Curse of Oil into a Blessing." Inter Press Service News Agency. http://www.ipsnews.net/2007/05/trade-africa-how-to-turn-the-curse-of-oil-into-a-blessing/ [Accessed 31 August 2018]

Nijar, G.S. 2017. "Finally, a Law to Curb Biopiracy in Malaysia," *The Green Watch*. Available at: https://greenwatchbd.com/finally-a-law-to-curb-biopiracy-in-malaysia/ [Accessed 10 July 2019]

Nurse, Angus. 2011. "Policing Wildlife: Perspectives on Criminality in Wildlife Crime." *Papers from the British Criminology Conference*. Volume 11, 2011, London: British Society of Criminology.

Nurse, Angus. 2013a. *Animal Harm: Perspectives on Why People Harm and Kill Animals*. Farnham: Ashgate.

Nurse, Angus. 2013b. "Privatising the Green Police: The Role of NGOs in Wildlife Law Enforcement." *Crime Law and Social Change* 59(3), 305–318.

Nurse, Angus. 2014, July. "Cleaning up Greenwash: The Case for Enforcing Corporate Environmental Responsibility," in Nurse, A. (ed.), *Critical Perspectives on Green Criminology, Internet Journal of Criminology*.

Nurse, Angus. 2015. *Policing Wildlife: Perspectives on the Enforcement of Wildlife Legislation.* London: Palgrave Macmillan.

Nurse, A. 2016. *An Introduction to Green Criminology and Environmental Justice.* London: Sage.

Nwilo, P.C. and Badejo, O.T. 2005. Oil Spill Problems and Management in the Niger Delta. International Oil Spill Conference Proceedings: May 2005, Vol. 2005, No. 1, pp. 567–570.

Obschonka, M., Andersson, H., Silbereisen, R.K., and Sverke, M. 2013. "Rulebreaking, Crime and Entrepreunership: A Replication and Extension Study with 37 Year Longitudinal Data." *Journal of Vocational Behaviour*, 83, 386–396.

Ofwat. 2019. *Ofwat's Final Decision to Impose a Financial Penalty on Southern Water Services Limited.* Birmingham: Ofwat.

O'Riordan, T. 1991. "The new environmentalism and sustainable development," *Science of the Total Environment*, 108(1-2): 5–15.

O'Riordan, T. 1994. *Interpreting the Precautionary Principle*, Abingdon: Routledge.

Ottinger, R. L. 1969. Legislation and the Environment Individual Rights and Government Accountability. *Cornell Law Review*, 55(5), 666–673.

Ozmy, J., and Jarrell, M. 2011. "Upset over Air Pollution: Analyzing Upset Event Emissions at Petroleum Refineries," *Review of Policy Research*, Vol, 28(4): 365–382.

Pantsios, A. 2015. "Confirmed: Oklahoma Earthquakes Caused by Fracking," *Ecowatch.* Online at: https://www.ecowatch.com/confirmed-oklahoma-earth-quakes-caused-by-fracking-1882034344.html [Accessed 13 November 2018].

Parker, C. 2004. "Restorative Justice in Business Regulation? The Australian Competition and Consumer Commission's Use of Enforceable Undertakings." *Modern Law Review* 67(2), 209–246. doi: 10.1111/j.1468-2230.2004.00484.x

Parry, R. L. 2001, August 2. "Bio-Pirates Raid Rrees in the Swamps of Borneo," *The Independent*, .

Paternoster, R. and Simpson, S. 1996. "Sanction Threats and Appeals to Morality: Testing a Rational Choice Model of Corporate Crime," *Law & Society Review* 30(3): 549–583.

Pearce, F. and Tombs, S. 1998. *Toxic Capitalism: Corporate Crime and the Chemical Industry.* Aldershot: Dartmouth.

Peeples, L. 2015. "Teens Take Politicians To Court Over Climate Change," *Huffington Post.* http://www.huffingtonpost.com/2015/01/17/climate-change-lawsuit-teens-oregon_n_6490036.html [Accessed 14 March 2015]

Penney, Terry L. 2014. "Dark Figure of Crime (Problems of Estimation)." In *The Encyclopedia of Criminology and Criminal Justice*, J. S. Albanese (Ed.). doi:10.1002/9781118517383.wbeccj248

Peterson, C.H., Rice, S.D., Short, J.W., Esler, D., Bodkin, J.L., Ballacjey, B.E., and Irons, D.B. 2003. "Long-Term Ecosystem Response to the Exxon Valdez Oil Spill," *Science*, Vol. 302 (5653): 2082–2086. DOI: 10.1126/science.1084282

Piatt, J.F., Lensink, C.J., Butler, W., Kendziorek, M., Nysewander, D.R. 1990. "Immediate Impact of the 'Exxon Valdez' Oil Spill on Marine Birds," *The Auk*, Vol. 107 (2): 387–397, https://doi.org/10.2307/4087623

Pirjatanniemi, E. 2009. "Desperately Seeking Reason—New Directions for European Environmental Criminal Law." *Scandinavian Studies in Law*, 54.

Potoski, P. and Prakash, M. 2004. "The Regulation Dilemma: Cooperation and Conflict in Environmental Governance," *Public Administration Review*, 64 (2) 152–163.

Powell R.A. and Single H.M. 1996. "Focus groups," *International Journal of Quality in Health Care* 8 (5): 499–504.

Preece, Rod. 1999. *Animals and Nature: Culture, Myths, Cultural Realities.* Vancouver: University of British Columbia.

Rachman, G. 2009. "The Crude Realities of Diplomacy." *Financial Times*, 8 September 2009, p. 13 (20 April 2015).

Reed, M. and Neubert, M. 2011. "General Electric: Ecomagination as a CSR Initiative," *Journal of Business Ethics Education* 8(1): 245–254.

Rees, E. 2011. "How oil and corruption have become so closely linked." *The Ecologist. http* ://www.theecologist.org/News/news_analysis/1092214/how_oil_ and_corruption_have_become_so_closely_linked.html (1 June 2015).

Rhodes, W.M., Allen, E. and Callahan, M. 2006. *Illegal Logging: A Market-Based Analysis of Trafficking in Illegal Timber.* Washington: ABT Associates/US Department of Justice.

Roberts, M., Cook, D., Jones, P., and Lowther, J. 2001. *Wildlife Crime in the UK: Towards a National Crime Unit.* Wolverhampton: Department for the Environment, Food & Rural Affairs/Centre for Applied Social Research (University of Wolverhampton).

Robinson, Daniel. 2010. *Confronting Biopiracy: Challenges, Cases and International Debates.* Abingdon: Routledge.

Roeschke, J.E. 2009. "Eco-Terrorism and Piracy on the High Seas: Japanese Whaling and the Rights of Private Groups to Enforce International Conservation Law in Neutral Waters." *The Villanova Environmental Law Journal* XX(1), 99–136.

Rosenstein, J. 2005. *Oil Corruption and Conflict in West Africa: The Failure of Governance and Corporate Social Responsibility.* Ghana: Kofi Annan Peacekeeping Training Institute. http://www.kaiptc.org/Publications/Monographs/Monographs/ mono-5_Rosenstein.aspx (1 June 2015).

Ruggiero, Vincenzo. 2015. *Power and Crime (New Directions in Critical Criminology).* Abingdon: Routledge.

Ruggiero, Vincenzo, & South, Nigel. 2010. "Green Criminology and Dirty Collar Crime." *Critical Criminology*, 18(4): 251. https://doi.org/10.1007/ s10612-010-9122-8

Ruggiero, Vincenzo, and South, Nigel. 2013. "Toxic State-Corporate Crimes, Neo-liberalism and Green Criminology: The Hazards and Legacies of the Oil, Chemical and Mineral Industries." *International Journal for Crime, Justice and Social Democracy,* 2(2): 12–26.

Ruhl, J. B. 1997. "The Case of the Speluncean Polluters: Six Themes of Environmental Law, Policy, and Ethics." *Environmental Law* Vol. 27: 343–374.

Runhaar, H. & Lafferty, H. 2009. "Governing Corporate Social Responsibility: An Assessment of the Contribution of the UN Global Compact to CSR Strategies in the Telecommunications Industry," *Journal of Business Ethics*, 84(4): 479–495. https://doi.org/10.1007/s10551-008-9720-5

Schaffner, J. 2011. *An Introduction to Animals and the Law.* Basingstoke: Palgrave Macmillan.

Schillemans, T. 2011. Does Horizontal Accountability Work? Evaluating Potential Remedies for the Accountability Deficit of Agencies. *Administration & Society*, 43(4), 387–416.

Schlosberg, D. 2007. *Defining Environmental Justice: Theories, Movements, and Nature.* New York, NY: Oxford University Press.

Schlosberg, D., and Collins, L. B. 2014. From Environmental to Climate Justice: Climate Change and the Discourse of Environmental Justice. WIREs Clim Change, 5: 359–374. doi:10.1002/wcc.275

Schnaiberg, A. 1980. *The Environment: From Surplus to Scarcity.* New York, NY: Oxford University Press.

Schnoor, Jerald. 2010. "The Gulf Oil Spill." *Environmental Science and Technology,* 44(13): 483.

Seba, Erwin. 2008. "Sierra Club Sues Shell over Refinery Pollution." Reuters/ Environmental News Network. Retrieved from www.enn.com/top_stories/article/28805 [Accessed 20 April 2013]

Senate Standing Committee on Legal and Constitutional Affairs. 1989. *Company Directors' Duties: Report on the Social and Fiduciary Duties and Obligations of Company Directors.* Canberra: AGPS.

Seyfang, Gill. 2006. "Ecological Citizenship and Sustainable Consumption: Examining Local Organic Food Networks," *Journal of Rural Studies*, 22(4): 383–395.

Sharpe, V. 1996. "Ethical Theory and the Demands of Sustainability." In C. Richard Cothern (ed.), *Handbook for Environmental Risk Decision Making.* Boca Raton: CRC Press.

Shell. 2008. *Sustainability Report 2007*, The Hague, Shell.

Shell. 2009. *Sustainability Report 2008*, The Hague, Shell.

Shell. 2012. *Sustainability Report 2011*, The Hague, Shell.

Shiva, V. 2007. "Bioprospecting as Sophisticated Biopiracy," *Signs: Journal of Women in Culture and Society* 32(2): 307–313.

Short, D., and Szolucha, A. 2019. "Fracking Lancashire: The Planning Process, Social Harm and Collective Trauma," *Geoforum*, Vol. 98: 264–276.

Simpson, S. S., Carole Gibbs, Melissa Rorie, Lee Ann Slocum, Mark A. Cohen, and Michael Vandenbergh. 2013. "An Empirical Assessment of Corporate Environmental Crime-Control Strategies." *Journal of Criminal Law & Criminology,* 103(1): 231–278.

Situ, Y. and Emmons, D. 2000. *Environmental Crime: The Criminal Justice System's Role in Protecting the Environment.* Thousand Oaks: Sage.

Skogan, Wesley G. 1977. "Dimensions of the Dark Figure of Unreported Crime." *Crime & Delinquency,* 23(1), 41–50. https://doi.org/10.1177/001112877702300104

Slapper, G., and Kelly, D. 2017. *The English Legal System* (eighteenth edition), Abingdon: Routledge.

Smith, J., Obidzinski, K., and Suramenggala Subarudi, I. 2003. "Illegal Logging, Collusive Corruption and Fragmented Governments in Kalimantan, Indonesia," *International Forestry Review* 5(3): 293–302.

Smith, Rhona. 2010. *Texts and Materials on International Human Rights* (Second Edition). Abingdon: Routledge.

Smith and Pangsapa 2009. "Corporate Environmental Responsibility and Citizenship" in Reynolds, M., Blackmore, C., and Smith, J. (eds). *The Environmental Responsibility Reader.* London: Zed Books/The Open University.

Sollund, R. 2012. "Introduction" in Rune Ellefsen, Ragnhild Sollund, and Guri Larsen, G. (eds) *Eco-global Crimes: Contemporary Problems and Future Challenges.* Farnham: Ashgate.

Sollund, R. (ed.). 2015. *Green Harms and Crimes: Critical Criminology in a Changing World.* Basingstoke: Palgrave Macmillan.

Solomon, G., and Janssen, S. 2010. "Health Effects of the Gulf Oil Spill." *JAMA*, 304(10), 1118–1119. doi:10.1001/jama.2010.1254.

South, Nigel. 2007. "The Corporate Colonisation of Nature: Bio-Prospecting, Bio-Piracy and the Development of Green Criminology." In Beirne, P and South, N. (eds.) *Issues in Green Criminology: Confronting Harms Against Environments, Humanity and Other Animals.* Willan, Devon, pp. 230–247.

South, N. and Wyatt, T. 2011. "Comparing Illicit Trades in Wildlife and Drugs: An Exploratory Study." *Deviant Behavior* 32: 538–561.

Spaargaren, Gert and Mol, Arthur. 1992. "Sociology, Environment, and Modernity: Ecological Modernization as a Theory of Social Change." *Society & Natural Resources*, 5:4, 323–344, DOI: 10.1080/08941929209380797

Spence, David B. 2011. "Corporate Social Responsibility in the Oil and Gas Industry: The Importance of Reputational Risk," *Chicago-Kent Law Review*, 86(1): 59–85. http://scholarship.kentlaw.iit.edu/cklawreview/vol86/iss1/4 [Accessed 20 March 2015]

Stallworthy, M. 2008. *Understanding Environmental Law.* London: Sweet and Maxwell.

Stapenhurst, R., and O'Brien, M. 2005. *Accountability in Governance.* Washington, DC: World Bank.

Starik, Mark. 1995. "Should Trees Have Managerial Standing? Toward Stakeholder Status for Non-human Nature." *Journal of Business Ethics* 14(3): 207–217. https://doi.org/10.1007/BF00881435

Steer, A. 1996. "Ten Principles of the New Environmentalism," *Finance and Development*, December 1996: 4–7.

Steiner, R. 2010. *Double Standard: Shell Practices in Nigeria Compared with International Standards to Prevent and Control, Pipeline Oil Spills and the Deepwater Horizon Oil Spill.* Amsterdam: Friends of the Earth Netherlands.

Stempel, J. 2019. "New York Plans to Sue EPA over GE's 'Incomplete' Hudson River Cleanup," Reuters. Available at: https://uk.reuters.com/article/us-new-york-epa/new-york-plans-to-sue-epa-over-ges-incomplete-hudson-river-cleanup-idUKKC-N1RN29W [Accessed 7 July 2019]

Stockdale, E., and Casale, S. (eds.) 1992. *Criminal Justice under Stress.* London: Blackstone.

Stone, Christopher. 1985. "Should Trees Have Standing? Revisited: How Far Will Law and Morals Reach? A Pluralist Perspective." *Southern California Law Review*, 59(1): 1–154.

Stone, Richard. 2010. *Textbook on Civil Liberties and Human Rights.* Oxford: Oxford University Press.

Subbiah, Sumathi. 2004. "Reaping What They Sow: The Basmati Rice Controversy and Strategies for Protecting Traditional Knowledge." 27 B.C. INT'L & COMP. L. REV. 529, 544.

Sudha, P. Sree. 2014. "Combating Biopiracy of Indian Traditional Knowledge (TK) A Legal Perspective." *Bharati Law Review,* October-December 2014: 42–62.

Sullivan, Ned and Schiavo, Rich. 2005. "Talking Green, Acting Dirty," New York Times.com.

SustainAbility. 2010. Shell Strategic Advisory. Retrieved from http://www.sustainability.com/case-studies/shell

Sutherland, E. 1949. *White-Collar Crime.* New York: Holt, Rinehart and Winston.

Sutherland, E. H. 1973. *On Analysing Crime.* Chicago: University of Chicago Press.

Sykes, G. M. and Matza, D. (1957). "Techniques of Neutralization: A Theory of Delinquency." *American Sociological Review, 22.* 664–673.

Taylor, D. E. 2000. "The Rise of the Environmental Justice Paradigm: Injustice Framing and the Social Construction of Environmental Discourses." *American Behavioral Scientist*, *43*(4), 508–580. https://doi.org/10.1177/0002764200043004003

Tempus, A. 2014. "Environmental Lawyers Gear Up for Fighting Climate Change in the Courts," *Vice News,* 21 October 2014. https://news.vice.com/article/environmental-lawyers-gear-up-for-fighting-climate-change-in-the-courts [Accessed 9 July 2019]

Tencer, D. 2011. "Monsanto, World's Largest Genetically Modified Food Producer, To Be Charged With Biopiracy In India," *Huffington Post Canada.*

Thomson, B. 2017. "'Determining Criteria to Evaluate Outcomes of Businesses' Provision of Remedy." *Business and Human Rights Journal*, Vol. 2(1), pp. 55–85.

Tombs, Steve and Whyte, David. 2012. "Transcending the Dderegulation Debate? Regulation, Risk, and the Enforcement of Health and Safety Law in the UK." *Regulation and Governance*, 7(1): 61–79. doi:10.1111/j.1748-5991.2012.01164.x

Tombs, Steve and Whyte, David. 2015. *The Corporate Criminal.* Abingdon: Routledge.

Tuller, D. 2015. "As Fracking Booms, Dearth Of Health Risk Data Remains." *Health Affairs* 34(6): 903–906.

Turley, S.L. 2016. "'To See Between': Interviewing as a Legal Research Tool." *Journal of Association of Legal Writing Directors*, Vol. 7, pp. 283–309.

Turner, R.K. 1992. *Environmental Policy: An Economic Approach to the Polluter Pays Principle.* Norwich: University of East Anglia.

Ubani, E. C., and Onyejekwe, I. M. 2013. "Environmental Impact Analysis of Gas Flaring in the Niger Delta Region of Nigeria." *American Journal of Scientific and Industrial Research*, 4, 246–252. https://doi.org/10.5251/ajsir.2013.4.2.246.252

Uhlmann, David M., 2009. "Environmental Crime Comes of Age: The Evolution of Criminal Enforcement in the Environmental Regulatory Scheme." *Utah Law Review*, No. 4, p. 1223, 2009; U of Michigan Public Law Working Paper No. 177. Available at SSRN: https://ssrn.com/abstract=1522506

Ukala, E. 2011. "Gas Flaring in Nigeria's Niger Delta: Failed Promises and Reviving Community Voices." *Washington and Lee Journal of Energy, Climate and the Environment*, 2(1): 97–126.

UN Global Compact. 2019. The Power of Princples. Available at: https://www.unglobalcompact.org/what-is-gc/mission/principles [Accessed 13 July 2019]

UN Human Rights Council. 2017. Report of the Special Rapporteur on the implications for human rights of the environmentally sound management and disposal of hazardous substances and wastes on his mission to the United Kingdom of Great Britain and Northern Ireland. http://www.srtoxics.org/wp-content/uploads/2017/09/Final-UK-mission-report.pdf [Accessed 6 October 2017]

United Nations. 2018. *United Nations Declaration on the Rights of Indigenous Peoples*. Retrieved from https://www.un.org/development/desa/indigenouspeoples/wp-content/uploads/sites/19/2018/11/UNDRIP_E_web.pdf

United Nations Environment Program. 2011. *Environmental Assessment of Ongoniland.* Nairobi: UNEP. Available at: https://postconflict.unep.ch/publications/OEA/UNEP_OEA.pdf

United Nations Human Rights Council. 2012. *Guiding Principles on Business and Human Rights: Implementing the United Nations "Protect, Respect and Remedy" Framework*, New York, The United Nations. Retrieved from http://www.businesshumanrights.org/media/documents/ruggie/ruggie-guiding-principles-21-mar2011.pdf

UNOHCHR. 2011. *Guiding Principles on Human Rights*. New York and Geneva: United Nations. http://www.ohchr.org/Documents/Publications/GuidingPrinciplesBusinessHR_EN.pdf [Accessed 12 February 2017]

US Department of Justice. 2013. Transocean Agrees to Plead Guilty to Environmental Crime and Enter Civil Settlement to Resolve U.S. Clean Water Act Penalty Claims from Deepwater Horizon Incident. Available at: https://www.justice.gov/opa/pr/transocean-agrees-plead-guilty-environmental-crime-and-enter-civil-settlement-resolve-us [Accessed 1 July 2019]

Vanhala, L. 2013. "Civil Society Organisations and the Aarhus Convention in Court: Judicialisation From Below in Scotland?" *Representation*, Vol 49(3), pp. 309–320.

Vaughan, A. 2018. "Fracking Firm Boss Says It Didn't Expect to Cause Such Serious Quakes," *The Guardian*. Online at: https://www.theguardian.com/

environment/2018/nov/11/fracking-firm-boss-says-it-didnt-expect-to-cause-such-serious-quakes-lancashire [Accessed 13 November 2018]

Vogel, D. 2005. *The Market for Virtue: The Potential and Limitations of Corporate Social Responsibility*. Washington, DC: Brookings Institution Press.

Voiculescu, A. and Yanacopulos, H. 2011. (Eds.), *The Business of Human Rights: An Evolving Agenda for Corporate Responsibility.* London, Zed Books/The Open University.

Vold, G. B., and Bernard, T. J. 1986. *Theoretical Criminology: Third Edition*. Oxford: Oxford University Press.

Walker, Kent, and Wan, Fang. 2012. "The Harm of Symbolic Actions and Green-Washing: Corporate Actions and Communications on Environmental Performance and Their Financial Implications." *Journal of Business Ethics* 109, 227–242.

Walters, Reece. 2007. "Crime, Regulation and Radioactive Waste in the United Kingdom," in Beirne, P. and South, N. (eds) *Issues in Green Criminology: Confronting Harms against Environments, Humanity and Other Animals.* Cullompton: Willan.

Werther, William B., and Chandler, David. 2005. "Strategic Corporate Social Responsibility as Global Brand Insurance." *Business Horizons*, Vol. 48(4): 317–324.

Weston, B., and Bollier, D. 2013. *Green Governance: Ecological Survival, Human Rights, and the Law of the Commons*. Cambridge: Cambridge University Press.

Wheeler, David. 2002. "Beyond Pollution Havens." *Global Environmental Politics* Vol. 2 (2): 1–10.

Wheeler, Stephen, and Beatley, Timothy. 2014. *The Sustainable Urban Development Reader*. Abingdon: Routledge.

White, Garry. 2011. "Caudrilla Admits Causing Blackpool Earthquakes," *The Telegraph*. Online at: https://www.telegraph.co.uk/finance/newsbysector/energy/8864669/Cuadrilla-admits-drilling-caused-Blackpool-earthquakes.html [Accessed 13 November 2018]

White, R. 2007. "Green Criminology and the Pursuit of Ecological Justice in Piers Beirne and Nigel South," in *Issues in Green Criminology*. Cullompton: Willan Publishing.

White, Rob. 2008. *Crimes Against Nature: Environmental Criminology and Ecological Justice*. Cullompton: Willan.

White, Rob. 2012a. "The Foundations of Eco-Global Criminology." In R. Ellefsen, R. Sollund, and G. Larsen, (Eds), *Eco-Global Crimes: Contemporary Problems and Future Challenges*, Farnham: Ashgate.

White, Rob. 2012b. "Land Theft as Rural Eco-Crime." *International Journal of Rural Criminology* V1(2): 203–217.

White, Rob. 2013. "Environmental Crime and Problem-Solving Courts." *Crime Law and Social Change*, 59 (3): 267–278.

White, Rob. 2017. "Carbon Economics and Transnational Resistance to Ecocide," in Hall, M., Maher, J., Nurse, A. Potter, G. South, N. Wyatt, T. (eds) *Greening Criminology in the 21st Century.* Abingdon: Routledge.

White, Rob. 2018a. "Carbon Criminals, Ecocide and Climate Justice," in Cameron Holley and Clifford Shearing (eds) *Criminology and the Anthropocene*. Abingdon: Routledge.

White, Rob. 2018b. *Climate Change Criminology*. Bristol: Bristol University Press.

White, Rob and Heckenberg, Diane. 2014. *Green Criminology: An Introduction to the Study of Environmental Harm*. Abingdon: Routledge.

Williams, Angela. 2011. "Climate Change Law: Creating and Sustaining Social and Economic Insecurity." *Social and Legal Studies* 20(4): 499–513.

Williams, Oliver. 2004. "The UN Global Compact: The Challenge and the Promise." *Business Ethics Quarterly 14*(4), 755–774. doi:10.5840/beq200414432.

Wilson, M., Foulger, G., Gluyas, J., and Davies, R. 2018. "Fracking causes earthquakes by design: Can regulation keep up?" *The Conversation.* Online at: https://theconversation.com/fracking-causes-earthquakes-by-design-can-regulation-keep-up-106183 [Accessed 13 November 2018]

Woolf, Harry. 1992. "Are the Judiciary Environmentally Myopic?" *Journal of Environmental Law* 4(1): 1–14. doi: 10.1093/jel/4.1.1.

World Health Organisation. 2014. "7 Million Premature Deaths Annually Linked to Air Pollution." Online at: http://www.who.int/mediacentre/news/releases/2014/air-pollution/en/ [Accessed 12 November 2018]

Wright, B. R. E., Caspi, A., Moffitt, T. E., & Paternoster, R. 2004. "Does the Perceived Risk of Punishment Deter Criminally Prone Individuals? Rational Choice, Self-Control, and Crime." *Journal of Research in Crime and Delinquency, 41*(2), 180–213. https://doi.org/10.1177/0022427803260263

Wyatt, Tanya. and Brisman, Avi. 2017. "The Role of Denial in the 'Theft of Nature': Comparing Biopiracy and Climate Change." *Critical Criminology* 25(3): 325–341.

Yanacopulos, H. (2011). "Foundations—Actors of Change?" In A. Voiculescu, and H. Yanacopulos, (Eds.), *The Business of Human Rights: An Evolving Agenda for Corporate Responsibility.* London, Zed Books/The Open University.

Index

About the Author

Angus Nurse is Head of Criminology and Criminal Justice at Nottingham Trent University. He was previously Associate Professor, Environmental Justice at Middlesex University School of Law. Angus has research interests in green criminology, criminality, critical criminal justice, animal rights, and human rights law. He is a member of the Wild Animal Welfare Committee and has previously worked in the environmental NGO field and as an Investigator for the Local Government Ombudsman. His books include *Policing Wildlife* (2015), *Animal Harm: Perspectives on Why People Harm and Kill Animals* (2013), *Miscarriages of Justice: Causes, Consequences and Remedies* (Policy Press, 2018) co-authored with Sam Poyser and Rebecca Milne, *The Citizen and the State* (Emerald, 2020), and *Wildlife Criminology* (Bristol University Press, 2020, co-authored with Professor Tanya Wyatt). He has co-edited a special edition of the journal *Crime, Law and Social Change* (with Erica von Essen) and co-edited two edited book collections on green criminology.